Transitions and Learning through the Lifecourse

Like m:
meanin
second:
further
an imp
unprod
and the
of inter

Tran:
range o
transiti
econom
more ef

Aim
across
feminis
togethe
a numb

- the
- the
- tra
- tra
- tra
- lea
- ap

Kathry

Gert Biesta is Professor of Education a ... on, University of Stirling, UK.

Martin Hughes is Professor of Education

Transitions and Learning through the Lifecourse

Edited by
Kathryn Ecclestone,
Gert Biesta and
Martin Hughes

Routledge
Taylor & Francis Group

LONDON AND NEW YORK

First published 2010
by Routledge
2 Park Square, Milton Park, Abingdon, Oxon OX14 4RN

Simultaneously published in the USA and Canada
by Routledge
270 Madison Avenue, New York, NY 10016

Routledge is an imprint of the Taylor & Francis Group, an informa business

© 2010 Kathryn Ecclestone, Gert Biesta and Martin Hughes for selection
and editorial material; individual chapters, the contributors.

Typeset in Goudy by
Bookcraft Ltd, Stroud, Gloucestershire

Printed and bound in Great Britain by
CPI Antony Rowe, Chippenham, Wiltshire

British Library Cataloguing in Publication Data
A catalogue record for this book is available from the British Library

Library of Congress Cataloging in Publication Data
Transitions and learning through the lifecourse / edited by
Kathryn Ecclestone, Gert Biesta, and Martin Hughes.
   p. cm.
   Includes index.
   1. Continuing education—Great Britain. 2. School-to-work
   transition—Great Britain. 3. Life cycle, Human—Great Britain.
   I. Ecclestone, Kathryn. II. Biesta, Gert. III. Hughes, Martin,
   1949 May 15-
   LC5256.G7T73 2010
   374'.941–dc22   2009016177

ISBN 10: 0-415-48173-2 (hbk)
ISBN 10: 0-415-48174-0 (pbk)
ISBN 10: 0-203-86761-0 (ebk)

ISBN 13: 978-0-415-48173-1 (hbk)
ISBN 13: 978-0-415-48174-8 (pbk)
ISBN 13: 978-0-203-86761-7 (ebk)

Contents

Figures

Tables

Contributors

Jane Andrews was previously Research Fellow at the Graduate School of Education, University of Bristol, before taking up a position as Senior Lecturer in Early Childhood Education at the University of the West of England. Jane has worked as a classroom teacher and has research interests in language education, children developing English as an additional language and learning in out-of-school contexts.

Phoebe Beedell worked as Research Fellow on two projects in the ESRC's Identities and Social Action Programme at the University of the West of England in both the Centre for Psycho-Social Studies and in the School of Education. She has a background in communications and community development work in both Britain and Southern Africa. Her published works include articles on commitment and motivation, school choice, and dialogical research methodology on which she contributed a chapter to *Researching Beneath the Surface* (2009). She is currently working in the voluntary sector on issues of community cohesion, conviviality and the use of public spaces.

Gert Biesta is Professor of Education at the Stirling Institute of Education, University of Stirling, UK, and Visiting Professor at Örebro University and Mälardalen University, Sweden. He is editor-in-chief of *Studies in Philosophy and Education*. He conducts theoretical and empirical research with a particular focus on the relationships between education, democracy and democratisation. Recent books include *Derrida and Education* (co-edited with Denise Egéa-Kuehne; Routledge, 2001); *Pragmatism and Educational Research* (co-authored with Nicholas C. Burbules; Rowman & Littlefield, 2003); *Beyond Learning: Democratic Education for a Human Future* (Paradigm Publishers, 2006); *Improving Learning Cultures in Further Education* (co-edited with David James; Routledge, 2007); *Democracy, Education and the Moral Life* (co-edited with Michael Katz and Susan Verducci; Springer, 2009); *Derrida, Deconstruction and the Politics of Pedagogy* (co-authored with Michael Peters; Peter Lang, 2009); *Contexts, Communities and Networks* (co-edited with Richard Edwards and Mary Thorpe; Routledge, 2009).

Jenny Bimrose is Professorial Fellow at the Institute for Employment Research, University of Warwick. With over thirty years' experience in higher education, researching, teaching and managing, Jenny's current interests include longitudinal research into the career trajectories of adults across Europe, integrating research findings into policy and practice, developing ICT systems to support the application of labour market information by end users, and the career development of women. She is a Fellow of the Institute of Career Guidance and a member of various national and international associations. Consultancy support has also been provided to organisations and a number of government departments.

Dan Bishop is Lecturer in Human Resource Development at the Centre for Labour Market studies, University of Leicester. With a background in the teaching profession, he previously worked as a researcher on ESRC-funded projects at the universities of Leicester and Cardiff. Dan has conducted and published research in areas connected to training, development and workplace learning, with a particular interest in learning processes within small businesses.

Alan Brown is Professorial Fellow at the Institute for Employment Research, University of Warwick. Since 2002 Alan Brown has been Associate Director of the ESRC Teaching and Learning Research Programme (TLRP) with responsibility for work-based learning and professional learning. (For further details of the TLRP see: www.tlrp.org). His current research, which has a strong international orientation, focuses mainly on changing occupational identities, continuing vocational training, skill formation, organisational performance, individual career development and supporting knowledge sharing, and development and learning in professional communities of practice. He is involved in the development of web-based knowledge-sharing sites that has considerable material on research and practice in careers guidance and research on lifelong learning and work-related learning.

Helen Colley is Senior Research Fellow at the Education and Social Research Institute, Manchester Metropolitan University, and a fellow of the National Institute for Careers Education and Counselling. She has researched and written widely on post-compulsory and lifelong learning, and has a particular interest in career guidance, mentoring, and lifecourse transitions. Her research draws on and develops critical feminist perspectives to investigate the influence of class and gender on learning. Key publications include her award-winning study *Mentoring for Social Inclusion* (RoutledgeFalmer, 2003) and, with Phil Hodkinson and Janice Malcolm, *Informality and Formality in Learning* (Learning and Skills Research Centre, 2003).

Harriet Dunbar-Goddet is Research Officer in the Policy and Communications Department at UCAS. Harriet gained her experience in research, and qualitative and quantitative data analysis, while studying for her PhD (1997–2002), and working as a Research Officer (2002–8) at both the University of Toulouse and the University of Oxford. Harriet carries out research, using both qualitative and quantitative research methods, in several topics including admissions processes and schemes.

Kathryn Ecclestone is Professor of Post-Compulsory Education at Oxford Brookes University. She has worked in post-compulsory education for the past 20 years, first as a practitioner in youth employment schemes and further education and as a researcher specialising in the principles, politics and practices of assessment and its links to learning, motivation and autonomy. Between 2002 and 2004 she was Associate Director for Further and Adult Education in the ESRC-funded Teaching and Learning Research Programme. She has published widely on assessment in post-compulsory education and on the rise of a 'therapeutic ethos' in education and assessment. She directs an ESRC seminar series on emotional well-being and social justice and is a member of the Assessment Reform Group, and the Access to Higher Education Assessment working group for the Quality Assurance Agency. She is on the editorial boards of *Studies in the Education of Adults, Assessment in Education* and the *Journal of Further and Higher Education*. Kathryn also works as a consultant to the National Board of Education in Finland on reforms to assessment.

Hubert Ertl is Lecturer in Higher Education at the Department of Education, University of Oxford. After completing his training in the German dual system of vocational education Hubert did his first degree in business studies, vocational education and English at the Ludwig-Maximilians-Universität (LMU) in Munich. He then studied comparative and international education at the University of Oxford, where he conducted research into the ways EU programmes in education and training are implemented in different European countries. This research was part of the EU-funded network PRESTiGE (Problems of Educational Standardisation and Transitions in a Global Environment). He taught at the LMU Institute of Vocational Education and Business Studies (Institut für Wirtschaftspädagogik) and completed his doctoral thesis on European aspects of vocational education and training. After his doctorate he worked for three years as a lecturer and researcher at the University of Paderborn (Germany) in the area of training teachers for German vocational colleges.

Karen Evans is Professor at the Institute of Education, University of London. Karen's main fields of research are learning in life and work transitions, and learning in and through the workplace. She has directed 16 major studies of learning and the world of work in Britain and internationally. Karen has published widely in these fields. Her books include *Learning, Work and Social Responsibility* (Springer, 2009); *Improving Workplace Learning* (Routledge, 2006); *Reconnection: Countering Social Exclusion through Situated Learning* (Springer, 2004); *Working to Learn* (Routledge, 2002); *Learning and Work in the Risk Society* (Palgrave/MacMillan, 2000). She is joint editor of COMPARE, the journal of comparative and international education.

Alan Felstead is Research Professor at Cardiff School of Social Sciences, Cardiff University. His research focuses on: training, skills and learning; non-standard forms of employment; and the spaces and places of work. He has completed over 30 funded research projects (including seven funded by the ESRC), produced six books and written over 150 journal articles, book chapters and research reports. His books include *Improving Working as Learning* (with A. Fuller, N. Jewson, and L. Unwin; Routledge, 2009) and *Changing Places of Work* (with N. Jewson and S. Walters; Routledge, 2005).

John Field is Professor in the Institute of Education, University of Stirling, where he directs the Centre for Research in Lifelong Learning. He also holds a visiting chair at Birkbeck, University of London. He has researched and written widely on social, economic and policy aspects of adult education and training and his work has been translated into German, Italian and Japanese. Recent books include *Social Capital and Lifelong Learning* (Policy Press, 2005) and he is editor with Jim Gallacher and Robert Ingram of *Researching Transitions in Lifelong Learning* (Routledge, 2009).

Alison Fuller is Professor of Education and Work in the School of Education, University of Southampton. Her research interests and publications include patterns of participation in education, training and work; education–work transitions; apprenticeship and workplace learning. Alison (with Felstead and Unwin) has recently co-directed the ESRC funded study 'Learning as Work'.

Pamela Greenhough is an honorary Research Fellow at the University of Bristol. She worked as a primary school teacher for more than 15 years, and before retirement in 2008 worked on a number of research projects concerned with learning in and out of school, including the Home–School Knowledge Exchange project.

Mary Hamilton is Professor of Adult Learning and Literacy at Lancaster University and Associate Director of the Lancaster Literacy Research Centre. She has written extensively on policy, practice and everyday learning in adult literacy. She is co-author of a number of books including *Local Literacies* (with David Barton; Routledge, 1998), *Powerful Literacies* (with Jim Crowther and Lynn Tett; NIACE, 2001) and *Changing Faces of Adult Literacy, Language and Numeracy: A Critical History* (with Yvonne Hillier; Trentham, 2006).

Geoff Hayward is Lecturer in Education at the Department of Education, University of Oxford, Associate Director of the ESRC Research Centre on Skills, Knowledge and Organisational Performance (SKOPE), a Director of the Nuffield 14-19 Review, and co-director of the Oxford Centre for Socio-cultural and Activity Theory (OSAT). He was a founder member of the Bath/Macmillan post-16 science education project which led to the publication of a large number of text books. Before returning to Oxford in 1993, Geoff taught at the Liverpool Institute of Higher Education where he worked with primary school teachers as they implemented the science National Curriculum. Originally appointed as a science teacher educator, in 1998 Geoff was seconded to work with the ESRC Research Centre SKOPE, becoming Associate Director of that centre in 2003. In 2003 he was also part of the team that set up the Nuffield 14–19 Review of Education and Training, the most systematic inquiry into this phase of education and training undertaken in the last thirty years.

Michael Hoelscher works at the University of Heidelberg. He has a background in sociology and cultural sciences. He did his DPhil at the Free University Berlin on the topic of 'Economic Cultures in the Enlarged EU'. As a research assistant he taught different courses at undergraduate and graduate level in the Department of Cultural Sciences, Leipzig University. He was involved in higher education research, first at the Wittenberg Institute for Research on Higher Education (Institut für Hochschulforschung (HoF)) and from 2006 onwards at the Department of Education at Oxford University.

Martin Hughes is Professor of Education at the University of Bristol. He has researched widely on learning in preschool and primary-aged children, with a particular focus on early mathematics and literacy, learning with computers, and the relationship between home and school. Previous books include *Young Children Learning* (with Barbara Tizard; Harvard, 1985), *Children and Number* (Blackwell, 1986), *Parents and their Children's Schools* (with Felicity Wikeley and Tricia Nash; Oxford, 1994) and *Numeracy and Beyond* (with Charles Desforges and Christine Mitchell). His most recent books are *Improving Primary Literacy: Linking Home and School* (Routledge, 2007) and *Improving Primary Mathematics: Linking Home and School* (Routledge, 2007), written with colleagues on the recently completed Home–School Knowledge Exchange project. He is currently working on out-of-school learning, funded by an ESRC professorial fellowship.

Roz Ivanič is Professor Emerita of Linguistics in Education at Lancaster University. From 2004 to 2008 she was the Director of the ESRC TLRP-funded Literacies for Learning in Further Education research project. She is the lead author for *Improving Learning in College: Rethinking Literacies across the Curriculum* (Routledge, 2009).

David James is Professor of Education and a Director of BRILLE, the Bristol Centre for Research in Lifelong Learning and Education at the University of the West of England, Bristol. He is also a Visiting Professor at the University of Latvia. His background includes working as a teacher in FE, and prior to that, as a local government officer and musician. His research encompasses pedagogy, curriculum, assessment and learner identity, and the links between education and social inequalities. His books include *Bourdieu and Education* (with Michael Grenfell; Falmer, 1998) and *Improving Learning Cultures in Further Education* (with Gert Biesta; Routledge, 2007).

Nick Jewson is Senior Research Fellow in the School of Social Sciences at Cardiff University. He has published widely on equal opportunities, non-standard forms of employment, spatial transformations in patterns of work and employment, and learning in the workplace.

Konstantinos Kakavelakis is Research Associate in the 'Learning as Work' research project hosted at the Cardiff School of Social Sciences. His research interests lie in the areas of knowledge management, workplace learning and organizational change.

Jocey Quinn is Professor of Education at the Institute for Policy Studies in Education, London Metropolitan University. Her work takes a cultural approach to higher education and lifelong learning, focusing on the relationships between knowledge transformations and social justice. She has published widely and conducted national and international research in this field. This includes research on the impact of the mass participation of women in higher education and on working-class 'drop out' from HE. She is currently writing two books, *Culture and Education* (Routledge) and *Learning Communities and Imagined Social Capital: Learning to Belong* (Continuum).

Sheila Riddell is Director of the Centre for Research in Education Inclusion and Diversity at the Moray House School of Education, University of Edinburgh. Her research interests are in the broad field of equality and social inclusion, with particular reference to gender, social class and disability in the fields of education, training, employment and social care. Sheila has published extensively in these areas and sits on policy advisory committees on disability and equal rights.

Candice Satchwell is Research Associate at the Lancaster University Literacy Research Centre where she has worked on the Literacies for Learning in Further Education research project funded by the ESRC Teaching and Learning Research Programme, and a project on homelessness and educational needs and provision funded by the NRDC. She is also Lecturer in English at Blackpool and The Fylde College where she teaches on the degree programme and is the adviser on HE in FE for the English Subject Centre of the HE Academy. She has published work on children's concepts of punctuation, and has recent papers in the *Journal of Applied Linguistics, Journal of Vocational Education and Training, The Teacher Trainer* and *Pedagogy, Culture and Society*.

Lorna Unwin is Professor of Vocational Education and Deputy Director of the ESRC-funded Centre for Learning and Life Chances in Knowledge Economies and Societies (LLAKES) at the Institute of Education, University of London. She was previously the Director of the Centre for Labour Market Studies at the University of Leicester and has held academic posts at the Open University and University of Sheffield. Her key research interests include workplace learning, vocational education and economic change, and apprenticeship.

Her recent books include *Communities of Practice: Critical Perspectives* (2007) and *Improving Workplace Learning* (2006), both published by Routledge.

Edmund Waite is Researcher at the Department of Lifelong and Comparative Education, Institute of Education, London University. His research interests and publications relate to the study of adult literacy in the United Kingdom and international contexts as well as the anthropological study of education in Muslim societies.

Elisabet Weedon is Deputy Director in the Centre for Research in Education Inclusion and Diversity at the Moray House School of Education, University of Edinburgh. Her main research interests are in the area of adult learning. She is currently working on a number of projects within the centre including disabled students' learning experiences in higher education, lifelong learning in Europe and learning in the workplace and has published research in this area.

Wan Ching Yee is Research Fellow and Departmental Research Ethics Co-ordinator at the Graduate School of Education, University of Bristol. Since 1990 she has worked on a wide range of research and evaluation projects including the Home–School Knowledge Exchange project, the EU-funded Citizenship Education project and the Becta-funded evaluation of 1:1 Mobile Learning. Her research interests include out-of-school learning, research ethics, ethnic diversity and transfer between primary and secondary school.

Acknowledgements

We would like to thank Andrew Pollard for his support for the project upon which this book is based. We also would like to thank Theo Blackmore (Disability Cornwall) and Regina Karousu (University of Nottingham) for their contributions to the project.

Chapter 6 has been published in *Research Papers in Education*, 23(2): 139–51 and is reproduced here with permission of Taylor & Francis. An earlier version of Chapter 9 was published in *International Studies in the Sociology of Education*, 17: 427–43, and is published here with the permission of Taylor & Francis.

Preface

John Field

Transitions are widely held to be fundamental features of social life. Today, it could be argued that they are one of the defining characteristics of everyday life in what has variously been called late modernity, second modernity or even postmodernity. Certainly, theorising about transition has become a hallmark of contemporary sociological thinking, as is illustrated by Zygmunt Bauman's writing on 'liquid life', Anthony Giddens' ideas of 'institutionalised reflexivity' or Ulrich Beck's notion of 'risk society' (Bauman 2000, 2001; Giddens 1991; Beck 1992). There is also a thriving policy debate about the best ways in which to prepare for and support transitions, not least because there is a widespread policy assumption that the frequency of transitions is increasing as a result of heightened requirements for flexibility and mobility, as well as a marked tendency for established transition routes to become ever more protracted and unpredictable (OECD 2000). Television soaps dramatise the variety of transitions that characterise everyday life and take viewers through the anxieties and risks of personal change. There is even a sub-genre of modern Gothic fantasies such as *Buffy the Vampire Slayer* (Jarvis and Burr 2005) or the film *Twilight*, which reworks adolescence as a transitional world inhabited by vampiric creatures, some of whom relate peaceably with young people and some of whom eat them.

Partly as a result of this heightened policy interest, accompanied by wider public attention, research into transitions is burgeoning. For many years, research on transitions was largely concerned with identifying and exploring what one scholar called the 'predictable' passages of youth and adult life (Sheehy 1976). In the case of educational studies, this often involved focusing on the transition from school to work – or from adolescence to adult status – as *the* central transition of people's lives. Much of this work tended to present transitions as unilinear, and as a staged process that was relatively standardised for all who undertook it. In recent years, though, researchers have responded to the changed circumstances of everyday life in Western societies, as well as developing new ways of examining transitions both 'from within', using methods drawn from the interpretative tradition of social research, and 'from without', often applying new statistical modelling techniques to large scale data sets such as the British cohort studies.

This collection is therefore timely and important. It draws together contributions that were originally presented and discussed at a series of seminars funded by the UK Economic and Social Research Council. While individual chapters pursue distinctive themes and approaches, the volume as a whole has benefited from the systematic debate and exchanges between authors that a coherent seminar series allows. This preface will not attempt to summarise the papers that follow, but will rather set out a few general themes, partly as a way of establishing the wider significance of this volume, and partly as a way of providing one possible contextual platform for interrogating the studies that follow.

Individualisation and the lifecourse

Many researchers have noticed a marked tendency towards the individualisation of transition routes (Evans 2002, Glastra, Hake and Schedler 2004, Walther, du Bois-Reymond and Biggart 2006). And it certainly seems as though, in Western countries, individuals' lifecourses are characterised by increasing variety and range of transition routes. Whereas lifecourse transitions in the industrial era were often collective experiences, shared by millions at more or less the same age span, and in more or less the same sequences, contemporary lifecourse transitions are increasingly pluralised and non-linear. They also involve increasing elements of individual choice. As Anthony Giddens has put it:

> In the increasingly global order which is the context of our daily activities, we all have to construct our lives more actively than ever was the case before.
> (Giddens 1996: 243)

In late modernity, Giddens reminds us, we have no alternative but to make choices (Giddens 1991). Habit and routine become less and less helpful as guides to the present, let alone as maps of the future. Moreover, responsibility for many choices, as well as for the active life planning of which Giddens speaks, lies with the individual. And of course, transition has itself become embedded as routine: we have learned to expect change, at an accelerating rate.

The paradox, then, is that individualised transition pathways have collective consequences. Our existing support systems are fragile and flawed, as other people – family, friends, colleagues – are themselves trying to negotiate transitions and changes of their own. From workers facing redundancy to divorcees facing lonely evenings, it is no use blaming someone else for one's predicament; it is your responsibility to improve your own prospects, unlock your own potential, and build a new you. The state has troubles of its own. The social welfare state has become the activation state (Rosanvallon 1995), aiming to reduce dependency and encourage among the precarious minority the values of autonomy and self-actualisation that drive the comfortable majority. In particular, it is social democratic and Christian democratic governments that are actively seeking inclusion by compelling their marginal citizens to undertake education and training, whether it is citizenship classes for people convicted of breaching anti-social behaviour orders or vocational preparation for people claiming welfare benefits.

Giddens poses the question of whether the radicalised reflexivity of modern societies amounts to a form of emancipation (as in the so-called Enlightenment scenario) or a source of anxiety and risk (Giddens 1996: 242–5). While Giddens suggests that both dimensions are always involved, the specific outcomes of transitions, and the nature of transitional experiences, will always be shaped by contexts. For some people, some experiences of transition are emancipatory, while for others the transition brings anxiety and risk. Unwanted changes in relationship can be felt as abandonment or betrayal for one partner and the chance to choose a new life for the other; retirement from a job can provide time to develop other roles (including unprecedented amounts of time learning new things) or a loss of identity as well as a disastrous collapse of income. If involuntary redundancy is still often associated with depression and other mental health problems, there are also workers who delight in changing their job from time to time, and even start to worry if they hold down one position for 'too long'. Some people even seem to enjoy adult education and survive entire semesters without needing to see a counsellor.

Liquid modernity is not all oppression and coercion wrapped up in the language of choice. If it were, then it would be unlikely to survive a week longer. People are not mere cultural dupes on whose bodies and minds can be inscribed any old nonsense. Quite the reverse: it is sustained, at least for the time being, because ideas of self-fulfilment through choice, self-development by continual reinvestment in the self, do offer people at least a degree of agency and some sense of control over their lives. People seem to value the existence of at least the potential for change, embracing the idea that who they are right now, what they are doing right now, is not how things always have been and always will be. Their future self is possibly an incomplete project – an idea that many people appear to find highly attractive, while others fear the anxieties and risks. This book discusses ideas of agency, including agency that is 'bounded' and circumscribed, in the context of transitions that may include more or less intentional shifts in identity (see also Evans 2002, Biesta and Tedder 2006).

Linearity

The idea of transition does not necessarily imply unilinear change, but that is how it has been predominantly studied. The literature on youth transition, for example, is really concerned with two linked processes of change, both of which have generally been understood as one-way streets: school to work, adolescence to adulthood. This is understandable, given the strong orientation towards policy that characterised much research into youth transitions. Adult life transitions, however, are not helpfully understood in this way.

Transitions are inevitably bounded in time and in space. What is happening to transitions in the lifecourse in societies like our own? Certainly there is broad agreement that the lifecourse is changing, and the nature of transitions is altering correspondingly. There is also broad agreement on the ways in which the lifecourse has changed in the long term – that is, in the last hundred to one hundred and fifty years. Let me outline four particularly relevant aspects of this long period of change.

First, there has been increasing standardisation of the lifecourse, largely brought about by public regulation (Kohli 2003). This trend is in tension with tendencies – discussed above – towards individualisation of the lifecourse. The state sets rigid limits on the ages at which people may undergo certain transitions. For example, most nineteenth century states laid down minimum ages at which people could leave school, enter the labour market, undertake military service, vote, have sex, and get married. This tendency was accentuated by the twentieth century welfare state, which tended to remove exceptions to the existing rules on school leaving, voting or labour market entry, while also laying down age-related regulations governing access to welfare benefits such as retirement benefits. So far, then, linearity can be said to have persisted into late modernity.

Second, there was a marked tendency for the major transitions – first entry to labour market, leaving home of origin, marriage, retirement – to converge around a relatively small age band (Shanahan 2000). The compression of significant transitions into standardised phases of the life cycle led to ideas of a 'normal' lifecourse, reflecting a situation where most young people made it to 20, marrying shortly thereafter, having children, and surviving as a couple until the husband reached his mid-fifties, the wife then living with her children for around ten more years. Again, this is consistent with ideas of a linear set of transitions.

Third, life has got a lot longer. This was partly the result of greater longevity, fuelled by reductions in infant mortality rates, so that people were more likely to see their children grow into adulthood, but wider changes in diet and healthcare, along with the eradication of epidemics, also affected the length of adult life. Much of this was achieved by the state, with a particularly significant period of change in the mid-nineteenth century, when it dawned on the urban middle classes that cholera was not confining itself to the poor. Much social analysis rather underplays the wider consequences of these demographic patterns, which have been dramatic in the extreme, and are entirely unprecedented in human history. Societal ageing has worked against linearity, not least because as people came to live longer, so they have tended to choose to end particular sets of arrangements, such as marriage, that no longer suit them.

Fourth, there have been striking changes in the amount of time spent in waged work, both for women and for men. For the population as a whole, the length of the average working year, and the proportion of the lifespan spent in work, have both fallen quite spectacularly (Gershuny 2000). This is sometimes couched as a primarily male experience, though this probably reflects a widespread ignorance of women's history – or at any rate, the history of the majority of women in Western societies, who belonged to the working class and therefore had paid jobs, often full time – which for men and often for women effectively meant a ten-hour day and a six-day week, with barely any holidays. By the mid-twentieth century, people were expecting to spend part of their life in retirement, and they expected short phases of leisure at intervals during their working lives. Again, this has worked against linearity, particularly as the division between work and retirement has started to blur for many individuals – some as a matter of choice and some as compulsion.

So how has the lifecourse fared in liquid modernity? Have postmodern conditions thrown the lifecourse into chaos? Are transitions experienced as coercion, a kind of eviction of the self, or do they represent people – either as individuals or as groups – achieving what they desire? From a broadly postmodern perspective, it has been argued that the life cycle has become increasingly elective and fragmented. Thus Glastra, Hake and Schedler recently suggested that:

> As is now well established, the standard biography has been replaced by the 'elective biography'... This development has two corollaries. One is that in certain periods of life, many different tasks must be combined. [...] The second is that given the individualization of lifecourses, coordination of life and work on an aggregate social level becomes problematic.
>
> (Glastra, Hake and Schedler 2004: 295)

While arguably this is an exaggerated claim, it does point to some aspects of non-linearity that seem to be characteristic of late modernity. Institutionalisation has by no means weakened, but is increasingly challenged by tendencies towards individualisation in a wider context where there are strong economic and cultural pressures favouring greater flexibility; these are experienced by a variety of actors as deeply contradictory tendencies, and they increasingly form the focus for a rather heated public debate over issues such as retirement age and pensions reform (Kohli 2003: 536).

Personal troubles and public issues

In attending to the diversity of individual experience, then, we should not neglect the collective dimensions to transition. In so far as transitions are seen as troubling, they are usually treated as personal troubles requiring individual responses. Glastra and his colleagues suggest that the flexibility and unpredictability of life have become deeply disturbing precisely because they are faced by individual actors who have access to few collective resources. As they put it,

> When flexibility constitutes the crucial capacity that work organizations and the unpredictability of life demand of individuals, having a stable identity can be a disadvantage. [...] Questions such as 'Who am I?' and 'Whom do I want to be?' can become quite haunting existential questions.
>
> (Glastra, Hake and Schedler 2004: 294)

Yet some of the most unsettling transitions are collective in nature – war, factory closure, the loss of farmland, the impact of terrorism, or the replacement of communism by capitalism. These large scale collective transitions are outside the scope of this collection, but they should serve to remind us that the individualisation thesis can easily be overstated. Equally, even the most intimate of troubles – a faithless loved one, child birth, illness or injury – can have causes and consequences that are rooted in the social. Transitions may also arise as the result of the cumulative impact of countless decisions made by others.

There are also different collective experiences of the same transition processes. If we take the example of retirement from one's paid job, then we can discern some clear differences between the experiences of different socio-economic groupings.

Start with gender: a range of existing social narratives exist for women which can shape and story the experience of moving out of waged work into a life centred on the home; there are fewer such narratives for men, whose social networks and identities have not been rooted in the domestic. But we can then examine differences between generations (Field and Malcolm 2007). Some, even many women born in the 1940s and 1950s, are likely to reject those conventional narratives of domesticity and are therefore faced with the challenge of co-creating a new narrative and identity after retirement from a career which has provided at least one store of significant meaning for much of their adult life.

And there are differences between socio-economic groups, which often translate into varied experience of health and well-being. A male manual worker in Scotland will be fortunate to survive to the age of seventy, whereas a middle-class Scottish woman retiring at the same age and on the same day is very likely to have an additional two decades of life. Social class differences have slipped down the social research agenda somewhat in recent years, not least because there is increasing recognition of other more or less structured forms of inequality, including ethnicity. These differences by gender, generation and socio-economic status may well vary over time, and may have different impacts in respect of different types of transition, but they appear to be strongly marked.

The collective dimension to transitions, and to the experience of transitions, has often been neglected in the literature. And it has also been largely neglected in policy, which tends to use either rather traditional age-bounded definitions, which were also often based on male models of the lifecourse (for example, of entry into the labour market, or retirement), or highly individualised models involving individual solutions. I neither can nor wish to claim that every individual remedy – therapeutic or remedial – is worthless; neither should we ignore the collective dimension, whether to the root causes or to the immediate consequences or transitions.

Conclusions

Where does this leave those concerned with studying transitions in relation to the learning that people undertake? First, I have argued that transitions are multi-level and multidirectional, which means that we can no longer simply follow the lines pursued by earlier research which mainly focused on transitions in relation to institutional pathways and relatively stable life trajectories. Second, I have argued for the need to recognise agency along with structure, which seem to me to imply a greater attention to the collective as well as the individual aspects of transition. While I accept that the nature and possibly the extent of transition are themselves undergoing change, with a shift towards flexibility and uncertainty, it is important to accept that there are also elements of continuity and institutionalisation in the lifecourse. Third, I have emphasised the multifaceted nature of transition as experienced by most individuals. We should be cautious in the face of those who wish to pathologise individuals, emphasising their vulnerability and anxiety in the face of change, and downplaying their agency and desire precisely to reassert and develop their sense of who they are and what they can do (see

Ecclestone 2004). If we see change as potentially pleasurable and emancipating, at least from the perspective of those who are involved, then we can also address people's aspirations and dreams in a more focused way. People imagine themselves otherwise, and indeed this imaginary alternative self is a necessary precondition for transformative learning. And, as Jocey Quinn has observed, imagined communities and imagined spaces can help people to underpin their collective learning and enable them to negotiate significant transitions that are both collective and personal (Quinn 2005).

This leaves us with some remarkably challenging and demanding tasks. The case for narrative-based research and analysis appears to be well-made, and it is hardly surprising that the biographical turn has been so important in empirical studies of transitions through the lifecourse, particularly in studies that seek to explore how learning interacts with identity work, across their lives and over time (Warren and Webb 2007, Tedder and Biesta 2009). Yet the implication of my argument is that we also need to examine systematically the sites in which learning occurs and the nature of locally experienced structures of opportunity; we need grounded studies of the organisational and institutional settings in which people experience and live particular transitions. Narratives are needed; but on their own they are simply not enough. They need to be complemented by systematic studies of transition at population level, of the kind currently being undertaken in Britain using longitudinal data sets such as the national birth cohort studies (Bynner and Joshi 2007).

Bibliography

Bauman, Z. (2000) *Liquid Modernity*, Cambridge: Polity Press.

—— (2001) *The Individualized Society*, Cambridge: Polity Press.

Beck, U. (1992) *Risk Society*, London: Sage.

Biesta, G.J.J. and Tedder, M. (2006) 'How is agency possible? Towards an ecological understanding of agency-as-achievement', *Learning Lives Working Paper 5*, Exeter: University of Exeter.

Bynner, J. and Joshi, H. (2007) 'Building the evidence base from longitudinal data', *Innovation*, 20: 159–79.

Ecclestone, K. (2004) 'Learning or therapy? The demoralisation of education', *British Journal of Educational Studies*, 52: 112–37.

Evans, K. (2002) 'Taking control of their lives? Agency in young adult transitions in England and the new Germany', *Journal of Youth Studies*, 5: 245–69.

Field, J. and Malcolm, I. (2007) 'Talking about my learning generation: the role of historical time and generational time over the life course', in M. Osborne, M. Houston and N. Toman (eds), *The Pedagogy of Lifelong Learning: Understanding Effective Teaching and Learning in Diverse Contexts*, London: Routledge.

Gershuny, J. (2000) *Changing Times: Work and Leisure in Post-industrial Societies*, Oxford: Oxford University Press.

Giddens, A. (1991) *The Consequences of Modernity*, Cambridge: Polity Press.

—— (1996) *In Defence of Sociology: Essays, Interpretations and Rejoinders*, Cambridge: Polity Press.

Glastra, F., Hake, B. and Schedler, P. (2004) 'Lifelong learning as transitional learning', *Adult Education Quarterly*, 54: 291–307.

Jarvis, C. and Burr, V. (2005) '"Friends are the family we choose for ourselves": young people and families in the TV series *Buffy the Vampire Slayer*', *Young*, 13: 269–83.

Kohli, M. (2003) 'Der institutionalisierte Lebenslauf: ein Blick zurück und nach vorn', in J. Allmendinger (ed.), *Entstaatlichung und soziale Sicherheit*, Opladen: Leske & Budrich.

OECD (Organisation for Economic Co-operation and Development) (2000) *From Initial Education to Working Life: making transitions work*, Paris: OECD.

Quinn, J. (2005) 'Belonging in a Learning Community: the re-imagined university and imagined social capital', *Studies in the Education of Adults*, 37: 4–17.

Rosanvallon, P. (1995) *La Nouvelle Question Sociale: repenser l'état-providence*, Paris: Editions du Seuil.

Shanahan, M.J. (2000) 'Pathways to adulthood in changing societies: variability and mechanisms in life course perspective', *Annual Review of Sociology*, 26: 667–92.

Sheehy, G. (1976) *Passages: Predictable Crises of Adult Life*, Dutton: New York.

Tedder, M. and Biesta, G.J.J. (2009) 'Biography, transition and learning in the lifecourse: the role of narrative', in J. Field, J. Gallacher and R. Ingram (eds) *Researching Transitions in Lifelong Learning*, London: Routledge.

Walther, A., du Bois-Reymond, M. and Biggart, A. (2006) *Participation in Transition: Motivation of Young Adults in Europe for Learning And Working*, Frankfurt-am-Main: Peter Lang.

Warren, S. and Webb, S. (2007) 'Challenging lifelong learning policy discourse: where is structure in agency in narrative-based research?', *Studies in the Education of Adults*, 39: 5–21.

1 Transitions in the lifecourse

The role of identity, agency and structure

Kathryn Ecclestone, Gert Biesta and Martin Hughes

Introduction

This book has its origins in a seminar series on transitions through the lifecourse which was part of the UK Teaching and Learning Research Programme (TLRP; see www.tlrp.org). It aims to bring together and evaluate insights about educational, life and work transitions from different fields of research and a range of theoretical orientations. The book responds to the injunction that researchers need to chart 'what individuals actually do and how this is changing' as a 'first step to understanding what it means' (Bynner quoted by Hayward *et al.* 2005: 115). In different ways, the chapters that follow explore the concept of transitions and its contemporary importance in policy and educational practices. In doing so they enable the book to address the following questions:

- What are the main characteristics of transitions depicted in policy, practice and research?
- How do different ideas and perspectives about transition, people's agency, identity and the effects of structural conditions help us to understand transitions better in research, policy and practice?
- Why are transitions a problem for some individuals and groups and, conversely, for whom are transitions not a problem?
- What interventions, activities or practices are seen as useful in dealing with transitions?
- What aspects of transitions are contested from different perspectives?

This book arose from a recognition that the research field around transitions is fragmented both historically and between disciplines and theoretical orientations. The book does not claim to represent a unitary view about transitions in the lifecourse. Rather, it brings together policy, professional and academic concerns about transitions in the lifecourse through the conceptual lenses of identity, agency and structure. The theorising and findings about transition, and the questions they raise about new forms of support, management and pedagogy, offered in the book, are meant to provide a basis for further thinking and empirical study.

We begin this chapter with a brief overview of the context in which the interest in transitions from policy makers and researchers has emerged. Next we discuss different meanings, conceptualisations of 'transition' and relate these to questions about identity (people's sense of self), agency (the capacity for autonomous, empowered action) and structure (factors such as class, gender, race and economic and material conditions). In the final section we introduce the contributions to this book.

The importance of transitions

Like many ideas that inform policy, practice and research, 'transition' has numerous everyday and theoretical meanings. Children make a transition to adulthood, pupils move from primary to secondary school, from school to work, training or further education. More broadly, major life events are seen as transitions when people change their sense of who they are, perhaps from single status to marriage or the other way round, take on a new occupational role or emigrate to a new country. Such transitions can lead to profound change and be an impetus for new learning, or they can be unsettling, difficult and unproductive. Yet, while certain transitions are unsettling and difficult for some people, risk, challenge and even difficulty might also be important factors in successful transitions for others.

Transitions have increasingly become a political concern in the UK, particularly through numerous policy initiatives that encourage organisations and individuals to manage and support transitions more effectively. A large number of formal transitions are currently the focus of political interest and initiatives to manage them. They include:

Early years to school:

- The move from home to nursery/family centres.
- The change from nursery to primary school.
- The daily transition between home and school, including the transfer of knowledge and experience between the two contexts.
- The move from primary to secondary school.
- Making new subject choices within secondary education.

Post-compulsory education:

- The move from compulsory education to work, training or further education (FE).
- The move from training or FE to work, training or higher education.
- Transitions into and out of prison.

Learning through the lifecourse:

- The move from family, social and work life into formal literacy and numeracy programmes.
- Transitions at work between job roles and responsibilities.
- Transitions caused by restructuring and economic change.

Higher education:

- Transitions for 'non-traditional' participants between further and higher education.
- Progression through a subject discipline.
- Progression from programmes into higher degrees and to work.

Taken together, initiatives to encourage and support these transitions reflect a serious political investment. In different and sometimes imaginative ways, a variety of initiatives focus on the role of educational content, support systems and qualifications in 'easing transitions' between educational sites, between different phases of education and from education to other social sites. Policy makers are encouraging institutions and educational agencies to support different activities and processes of formal transitions through a growing range of assessment, guidance and support activities, including diagnostic assessment and systems of monitoring and review and 'blended' forms of teaching and assessment (IT, distance and face to face). These activities all aim to improve participation, retention, engagement and achievement.

In some respects, political interest in transitions is not new. The 1959 Crowther Report, for example, analysed the nature of risk, change and opportunity for 15- to 18-year-olds. Since 1997, initiatives to deal with transitions across the education system have reflected political concerns to ease transitions between educational sites, different phases and requirements, from education to other social sites, such as welfare, health and social work, and to minimise the difficulties that they cause for students. Particular concerns focus on the transition from nursery to primary school, the dip in achievement and motivation in the move to secondary school, a drop in retention in further/tertiary education at 17, and rising rates of dropout in higher education.

Political attempts to manage transitions more effectively emerge, in part, from the de-standardisation and increasing non-linearity of youth transitions, together with the individualisation and complexity of many lifecourse transitions for adults. Initiatives to deal with transitions also arise from other policies, such as targets for participation, achievement and engagement, proposals to raise the compulsory school leaving age to 18 and the creation of a new formal transition at 14. Policy therefore both stimulates concerns about success, failure and dropout and the role of transitions in these outcomes and creates normative expectations about appropriate processes, outcomes and dispositions.

Attempts to manage transitions are reinforced by pressures across Europe to deal with the ways in which globalisation is bringing about: the deregulation of labour markets; privatisation; technological advances; changing employment patterns; changing organisational forms and structures; demographic and labour market changes; new tensions between work and non-work life; lack of job security; changes in educational goals and systems for assessing them. A review of careers guidance policies in 37 countries, funded by the OECD and the World Bank, highlighted concerns about social exclusion and disadvantage caused by the inability to move easily through education and labour markets (see OECD 2004 and for a critical discussion see Watts and Sultana 2004).

Similar political concerns and responses also feature in the UK, embellished by a view that better management of specific social, educational and career transitions is crucial for breaking cycles of social and economic disadvantage. This view, first presented in an influential report 'Bridging the Gap' by the Social Exclusion Unit in 1999 is reinforced through 'Every Child Matters' (ECM) which promotes outcomes for health and well-being, leisure, and economic and educational achievement and requires different agencies to work together to achieve them (for critical evaluation of 'Bridging the Gap' see Colley and Hodkinson 2001). It also features in policies to raise achievement and increase participation for 'non-traditional' groups where better management of transitions into higher education for working-class young people is supposed to realise benefits of social cohesion and the creation of 'engaged citizens' (see Quinn et al. 2005; Biesta and Lawy 2006).

Supporting and managing transitions has become the focus of growing interest amongst policy makers, social service and education practitioners and researchers in the UK. From early years to widening participation initiatives in higher education, to continuing professional development and workplace learning, a dominant theme in policy texts, practical strategies and research reports is that transitions are problematic and need 'support', particularly for children, young people and adults deemed to be vulnerable, disaffected or 'at risk'.

Interventions and associated research activities have grown around this idea. A rapid increase in peer mentoring and buddy schemes in primary and secondary schools, colleges and universities runs alongside calls for closer alignment between home, school and life knowledge and learning, and between different institutional and assessment systems, curriculum content, pedagogy and assessment, and between the norms and expectations of different learning cultures. Notions of 'bridging' and 'blurring' divisions and differences between these aspects of educational experience are now commonplace in debates around transitions.

In parallel to the rise in concern about people's ability to navigate the norms, practices and expectations of institutional systems, broader concerns about the nature of change, progress and identity are leading to a huge growth of popular interest in work, social and personal transitions. Responses such as 'life coaching' and personal mentoring suggest that more people are seeking or being offered help in managing transitions. In educational and careers guidance this has produced a huge increase in formal mentoring schemes and, in particular, in 'engagement mentoring' and forms of mentoring that can be characterised as 'therapeutic' (Colley 2004; Ecclestone and Hayes 2008; also Cullingford 2006).

Despite the dominance of policy depictions and responses, some of the critiques cited above show profound tensions between images of flexible, self-managing, self-aware 'portfolio' workers who choose rationally to maximise their human capital, can deal with unpredictability and risk and move easily between transitions through life. Policy debate about transition is also based on very pessimistic assumptions about the negative effects of globalisation, risk and social upheaval. Notions of risk, a perceived need to ameliorate the emotional difficulty of transitions and concerns about people's ability to deal with transitions without professional help sit uneasily with the possibilities of creative risk, opportunity and change that transitions can create (see also Biesta 2006a).

It is therefore important to note at the outset that a great deal of concern, with subsequent calls for easing, smoothing and supporting transitions, arises from the idea that they are inherently unsettling, daunting and risky. This, as will also become clear in the contributions to this book, is an inherently problematic, and contested, premise for debating the nature and management of transitions.

Understanding transitions

Since the idea of transitions functions in different practical and theoretical contexts, it should not come as a surprise that there is no agreed-upon definition of what constitutes a transition. Different practical and academic interests result in different conceptualisations and theories which, in turn, lead to different ideas about how to manage or support transitions. In this section we map some of the main definitions and theoretical orientations and relate the idea of transitions to questions about identity, agency and structure.

Navigating pathways, structures and systems

Two especially influential areas for the study of transitions are lifecourse research and careers and guidance research. For example, Elder *et al.* (2003) depict lifecourse as a theoretical orientation that focuses on 'age-graded patterns that are embedded in social institutions and history' and in which it is assumed that 'lives are influenced by an ever-changing historical and biographical context' (Elder *et al.* 2003: 8). Lifecourse research emerged from social pathway studies, which focused on lifecourse as a system of statuses (the work of Cain 1964, cited by Elder *et al.* 2003) and work on career, particularly role histories in education, work and family. Lifecourse research tends to reinforce an institutional or context-specific image of transitions, suggesting that 'individuals generally work out their own lifecourse in relation to institutionalized pathways and normative patterns' (Elder *et al.* 2003: 8). This suggests that transitions are not only the product of social institutions but are also produced by social expectations (although it can, of course, be argued that institutions are nothing but the embodiment of social expectations).

From a lifecourse perspective it is therefore possible to make a distinction between (1) transitions in relation to institutionalised pathways which are about transitions as 'changes in state or role [which] often involve changes in status and identity, both personally and socially, and thus open up opportunities for behavioral change' (Elder *et al.* 2003: 8), and (2) transitions in relation to more general normative patterns and social expectations. The idea of social expectations suggests that every society has a system of social expectations regarding age-appropriate behaviour. There are not only age-linked expectations but also age-linked sanctions and options. Lifecourse research thus makes use of a 'normative concept of social time' which specifies 'an appropriate age for transitions' and thus makes it possible to say that individual transitions occur as relatively 'early' and 'late' transitions (Elder *et al.* 2003: 10). Research shows that age norms are different in different countries/cultures/times and differ in strictness, which implies that what counts as a lifecourse transition is closely connected to contextual and historical factors.

The notion of transitions as the navigation of institutionalised pathways or systems is supported by research on career by Pallas who describes transitions as attributes of social systems rather than as attributes of an individual's lifecourse. 'Pathways are well-travelled sequences of transitions that are shaped by cultural and structural forces. [...] A trajectory is an attribute of an individual, whereas a pathway is an attribute of a social system' (Pallas 2003: 168). From this perspective, educational attainment is determined by movement through 'an ordered sequence of educational transitions' (Pallas 2003: 172–3).

Other research on careers and guidance draws on influential studies by Super and Ginzberg, amongst others, using perspectives from developmental psychology to explore lifecourse transitions (see Collin and Young 2000 for an overview). An important and often overlooked counter to perspectives summarised here comes from feminist critiques of the profound differences and inequalities of work and life transitions for women, particularly through motherhood and career patterns (see, for example, Gatens and McKinnon 1998; Hughes 2002).

Navigating cognition, emotion and sense of self

Researchers agree that transition is not the same as 'movement' or 'transfer', although it involves both. Instead, some research focuses on transitions and shifts in identity and agency as people progress through the education system. For example, Lam and Pollard analyse the transition of children from home to nursery school and they differentiate between transition as the movement from one institutional setting or from one activity to another, namely as a change of context. They differentiate further between horizontal transitions as 'movement between various settings that a child and his/her family may encounter within the same time frame' while vertical transitions refer to 'movement among education/care programmes, health and social services across time' (Lam and Pollard 2006: 124).

From this perspective, transition is a change process but also a shift from one identity to another.

> [Transition is] the process of change that is experienced when children (and their families) move from one setting to another ... to when the child is more fully established as a member of the new setting. It is usually a time of intense and accelerated development demands that are socially regulated.
>
> (Lam and Pollard 2006: 125)

This depiction means that managing transitions requires more than facilitating changes in context or easing transfer between them: effective transitions require a better understanding of how people progress cognitively, emotionally and socially between different subjects at different stages of their learning, and how they navigate the complex demands of different contexts. A number of studies examine the psychological and sociocultural factors that affect how children manage, influence and adapt to, the transition from home to nursery, home to primary school, primary school to secondary or from national settings for compulsory schooling to institutions in other countries (Lam and Pollard 2006; Pollard and Filer 1999; Hughes this volume; Fabian and Dunlop 2002; Fabian 2006).

'Becoming somebody'

Some research from the fields of careers, guidance and life transitions challenges the depiction of transition as change brought about through navigating institutional norms and procedures, focusing instead on processes of 'being' and 'becoming'. Work on 'careership' by Hodkinson *et al.* (1996) has developed new thinking about the ways in which people make social and cultural transitions, individually and collectively, in response to a broader context of structural change, such as opportunities in the labour market or changes in work structures and organisation. This contribution arises from an influential body of work on 'pupil career' and the 'learning careers' of young people (see Pollard 1985; Bloomer and Hodkinson 1997).

Numerous studies show how transitions combine turning points, milestones or life events with subtle, complex processes of 'becoming somebody' personally, educationally and occupationally (see Banks *et al.* 1992; Ball *et al.* 2000; Reay 2005; Hodkinson *et al.* 1996; Evans 2002; Hughes 2002; Felstead *et al.* this volume; Colley 2006; Hodkinson *et al.* 2007). Some researchers define transition as 'personal transition between two states of "being" – the before and after of specified learning experiences' (Gallacher and Cleary 2007). Blair (2007) defines it as a 'discontinuity in a person's life-space'. Processes of 'becoming somebody' are sometimes a response to particular events, and sometimes events arise out of shifts and developments in identity and agency. For example, the evolution of a professional or occupational identity in a particular field, navigating uncertain labour and educational systems, changes in cultural identity for asylum seekers or migrants taking up educational opportunities in a new culture or for women returning to education after time at home might trigger a turning point or life event, or arise from one.

Such transitions, which also involve setbacks or processes of 'unbecoming' over time, are located and enacted within specific fields rather than emerging from a fixed series of rational decisions and they emerge through periods of routine and stability as well as from change. They are influenced by elements of a person's whole life rather than merely through their involvement with education systems. Transitions are therefore not always discernible events or processes and a transition may happen long after subtle, subconscious changes in feelings and attitudes.

Life-as-transition

Post-modern, post-structural and some feminist perspectives challenge transition depicted as rites of passage, movement through life stages, bridges that connect old and new, 'crisis events' or 'critical incidents' and life change rooted in theories of discernible processes of 'typical' adult maturation. In contrast to movements from one life stage to another, bounded by periods of stability, many women argue that they have been psychologically in transit almost all their adolescent and adult lives. From this perspective, many depictions of transition ignore the particular distinctiveness of women's transitional experiences and use, instead, androcentric lenses that overlook how certain transitions create emotional conflict that is crucial to their outcomes and management, whilst also reproducing inequalities of class and gender (see Hughes 2002; Skeggs 1997; Colley 2006). Such perspectives illuminate transition as something much more ephemeral and fluid, where the whole of life is a form of transition, a permanent state of 'becoming' and 'unbecoming', much of which is unconscious, contradictory and iterative.

This work not only challenges notions of linearity, chronology, time and change (see Colley in this volume), it also questions the assumption that people can generate a coherent narrative about themselves. According to Quinn and colleagues' study of working-class students leaving higher education early, individuals construct multiple identities that draw on many interlocking cultural narratives and these are often classed and gendered (Quinn et al. 2005; see also Quinn in this volume). This work shows how working class young men combined narratives of masculinity, nostalgia for extinct employment opportunities and hedonism as reasons to leave university.

A feminist or post-structuralist perspective therefore undermines assumptions that 'becoming somebody' involves a unified subject capable of being transformed: 'a subject is not an "entity" or thing, or a relation between mind (interior) and body (exterior). Instead, it must be understood as a series of flows, energies and movements and capacities, a series of fragments or segments capable of being linked together in ways other than those that congeal it into an identity' (Grosz, quoted by Quinn, this volume). A similar view is expressed in post-structural understandings of subjectivity as that which is always at stake in our relationships with others rather than as what can be taken for granted in such relationships (see Biesta 2006b). From this standpoint, 'we are always lost in transition, not just in the sense of moving from one task or context to another, but as a condition of our subjectivity' (Quinn, this volume).

Transition, identity, agency and structure

Perspectives on transition, summarised above, show that political, academic and practical interests in transition are underpinned both explicitly and implicitly by different views about the extent to which people's identity and agency and the effects of structure affect assumptions about the processes and outcomes of different types of transition in the education system, and the best ways to deal with them. While the three concepts are inextricably connected, researchers explore transitions in different ways, depending on the emphasis they place on each or all of the concepts.

Identity

Broadly, identity can be defined as the ways in which the self is represented and understood in dynamic, multidimensional and evolving ways. Stuart Hall defines identity as 'the unstable point at which the unspeakable stories of subjectivity meet the narratives of history and of a culture' (Hall quoted by Wetherall 2005). Contemporary studies of identity explore the ways in which the social, personal and cultural meet, the subsequent ways in which people are 'stitched into' social relations, how identities are made within this psycho-social nexus, and the possible actions that flow from understanding one's place in a system of social relations (Wetherall 2005, see also 2006). Identity is therefore constructed through complex interactions between different forms of capital (cultural, social, economic and emotional), broader social and economic conditions, interactions and relationships in various contexts, and cognitive and psychological strategies.

Successful creation of a viable identity in navigating transitions into school and between home and school is a central theme in the Home–School Knowledge Transfer project in the TLRP. This develops insights from longitudinal, ethnographic studies of children and young people's learning/schooling careers through primary and secondary education and post-education careers (Pollard 1985; Pollard and Filer 1999). This work depicts identity as having a narrative structure that enables children to tell viable, coherent stories about themselves and their lives in order to achieve a viable way of 'being' in a particular context. Brookes argues that:

> Individual learners are active agents constructing understanding and 'making sense' of new experiences and challenges by drawing on various cultural resources at their disposal. In the case of transition, pupils' relationships with their parents, siblings, teachers and peers will affect the types of support received as new learning challenges are encountered.
>
> (Brookes 2006: 5)

From this perspective, transitions become problematic if a viable identity in one context does not transfer to another. Having to reconstruct an identity narrative can disrupt a viable way of being in a context, making transitions demotivating and stressful (see Pollard and Filer 1999; Lam and Pollard 2006; Osborn *et al.* 2006).

Some researchers argue that the socially constructed components of identity should be of special interest.

> Such constructions [of identity] happen in relation to horizons of interpretation opened by the society and by interaction with significant others. They involve configurations of the past, perceptions of the present and imagined futures. 'Ideal identity' is part of such projections of the individual in the future and their might be a mismatch between the ideal identity as harboured by an individual and the externally imposed models received as pressures from school, family or peers.
>
> (Hayward *et al.* 2005: 116)

Agency

In the most general sense 'agency' refers to people's ability or capacity for action. A more precise definition sees agency as the extent to which human action is considered *not* to be determined by 'inner' or 'outer' factors. It thus refers to the underdetermined nature of human action in relation to material (e.g. biological) or social structures, processes and conditions. Philosophically the idea of 'agency' is connected to the notion of 'free will' and voluntary action. This helps to explain why discussions about agency are not exclusively empirical but contain normative ideas about the extent to which one believes that human beings ought to be seen as capable of voluntary action.

A complication with the notion of 'agency' is that it functions in two radically different theoretical contexts or 'language games'. On the one hand 'agency' refers to a particular *phenomenon* – the human capacity for voluntary action – that can be studied and theorised in its own right (for an extensive overview of work in this tradition see Emirbayer and Mische 1998). On the other hand 'agency' plays a central role as an explanatory concept in sociological theory and research that aims to understand or explain human action. The guiding question for such work concerns the extent to which human action – either individual action or social action – can be understood or explained by referring to the agentic actions of individuals and the extent to which human action can be understood or explained by referring to the influence of social structures. The 'structure–agency debate' came to the fore in sociology in the 1970s and 1980s in the context of increased attention to practice and an increased concern for the analysis of power relations and conflict. It can even be argued that 'structure' and 'agency' have become *the* framing concepts of modern sociology.

In order to reduce the confusion about the different theoretical contexts in which the same concept, 'agency', figures, Martin Hollis (1994) has made the helpful distinction between individualistic and holistic strategies in understanding and explaining human action. Whereas structural and cultural approaches count as holistic strategies in that they seek to account for human action through reference to wider, more encompassing structures and processes, rational choice theory is an example of an individualistic strategy, just as, for example, psychological theories which focus on the 'ego' as the main driver of agentic action (see Levine 2005, see also Biesta and Tedder 2006).

Consideration of agency, understood as the capacity to give direction to one's life through interaction with social and material conditions, both individually and collectively, requires self-direction, self-efficacy, opportunities to exercise autonomy and perhaps a desire to shape a specific field or context. The idea that education can, and should, help people develop their capacities for agentic and autonomous action has been a long-standing tradition in Western societies, at least since the Enlightenment.

Yet, the rhetoric of agency often elides 'choice', 'action' and 'autonomy' in confusing ways and therefore suggests that people can 'navigate' transitions without regard for factors that influence, structure and limit their actions and choices. Such an 'over-agentic' view of human action has played an influential role in forms of lifecourse theory and research. Elder, for example, presents agency as the way in which 'individuals construct their own lifecourse through the choices and actions they take within the opportunities and constraints of history and social circumstance' (Elder *et al.* 2003: 11). As Emirbayer and Mische (1998) have shown, such teleological and voluntaristic views have also played an important role in the work on agency more generally, for example, in the writings of Parsons, Coleman and Habermas (see Emirbayer and Mische 1998: 964–7). They identify pragmatism, and more specifically the work of George Herbert Mead, as the first approach that did not perceive human action 'as the pursuit of preestablished ends' (Emirbayer and Mische 1998: 967; see also Joas 1996). Against this background they suggest defining agency as

> *the temporally constructed engagement by actors of different structural environments – the temporal-relational contexts of action – which, through the interplay of habit, imagination and judgement, both reproduces and transforms those structures in interactive responses to the problems caused by changing historical situations.*
> (Emirbayer and Mische 1998: 970; emphasis in original)

Such a definition helps to explain why agency should not be seen as a capacity that individuals possess, but should rather be understood as something that individuals *do*, that is, as something that can be *achieved* in particular contexts and situations and at particular points in time (see also Biesta and Tedder 2006, 2007).

Combining agency, identity and structure

The importance of the contribution from sociology to questions of agency is to highlight the effects of structural factors such as class, race and gender, and economic and occupational conditions in understanding and explaining individual and social action. For example, studies of working-class participation and 'dropout' from higher education show the extent to which agency is affected by the ways in which working-class and middle-class young people and adults are attracted to, and have access to, very different courses and 'types' of institution. In addition, the apparent exercise of agency in deciding to drop out is often presented by careers and other agencies as confirming 'helpless failure': dropout becomes a self perpetuating narrative and this discourse is more important than individual choice or even structure (see Quinn this volume; see also Ball *et al.* 2005). This perspective reveals the role of structural factors in the achievement of agency by identifying how different access to economic, social and symbolic forms of capital arises from key social divisions, framing possibilities and restricting social mobility (see, for example, Skeggs 1997; Reay 2005; Ball *et al.* 2005).

The TLRP's Transforming Learning Cultures in Further Education project also explored identity but embedded it in consideration of agency and structure by connecting it to Bourdieu's interlinked notions of 'habitus' and 'field' (see James and Biesta 2007). The project showed that transition by students and their teachers through the demands of a learning programme and the evolution of an acceptable occupational identity was a gradual process of *orientation*, navigated between the tensions of idealised and realised identities in different vocational cultures (see Colley *et al.* 2003). Identity and habitus that embody and enact past and current dispositions and horizons for action interact in complex and subtle ways with the practices, expectations, norms and relationships of specific learning cultures. The unpredictable and idiosyncratic features of this interaction in different learning cultures shape identity and habitus and create new practices (see James and Biesta 2007, and, for discussion of the limitations of Bourdieu's ideas, particularly with regard to questions about social justice, see Avis 2007).

Many researchers argue, therefore, that it is only possible to understand transitions through a focus on agency and identity together with an account of how these are shaped, constrained and sometimes determined by the material conditions and normative expectations of different structural factors. Considerations of structure also reveal the day-to-day interactions between habitus, adaptation and progression through specific transitions which shape identity and agency in both exploitative and transforming ways. In her analysis of vocational habitus of young women learning to become nursery nurses, Colley, for example, explores how gendered notions of caring for others and the deployment of emotional labour are crucial to the development of that habitus within particular fields that both offer and constrain what Bourdieu calls 'horizons for action':

> As students talked about what they have learned as they participated in their work placements, their narratives centred on coping with the emotional demands of the job, and revealed a vocational culture of detachment in the workplace which contrasts somewhat with the nurturing ideal that is officially promoted.
>
> (Colley 2006: 15; see also Bates 1991)

Conflict between the 'nurturing ideal', formalised in the childcare curriculum and the 'vocational detachment of the job', produces coping strategies, but also frictions as students move between the two contexts, particularly in relation to the cultivation of 'acceptable' forms of emotional labour as part of becoming 'respectable' young women. This emotional element of the transitional process, as students move into and out of different settings is not only problematic emotionally for some students; it also reinforces class and gendered exploitation because cultural resources in the form of emotional labour can only be deployed as capital in a field of low status, low pay and poor conditions. Yet, it is also a means of escape from what young people and their tutors see as the 'mass of the non-respectable' (Colley 2006).

Transitions in the lifecourse

While some researchers do not separate the effects of structural conditions from the construction and shaping of identities and agency in understanding the complexities of transitions in the lifecourse, others focus their efforts more explicitly on one of these dimensions. Some do this for methodological reasons in order to pay specific attention to one of the dimensions without claiming that it can be isolated from the other two. Others bring different theoretical framings to the research on transitions and therefore see the interrelationships between identity, agency and structure in a different light. The chapters that follow represent clearly the range of different methodological and theoretical approaches in the emerging field of research on transitions in the lifecourse. In doing so, they not only shed light on a wide range of lifecourse transitions, but also show the strengths and weaknesses of particular methodological approaches and theoretical framings. Taken together the chapters make an important contribution to our understanding of transitions and learning in the lifecourse.

Acknowledgement

We are extremely grateful to Theo Blackmore (Disability Cornwall) and to Helen Colley (Manchester Metropolitan University) for extensive contributions to the literature review and for comments on various drafts of this chapter and the working paper it came from.

Bibliography

Avis, J. (2007) *Education, Policy and Social Justice: Learning and Skills*, London: Continuum.

Ball, S.J., David, M. and Reay, D. (2005) *Degrees of Difference*, London: RoutledgeFalmer.

Ball, S.J., Maguire, M. and Macrae, S. (2000) *Choices, Pathways and Transitions Post-16: New Youth, New Economies in the Global City*, London: RoutledgeFalmer.

Banks, M., Bates, I., Breakwell, G., Bynner, J., Emler, N., Jamieson, L. and Roberts, K. (1992) *Careers and Identities*, Buckingham: Open University Press.

Bates, I. (1991) 'Closely observed training: an exploration of links between social structures, training and identity', *International Studies in Sociology of Education*, 1: 225–43.

Biesta, G.J.J. (2006a) 'What's the point of lifelong learning if lifelong learning has no point? On the democratic deficit of policies for lifelong learning', *European Educational Research Journal*, 5: 169–80.

Biesta, G.J.J. (2006b). *Beyond Learning: Democratic Education for a Human Future*, Boulder, CO: Paradigm Publishers.

Biesta, G.J.J. and Lawy, R.S. (2006) 'From teaching citizenship to learning democracy. Overcoming individualism in research, policy and practice', *Cambridge Journal of Education*, 36: 63–79.

Biesta, G.J.J. and Tedder, M.T. (2006) 'How is agency possible? Towards an ecological understanding of agency-as-achievement', Working Paper 5 for the Learning Lives project, Exeter: University of Exeter.

Biesta, G. and Tedder, M. (2007) 'Agency and learning in the lifecourse: towards an ecological perspective', *Studies in the Education of Adults*, 39: 132–49.

Blair, S. (2007) 'The prevailing discourse of lifelong learning and the contrasting narrative from older people', paper presented at the Researching Transitions in Lifelong Learning Conference, University of Stirling, June 2007.

Bloomer, J.M. and Hodkinson, P. (1997) *Moving into FE: the Voice of the Learner*, London: FEDA.

Brookes, J. (2006) 'Exploring the secondary transfer of gifted and talented pupils', paper from the TLRP Home–School Knowledge Transfer project, Bristol: University of Bristol.

Colley, H. (2004) *Mentoring for Social Inclusion: a Critical Approach to Nurturing Mentoring Relationships*, London: Routledge.

Colley, H (2006) 'Learning to labour with feeling: class, gender and emotion in childcare education and training', *Contemporary Issues in Early Childhood*, 7: 15–29.

Colley, H. and Hodkinson, P. (2001) 'Problems with "Bridging the Gap": the reversal of structure and agency in addressing social exclusion', *Critical Social Policy*, 21: 337–61.

Colley, H., James, D., Tedder, M. and Diment, K. (2003) 'Learning as becoming in vocational education and training: class, gender and the role of vocational habitus', *Journal of Vocational Education and Training*, 55: 471–96.

Collin, A and Young, R.A. (eds) (2000) *The Future of Career*, Cambridge: Cambridge University Press.

Cullingford, C. (2006) *Mentoring: an International Perspective*, Aldershot: Ashgate Publishing.

Ecclestone, K. and Hayes, D. (2008) *The Dangerous Rise of Therapeutic Education*, London: Routledge.

Elder, G.H., Kirkpartrick Johnson, M. and Crosnoe, R. (2003) 'The emergence and development of lifecourse theory', in J.T. Mortimer and M.J. Shanahan (eds) *Handbook of the Life Course*, New York: Plenum.

Emirbayer, M. and Mische, A. (1998) 'What is agency?', *American Journal of Sociology*, 103: 962–1023.

Evans, K, (2002) 'Taking control of their lives? Agency in young adult transitions in England and the new Germany', *Journal of Youth Studies*, 5: 245–69.

Fabian, H. (2006) 'Secondary school transitions', paper presented at the ESRC/TLRP seminar series Transitions through the Lifecourse, University of Exeter, January 2006.

Fabian, H. and Dunlop, A.-W. (2002) *Transitions in the Early Years: Debating Continuity and Progression for Children in Early Education*, London: Routledge.

Gallacher, J. and Cleary, P. (2007) 'Learning careers: exploring transitions between community-based further education to main college campuses', paper presented at the Researching Transitions in Lifelong Learning Conference, University of Stirling, June 2007.

Gatens, M. and McKinnon, A. (eds) (1998) *Gender and Institutions: Welfare, Work and Citizenship*, Cambridge: Cambridge University Press.

Hayward, G., Hodgson, A., Johnson, J., Oancea, A., Pring, R., Spours, K., Wilde, S. and Wright, S. (2005) *The Nuffield Review of 14-19 Education and Training: annual report 2004–2005*, Oxford: University of Oxford.

Hodkinson, P., Sparkes, A.C. and Hodkinson, H. (1996) *Triumphs and Tears: Young People, Markets, and the Transition from School to Work*, London: David Fulton Publishers.

Hodkinson, P., Hawthorne, R., Ford, G. and Hodkinson, H. (2007) 'Learning careers, learning lives and informal learning', paper presented at the Researching Transitions in Lifelong Learning Conference, University of Stirling, June 2007.

Hollis, M. (1994) *The Philosophy of Social Science*, Cambridge: Cambridge University Press.

Hughes, C. (2002) *Feminist Theory and Research*, London: Sage Publications.

Joas, H. (1996) *The Creativity of Action*, Chicago: University of Chicago Press.

James, D. and Biesta, G.J.J. (2007) *Improving Learning Cultures in Further Education*, London: Routledge.

Lam, M. and Pollard, A. (2006) 'A conceptual framework for understanding children as agents in the transition from home to kindergarten', *Early Years*, 26: 123–41.

Levine, C. (2005) 'What happened to agency? Some observations concerning the post-modern perspective on identity', *Identity: An International Journal of Theory and Research*, 5: 175–85.

OECD (2004) *Career Guidance and Public Policy: Bridging the Gap*, Paris: Organisation for Economic Cooperation and Development.

Osborn, M., McNess, M. and Pollard, A. (2006) 'Identity and transfer: a new focus for home–school knowledge exchange', *Educational Review*, 58: 415–33.

Pallas, A.M. (2003) 'Educational transitions, trajectories, and pathways', in J.T. Mortimer and M.J. Shanahan (eds) *Handbook of the Life Course*, New York: Plenum.

Pollard, A. (1985) *The Social World of Primary School*, London: Cassell.

Pollard, A. and Filer, A. (1999) *The Social World of Pupil Career: Strategic Biographies through Primary School*, London: Cassell.

Quinn, J., Thomas, L., Slack, K., Casey, L., Thexton, W. and Noble, J. (2005) *From Life Crisis to Lifelong Learning: Rethinking Working Class 'Drop Out' from Higher Education*, York: Joseph Rowntree Foundation.

Reay, D. (2005) *Beyond Consciousness: The Psychic Landscape of Social Class*, London: Sage Books.

Reay, D. and William, D. (1999) '"I'll be a nothing": structure, agency and the construction of identity through assessment', *British Educational Research Journal*, 25: 343–54.

Skeggs, B. (1997) *Formulations of Class and Gender: Becoming Respectable*, London: Sage Books.

Watts, A. and Sultana, R. (2004) 'Careers guidance policies in 37 countries: contrasts and common themes', *International Journal for Educational and Vocational Guidance*, 4: 105–22.

Wetherall, M. (2005) 'Identity and the ESRC identities programme', paper presented at the Teaching and Learning Research Programme Annual Conference, University of Warwick, November 2005.

Wetherall, M. (2006) 'Identities and transitions', paper presented at the ESRC/TLRP seminar series Transitions through the Lifecourse, University of Nottingham, October 2006.

2 The daily transition between home and school

Martin Hughes, Pamela Greenhough,
Wan Ching Yee and Jane Andrews

Introduction

This chapter is concerned with the daily transition between home and school that is made by children of primary school age (5–11 years). This transition is so commonplace that it might seem unremarkable, and indeed, it has received little explicit attention from educational policy makers in the UK and elsewhere. Yet, as we shall see in this chapter, it is a transition that raises questions of fundamental importance concerning the educational attainment of different groups of children. Moreover, as we shall also see, attempts to manage this transition by exchanging information between home and school raise major ethical and political questions about the appropriate boundaries between the two contexts, and about the underlying relationship between public and private lives.

The daily transition between home and school differs in some important ways from most of the transitions considered elsewhere in this book. In particular, it is an ongoing and oft-repeated transition between two simultaneously coexisting contexts in a child's life, rather than a single transition between two successive contexts (as in the transition from primary to secondary school, for example, see Chapter 3 by James and Beedell, this volume). This difference has been conceptualised in various ways by different authors. For example, Lam and Pollard (2006) have talked in terms of 'horizontal' and 'vertical' transitions. Lam and Pollard use the term 'horizontal transitions' to refer to the 'movement across various settings which a child and his/her family may encounter within the same time frame'. In contrast, they use the term 'vertical transitions' to refer to 'movement among care/education programmes, health and social services across time' (Lam and Pollard 2006: 124). An alternative terminology is provided by Bransford *et al.* (2006) who use the distinction between 'synchronic' and 'diachronic' transitions. Bransford *et al.* (2006) argue for the need to study transitions along temporal dimensions that are both synchronic (e.g. as children move from home to school on a particular day) and diachronic (e.g. as people move from post-secondary 'training' to occupational work).

While the 'horizontal' or 'synchronic' transition between home and school clearly differs in some fundamental ways from other 'vertical' or 'diachronic' transitions, it also raises many of the same underlying questions about transitions highlighted by Ecclestone, Biesta and Hughes in Chapter 1 of this book.

The notion of identity is clearly salient: as part of their daily transition children must develop and negotiate a 'school identity', which may differ in important respects from their 'home identity'; they may also need to maintain two (or more) contrasting identities at the same time. The notion of agency is also salient, as children discover and come to terms with the realisation that their options, roles and personal potency are not the same in the two locations. Aspects of structure are also important: we shall see later in this chapter how the nature of home–school transitions may be fundamentally shaped by factors such as ethnicity, gender and social class. There are also questions about what happens when attempts are made to 'manage' children's daily transitions, particularly through the two-way flow of information between home and school.

In this chapter we will draw on data from the ESRC/TLRP funded Home–School Knowledge Exchange project to explore these issues. We start by looking at the way in which the relationship between home and school has been conceptualised in recent English policy documents, and at research that illuminates this relationship. We then propose a way of conceptualising the daily transition between home and school in terms of Lave and Wenger's work on communities of practice, and particularly Wenger's work on boundaries. We next provide a short description of the Home–School Knowledge Exchange project and present data from the project relevant to the issues of identity, agency and structure outlined above. This leads on to an account of attempts to manage the transition between home and school through a process of home–school knowledge exchange, based on the increased flow of information between the two contexts, and at the wider ethical and political concerns that this raises. The chapter ends by looking at the implications for transitions more generally.

The policy context

While there is growing interest among UK policy makers in transitions in general, there is little specific attention paid to the daily transition between home and school. In England, for example, the recent Children's Plan (Department for Children, Schools and Families 2007) states that one of its key targets for 2020 is 'to enhance children and young people's well-being, particularly at key transition points in their lives' (ibid., summary, para. 35). However the main transitions addressed within the Plan itself are the initial transfer from preschool or early years settings into primary school (ibid., para. 3.51) and the transition from primary school into secondary school (ibid., para. 3.78). In the same way, the earlier Every Child Matters proposals (see Department for Education and Skills 2004) also prioritise the transitions into and out of primary school and make little or no mention of the daily transition between home and school.

While little explicit attention is currently being paid to children's daily transitions between home and school, the same cannot be said for home–school relationships in general. Indeed, there is a long tradition in the UK, dating back to the Plowden Report of 1967 and beyond, of schools and teachers being urged to involve parents more closely in their children's education. While the specific rationale for such involvement has varied over the years, its desirability in the eyes of policy makers has remained unchanged (see for example Docking 1990; Hughes, Wikeley and Nash 1994; Vincent 1996).

In England, current policy documents emphasise the importance of schools promoting 'parental engagement' in their children's learning. As a recent guide for school leaders (Becta 2008: 2) puts it: 'If there was any doubt, recent research has shown that parental engagement is a decisive factor in determining learner achievement. What really matters is that learners feel their parents are paying attention, engaged in their learning and care about their performance'. Similarly, the 2007 document 'Every Parent Matters' (Department for Education and Skills 2007) refers approvingly to an earlier review entitled '2020 Vision', and notes 'the fundamental contribution parental engagement can make to improving educational attainment'. Specific recommendations from these documents for engaging parents include improved two-way communication with parents based around easier to understand information about their child's progress and regular parental access to a 'learning guide' – a member of staff who works with individual children to review their learning goals and achievements.

Parental engagement, then, is being promoted as a means of raising attainment in school. However, attempts to involve parents in the work of the school have been criticised in some quarters as representing a major shift in the power relations between home and school, what Edwards and Warin (1999) call the 'colonisation' of the home by the school. A similar critique has been made by Dyson and Robson (1999), who argue that parental involvement can be seen as a 'form of cultural imperialism, devaluing the practices and values of families who might already be marginalised'. Moreover, the two-way exchange of information between teachers and parents, and the consequent blurring of boundaries between home and school, might be seen as a further example of the unnecessary and unwelcome intrusion of the state into the private lives of children and their families (e.g. Ecclestone and Hayes 2009). We will revisit these important concerns later in the chapter.

Home, school and attainment

One research study that is frequently quoted as showing the importance of parental engagement is a review carried out for the DfES in 2003 by Desforges and Abouchaar. Desforges and Abouchaar's main conclusion was that, what they termed, 'at-home good parenting' had a significant positive effect on children's achievement and adjustment even after all other factors had been taken out of the equation. By 'at-home good parenting', they included factors such as parental values and educational aspirations and the way these are manifested in discussion with their children and other shared activities. Desforges and Abouchaar also noted that differences between parents in their levels of parental involvement were associated with factors such as social class, poverty and health.

Desforges and Abouchaar's conclusions can be seen as an example of what has been termed a 'deficit' position. Essentially such a position assumes that some groups of parents or families – such as those from particular social class groups – lack certain parenting abilities or aptitudes and that this explains their children's relative underachievement in school. In contrast, other researchers in the home–school area have adopted what might be termed a 'difference' position (e.g. Heath 1983; Lareau 2000). These authors argue that the ways in which different groups of parents relate to their children reflect deeply rooted differences in cultural beliefs and values. For some groups, these cultural beliefs and values are closer to those of the school than for other groups, and hence their children are more likely to achieve educational success.

One recent example of such a 'difference' perspective is provided by Street *et al.* (2005). In addressing the issue of why children of lower social classes have generally lower attainment in mathematics, Street *et al.* explicitly stress that they are not adopting a 'deficit' position. Rather they argue that children from all backgrounds have access to 'cultural resources' at home, but that these resources are not all the same. For some children, Street *et al.* argue that their cultural resources are 'more consonant' with those of the school, while for others their cultural resources may be more 'dissonant'. Indeed, for some children the dissonance may be so great that they can hardly engage with school practices at all.

These issues are clearly important for considering the daily transition between home and school. If the differences between home and school values, beliefs and practices are wider for some groups of children than they are for others, then the daily transition may be harder for these children to negotiate than for others – with potentially highly significant consequences for their school achievement.

Transitions as movements between communities of practice

In thinking about the daily transition between home and school, we have found it helpful to draw on ideas put forward by Wenger (1998) when describing movements between different *communities of practice*. This term refers to the communities which are formed over time when people engage in the sustained pursuit of shared purposes or enterprises (e.g. Lave and Wenger 1991; Wenger 1998).

In their earlier work, Lave and Wenger focus on the changes that take place within – rather than across – particular communities of practice. For example, a central theme of their 1991 collaboration is that learning can be seen as a process of *legitimate peripheral participation*, a process through which newcomers to a community of practice progress to becoming full and central members of that practice. However, Wenger's recent work has focused more clearly on individuals being simultaneously members of multiple communities of practice, and on the ways in which individuals move between them. For example, Wenger (1998) pays particular attention to the *boundaries* between communities of practice and looks at ways in which continuities across these boundaries can be maintained. One way he suggests this is done is through *boundary objects*, a term originally used by Star and Griesemer (1989) to describe 'objects that serve to coordinate the perspective of different constituencies for some purpose' (Wenger 1998: 106). A second way of maintaining continuity is through the practice of *brokering*, which occurs when individuals use their membership of multiple communities of practice 'to transfer some element of one practice into another' (Wenger 1998: 109). Wenger points out that 'the job of brokering is complex. It involves processes of translation, coordination and alignment between perspectives' (Wenger 1998: 109).

The multiple membership of different communities of practice is also central to Wenger's conceptualisation of identity. He argues that an identity should not be regarded as a static or singular entity, but instead should be viewed as '*a nexus of multimembership*'. This notion of identity as a nexus means that work frequently has to be done to bring about a *reconciliation* of the different forms of membership forming the nexus. Indeed, Wenger proposes that:

> The work of reconciliation may be the most significant challenge faced by learners who move from one community of practice to another. For instance, when a child moves from a family to a classroom, when an immigrant moves from one culture to another, or when an employee moves from the ranks to a management position, learning involves more than appropriating new pieces of information. Learners must often deal with conflicting forms of individuality and competence as defined in different communities.
>
> (Wenger 1998: 160)

Wenger suggests that this process of reconciliation may not be easy, and that membership of multiple communities of practice may involve tensions and conflicts that are never fully resolved. At the same time, he makes clear that in his view 'multimembership and the work of reconciliation are intrinsic to the very concept of identity' (Wenger 1998: 161).

As the above quote from Wenger suggests, the notion of movement between communities of practice can usefully be applied to the daily transition between home and school. However, this does not imply that home and school are simple, unitary communities of practice. Rather, as Wenger himself suggests (e.g. 1998: 6), there may be several different and overlapping communities of practice in each location. At school, for example, a child might be a member of a classroom group, a football team, a drama club and a playground clique, while out-of-school they may be members of an immediate family, a wider or extended family, a cultural or religious group, and a neighbourhood chess club. In other words, a child may simultaneously be a member of, and make regular transitions between, a number of different communities of practice.

From this perspective we can draw on Wenger's ideas about moving between communities of practice to ask critical questions about the daily transition from home to school. We can look at the boundaries between different home and school practices, at how they are constituted and maintained, and at how easy or difficult it is for different children to cross them. We can try to identify boundary objects that are intended to coordinate different communities of practice, and ask whether and how they do so in practice. We can look at whether parents, teachers or children engage in the activity of brokering, and with what results. Finally, we can look at the ways in which membership of different communities of practice shapes children's identities, and whether they are carrying out acts of reconciliation between these different aspects of their identities.

The Home–School Knowledge Exchange project

In this chapter we address some of these issues by drawing on the work of the Home–School Knowledge Exchange project. This project, which took place between 2001 and 2006, worked closely with teachers, parents and children to develop, implement and evaluate the impact of home–school knowledge exchange activities. The project had three main strands, one focusing on literacy at Key Stage 1 (5–7 years), one focusing on numeracy at Key Stage 2 (7–11 years) and one focusing on primary/secondary transfer. Within each strand an experienced teacher was seconded to work part-time on the project developing and implementing knowledge exchange activities.

The project took place in the two cities of Bristol and Cardiff. Within each strand, four primary schools were involved in the 'action' side of the research, two in Bristol and two in Cardiff. In each city, one school had a high proportion of children who were eligible for free school meals, while the other school had a low proportion of such children. In each city, the intake to the schools reflected the ethnic diversity present in both cities.

Within each strand, a cohort of between 250 and 350 children were assessed at regular intervals using standardised measures of attainment and learning disposition. In addition, a smaller group of around 24 'target' children in each strand were selected for more intensive study. These target children, their parents and teachers were periodically interviewed and observed in the classroom; they also made videos about their out-of-school lives. A smaller group of four children in each strand were selected from each target group to serve as more intensive 'case study' children. The project's final report can be found at www.esrc.ac.uk/ESRCInfoCentre, while more detailed accounts of the work within each strand can be found in Feiler *et al.* (2007), Greenhough *et al.* (2007) and Winter *et al.* (2009).

Children's perceptions of home and school

Towards the end of the project, all the target children in the literacy and numeracy strands were asked whether they felt they were 'different at home from what they were like at school'. At this point in time, the children in the literacy strand were aged about 7 years and those in the numeracy strand about 10 years. The children were asked these questions at home, often with other family members present. Their answers provide some insights into how they perceived the two locations of home and school. They also give some indications about how they perceived their own identity and agency in the two locations.

The great majority of the children (32 out of 45) said they felt different in the two places. Only five said they did not, with the remainder saying they weren't sure or didn't know. The most common theme to emerge from their answers was that school was a place with more rules and restrictions on their behaviour than home. On the whole the children went along with these rules and restrictions and said they were more sensible and less naughty at school. Home, in contrast, was a place where there were fewer rules and restrictions and where they felt freer and less constrained: For example:

When I'm at home I'm free to be naughtier ... not as good, much naughtier ... because I feel like school's a place to be good and learn to be polite, but then when its home its like being free.

(girl, numeracy strand, Bristol school)

At home I feel more relaxed and more like myself than at school. And there I've got to do this and got to do that (Q: so does that mean you like being at home more than at school?) Yes, but I like going to school to see my friends as well.

(boy, numeracy strand, Bristol school)

I'm really sensible at school. But like you're not worried at home, because it's not like there's rules or anything, it's more comfy at home ... at home if you want to play outside you play outside, but in school you're not allowed to stay in if it's playtime. There's no rules here [at home], I can just be normal here.

(girl, numeracy strand, Bristol school)

Yes! At home it's more fun, in school you can't play with PlayStation or Gameboy or film no-one ... at home you can watch TV, in school you have to watch what the teacher chooses.

(boy, literacy strand, Cardiff school)

One area in which the children felt more freedom at home was in expressing their feelings. They said they were more likely to have arguments with their siblings, or to lose their temper, or to express sadness.

At school I'm probably definitely quieter. At home my temper kind of comes out a bit more than at school. But I kind of shout at my brother if he gets unruly, as they do! (Q: So you sound as if you're a bit louder at home?) Yes, I'm kind of not, erm, I'm just, well at school you have to be quiet at school to let teachers talk, but at home you can kind of just not go wild but you don't have to be silent. You just have to kind of be in the middle really. Do what you want but make sure you listen to people.

(girl, numeracy strand, Bristol school)

When I'm sad, at home I tell my mum when I'm sad, at school mostly I don't tell my nasty teacher.

(girl, literacy strand, Cardiff school)

I'm probably a bit ... a bit more whiny at home than school, cos I'm not whiny at all at school.

(girl, literacy strand, Bristol school)

Some of the children were aware, however, that while school was a place with more rules and restrictions, it also opened up more possible roles for them to play:

Yes, at school I'm very funny, I'm like the official class joker. And when I get home my mum and dad have probably heard about a hundred jokes, they'll know them all, so I'm not as funny as I was back there.

(boy, numeracy strand, Bristol school)

The children's responses to these questions suggest they have some insight into the different rules, expectations and practices present at home and at school. The children also seem to think that they have less agency at school, and that there are important differences between their home and school identities. However, their responses do not tell us much about the detailed nature of these identities, and the ways in which they might relate to each other. For a more nuanced account we need to look at the more detailed case studies. In the next section we, therefore, compare the case studies of two children, Nadia and Ryan, from the numeracy strand of the project.

Case study 1: Nadia

Nadia was a high-achieving girl attending school in Cardiff. Her family came originally from Bangladesh and the family paid regular visits to their home village. Nadia's father was the chef and deputy manager of an Asian restaurant in Cardiff. She had an elder brother and sister, and her mother was responsible for the home and was the main contact with the school. Her mother, however, did not speak much English so Nadia often had to act as translator of home–school communications.

When asked if she was different at home and at school, Nadia replied that she was. She justified this in terms of the different adults and activities in each place: 'At school I have "sir" and at home I have my mum and I do work and watch telly. That's all really'. On closer inspection, however, there appeared to be a great deal of consonance between Nadia's school identity and her home identity. At school she was quiet, conscientious and worked hard at most subjects, especially maths. Being good at maths was an important part of her school identity. But it was an important part of her home identity too. The family placed great stress on educational achievement and were very proud of the fact that Nadia was successful at school. They had many cultural resources, which they mobilised to support school learning, particularly through the extended family networks and her father's professional networks. For example, many Asian students ate at his restaurant and he told us they would give Nadia extra tuition – without charge – if she needed it.

There was also a lot of mathematics going on at home, both formal and informal. Nadia and her sister gave each other maths problems to solve – indeed one of their favourite games was playing 'school' at home – and there was general support from the family for her maths homework. She used a calculator to check her answers and had a whiteboard in her room, which she used for school work. At the same time there was a lot of more informal maths going on. Nadia gave her father a weekly 'bill' for her pocket money and he would test her by giving her part of the money and asking what he still owed her. Nadia also went shopping with her mother and her job was to check the shopping list, read the labels and check that her mother had received the right change.

Like many Asian families, Nadia's family used a method of finger counting which involved counting on the knuckles of each finger. There are several ways to do this – Nadia counted in threes while her mother counted in fours. Nadia, however, did not use this method in school. She didn't know if her teacher was aware of this method and didn't want to show it to him. In this respect, then, there was a separation between her home and school maths.

Overall, it seems there is a general consonance between Nadia's home and school identities. Her family and home environment are strongly supportive of her achievements at school and there are several school-like activities and artefacts in the home. Nadia is also actively involved in brokering between home and school, as when she translates home–school communications for her mother. At the same time, the boundaries between home and school are not totally porous, for example, Nadia is keen to keep her culturally-based finger counting hidden from her teacher.

Case study 2: Ryan

Ryan attended a different school in Cardiff. He lived with his Welsh father, Scottish mother and younger brother on an estate on the outskirts of the city. His father worked as a supervisor on the railways and his mother used to work as a playground assistant. The family seemed quite isolated, and indeed, during the first year of the project Ryan's mother took both children out of school and returned to Scotland for a couple of months. They took some schoolwork with them but it didn't appear that Ryan did very much.

At school Ryan was a low achiever who had problems across the curriculum. We observed him during a maths lesson where he seemed to have serious difficulties understanding what the lesson (on percentages) was about. He also seemed tired and yawned a lot. At the same time, he tried to be helpful in the classroom, operating as the 'unofficial class technician' by plugging in and unplugging the lead for the OHP.

His teachers seemed to be quite fond of him, but thought that he had limited ability: as one of them put it, 'there isn't much there'. The only time he seemed happy at school was when he was playing outside. At home, Ryan also spent a lot of time playing outside with his brother and other friends on the estate.

When asked if he was different at home and school, Ryan replied 'Loads. When I'm at home I just forget about school and play. In school I'm one person but when I come home I'm another person ... I'm naughtier at home.'

Like Nadia's parents, Ryan's mother thought it was important that he did well at school and was obviously concerned that this was not the case. She tried to make sure he did his homework and wanted to help him with maths. However, she lacked confidence herself in maths and was also aware that she had been taught different methods at school. Ryan himself was aware of this and seemed regularly to criticise his mother's attempts to help him.

The tension and conflict between Ryan and his mother came over particularly clearly on a videotape that Ryan's mother made of him doing his maths homework. On the tape, Ryan does not appear to be enjoying his homework and at one point asks to go out to play, but his mother says he has to finish his work. He is doing a page of subtraction problems and he keeps using a faulty method to end up with incorrect answers. His mother tries to help by pointing out other ways of doing the problem, but he criticises her methods and rebuffs her on several occasions by saying 'we do it different at my school' (see Hughes and Greenhough 2007 for an extended analysis of this episode).

Overall, there appears to be considerable dissonance between Ryan's identities at home and at school. His main school identity – that of a low attainer – is not a happy one, and one that he would prefer to leave at the school gate. Having to do homework brings it back into play at home and is therefore unwelcome. As we have argued elsewhere (Hughes and Greenhough 2007), the piece of homework is potentially a boundary object, but Ryan resists this attempt to bring home and school closer together. He also appears to have little interest in acting as a broker between home and school practices, and indeed tried to draw on the legitimacy of his school as a means of discrediting and rejecting his mother's attempts to engage with the homework.

Taken together, these two case studies suggest that children's identities at home and school can intersect in different and diverse ways. For children like Nadia, who appear to have a degree of consonance between their home and school identities, there is little to be done in the way of 'reconciliation' work. For children like Ryan, however, where there seems to be a greater dissonance between home and school identities, the picture is more complex. In his case, the introduction of a potential boundary object such as homework is a source of tension and conflict rather than one of reconciliation.

These two cases have strong resonances with the more extensive longitudinal case studies which form the basis of Pollard's 'Identity and Learning' research programme (e.g. Pollard 1996; Pollard and Filer 1999; Filer and Pollard 2000). As Pollard's work makes clear, extensive study of children in a range of social settings reveals the complex processes through which, what Pollard terms, their 'learning identities' are shaped and maintained. Like Pollard's work, these case studies also suggest that the relationship between home and school identities is a complex and transient process, which may be strongly influenced by structural factors such as social class, gender and ethnicity. The relationship may also be affected by attempts to manage it through the exchange of information, as we shall see in the next section.

Exchanging knowledge across the home–school boundary

As we saw earlier, schools in England are currently being urged to provide parents with more information about what is happening to their children at school. There are, moreover, calls for this exchange of information to be 'two-way', with parents providing schools with information about their children's out-of-school lives. These proposals are made on the grounds that they will help parents become more engaged with their children's learning, and also help children become more motivated and engaged with their school work. In other words, it is assumed that increasing two-way information flow between home and school will lead to higher educational attainment. At the same time, however, concerns have been expressed about this deliberate blurring of the boundary between home and school. Some commentators have suggested that this represents a further intrusion by the education system into the personal lives of children and their families (e.g. Ecclestone and Hayes 2009). Others have questioned whether children's right to a private 'safe haven' at school is also being eroded by such proposals.

The Home–School Knowledge Exchange project provided evidence relevant to these questions. The teacher-researchers seconded to the project spent time working with parents, teachers and children to develop activities that would allow knowledge and information to be exchanged across the home–school boundary. Some of these activities encouraged information flow in the school-to-home direction. For example, schools in all three strands of the project made videos of classroom life with the explicit purpose of informing parents about the curriculum and teaching methods being used. Other activities encouraged information flow in the opposite direction, from home-to-school. For example, all four schools in the literacy strand developed a 'shoebox' activity, in which children were asked to bring into school in their shoeboxes important artefacts from their out-of-school lives. These artefacts were used for a range of purposes in the classroom – one school, for example, used them to encourage the children's creative writing (more details of the activities can be found in Feiler *et al.* 2007 and Winter *et al.* 2009).

Both the videos and the shoeboxes can be seen as boundary objects (Wenger 1998) in that they aimed to 'coordinate the perspectives' of individuals on different sides of the boundary – in this case parents and teachers. The videos made visible to parents aspects of classroom life, which had hitherto been invisible to them – in the words of one parent, they 'opened up the world of school to us'. In particular, they revealed aspects of their children's school identity, which previously they had only guessed at. One parent, for example, described how she underwent a range of different emotions as she watched her child on the video:

> I didn't watch it with him, I watched it on my own, and I could feel myself thinking 'oh he's not listening [mimics worried disappointed voice], he's not listening' and then 'oh good [excited] he's ans..., he's got his hand up, he's answering a question, oh yes he got it right', and that sort of thing, and then concern cos he was the only one standing up and he just wasn't doing his work, but I didn't say anything to him about it. And it was also funny as well, you know … and the fact … in a way it was reassuring because he was kind of gazing at the books on the … in the library … in the book corner for ages, and then he kind of became focused and contributed so … it was quite nice to see that even though he was distracted he was focused at parts as well.

The shoebox activity, in contrast, enabled aspects of the children's home identities to become more visible in the classroom, not only for the teacher but for the other children as well. For example, a boy called Douglas placed photographs of his two pet budgerigars in his shoebox. In the classroom, he gave a short presentation to the rest of the class about his birds, which he had called 'Harry' and 'Potter'. As a result of this activity Douglas became the class authority on birds, and the other children would consult him when they wanted to know something about birds. He had thus acquired an identity in school that was more consonant with the one he had at home.

The Home–School Knowledge Exchange project provided evidence that knowledge exchange activities could lead to improved educational attainment, although this was not found uniformly across every strand of the project. On the primary–secondary transfer strand, for example, we found that children who had attended schools where knowledge exchange activities had taken place made significantly better progress in reading than children who had not. Children from knowledge exchange schools were also more positive about their own learning and appeared to have adjusted more quickly to life in secondary school (Greenhough *et al.* 2007). On the literacy and numeracy strands, learning gains associated with particular knowledge exchange activities were reported by parents, teachers and children (Feiler *et al.* 2007; Winter *et al.* 2009).

At the same time, the knowledge exchange activities opened up some wider political, moral and ethical questions raised by the blurring of boundaries between home and school. For example, although the classroom videos were intended to convey to parents the impersonal aspects of classroom life such as the curriculum and teaching methods, they were usually interpreted by parents in terms of what they revealed about their own children. This process, which we have described elsewhere as 'personalisation' (Hughes and Greenhough 2006), is well illustrated by the commentary provided by the parent (see above) as she watches her child during his literacy lesson. While many parents might identify strongly with this mother's desire to see how her child is behaving in an unfamiliar context, others might see it as unnecessary parental monitoring of a child's school life. It is often suggested that school can provide a 'safe haven' where children can feel protected from some of the harsher realities of out-of-school lives, and it might well be asked whether this is being put in jeopardy by school-to-home knowledge exchange activities.

Similar questions may be asked about home-to-school knowledge exchange using activities like the shoebox. As we have pointed out elsewhere, such activities can turn the children's personal and intimate possessions into props for the curriculum, a process we have referred to as 'curricularisation' (Hughes and Greenhough 2006). Again we need to ask whether this represents an infringement of the rights of children – and their families – to a personal life which is not being monitored by the school. It should also be noted that bringing in artefacts or photographs from home might make visible inequalities between children in their home and family circumstances. Do children have the right to keep their home and school lives separate?

In practice, we noted that while the children in the Home–School Knowledge Exchange project engaged readily and enthusiastically with activities like the shoebox, they would occasionally make clear that they did not want the boundaries between home and school to be totally transparent. We saw this in both the case studies: Nadia did not want her teacher to know about her finger counting methods, while Ryan did not want his mother to 'interfere' with his homework. This ambivalence was also present in the comments of some of the other children, particularly when asked if they would like their teacher to know more about what they were like at home. For example:

> It depends on the teacher really ... if it's someone who's quite a nice teacher, not who I can, she's not going to be annoying and always tell me off or something like that, then yes, it would be fine. But if it's someone who's telling me off or can be quite stressy then probably not.
>
> (boy, numeracy strand, Bristol school)

> Sometimes and sometimes not. Because sometimes you have a kind of bad side and sometimes you have a good side and sometimes you don't want them to know, say if you've got like verrucas, you don't want them to know that. But sometimes you do want to tell them that I have that many beanies or something. Or I've just made a website.
>
> (girl, numeracy strand, Bristol school)

or more simply:

> I like to keep some things a secret from my teacher.
>
> (boy, literacy strand, Bristol school)

These examples suggest that children may be aware of the important role that boundaries can play in keeping aspects of their lives separate. They also suggest an awareness that boundaries are not simple and straightforward but are complex and multifaceted, and that some kinds of boundary crossing are acceptable while others are not. This in turn suggests that a useful way forward in this area might be through a more detailed and finely grained mapping of the different types of boundaries in operation, and of the legitimacy (or otherwise) of different crossing points.

Conclusions and implications

In this chapter we have looked at the daily transition which children make between home and school. This transition is often ignored by educational policy makers and researchers, yet it is of fundamental importance in understanding the differential educational attainment of different groups of children. Our data suggests that most primary school children feel they are different in the two locations, and that these differences are related to the more rule-governed and restraining nature of school. At the same time, the two case studies presented here suggest that the relationship between children's home and school identities can be subtle and complex, and that the degree of consonance or dissonance between home and school is likely to be related to factors such as social class, ethnicity and cultural resources.

We also looked at current policy proposals to increase the two-way flow of information between home and school. The work of the Home–School Knowledge Exchange project suggests that a greater exchange of knowledge between home and school is often welcomed by parents and teachers, and in some circumstances can have a positive impact on children's learning and attainment. At the same time, knowledge exchange activities that open up home to school, and vice versa, raise some contentious issues about the blurring of boundaries between public and private lives, and about the rights of children to keep their home and school lives separate.

What, then, are the implications of this 'horizontal' transition for the kinds of 'vertical' transitions that are discussed elsewhere in this book – such as the transition from primary to secondary school, from school to further or higher education, or within the world of work? We would suggest three points in particular stand out.

The first is the recognition that all vertical transitions also take place within a web of horizontal transitions. For example, when children move from primary to secondary school, they still make the daily journey from home to school. The nature of this daily transition, moreover, is likely to affect – and be affected by – the nature of the transition between the two phases of school. At a more superficial level it may involve travelling with friends on the school bus rather than walking or being driven in the parents' car; at a deeper level it may involve changing roles within the family, and a changing relationship between home and school, which are associated with having made a major transition in life. In Wenger's terms, we do not simply move from one community of practice to another; rather we are simultaneously members of multiple communities of practice whose properties – and boundaries – are constantly in a state of negotiation and flux.

This relates directly to the second point. In this chapter, Wenger's ideas about communities of practice have provided a useful perspective through which to look at transitions. In particular, his ideas about boundaries, boundary objects and brokering have been useful in drawing attention to what happens 'at the borderline' between different practices, while his ideas about identity work and the 'reconciliation' of identities is helpful in reminding us of the dynamic and changing nature of identity. These ideas can be usefully applied to other transitions too. For example, the recent independent review of the English primary curriculum (Department for Children, Schools and Families 2008) suggests that the secondary 'learning guides' referred to above might also spend time with pre-transition children in the final term at primary school, thus acting as a broker between the two settings.

Finally, we return to the question of how transitions might best be 'managed' for the benefit of those making the transition. In this chapter we have looked at information flow – or knowledge exchange – as one possible approach. At one level, it seems common sense that individuals should have as much knowledge as possible about the different regimes that they are moving between. However, as we have seen here, passing information between different communities of practice is by no means a straightforward matter and can raise some deeper ethical, moral and political questions.

Acknowledgements

This chapter draws on data collected by the Home–School Knowledge Exchange project which was funded by the UK Economic and Social Research Council through its Teaching and Learning Research Programme (ref no. L139 25 1078). The HSKE project team consisted of Martin Hughes (project director), Jane Andrews, Anthony Feiler, Pamela Greenhough, David Johnson, Elizabeth McNess, Marilyn Osborn, Andrew Pollard, Mary Scanlan, Leida Salway, Vicki Stinchcombe, Jan Winter and Wan Ching Yee. The chapter was written while the first author was supported by an ESRC professorial fellowship (ref no. RES 051 27 0092) on Learning out of School.

Bibliography

Becta (2008) *Parental Engagement: a Guide for School Leaders*, Coventry: Becta.

Bransford, J., Stevens, R., Schwartz, D., Meltzoff, A., Pea, R., Roschelle, J., Vye, N., Kuhl, P., Bell, P., Barron, B., Reeves, B. and Sabelli, N. (2006) 'Learning theories and education: toward a decade of synergy', in P. Alexander and P. Winne (eds) *Handbook of Educational Psychology*, New Jersey: Erlbaum.

Department for Children, Schools and Families (2007) *The Children's Plan: Building Brighter Futures*, London: The Stationery Office.

—— (2008) *The Independent Review of the Primary Curriculum: Interim Report*, London: Department for Children, Schools and Families.

Department for Education and Skills (2004) *Every Child Matters: Change for Children*, London: Department for Education and Skills.

—— (2007) *Every Parent Matters*, London: Department for Education and Skills.

Desforges, C. with Abouchaar, A. (2003) *The Impact of Parental Involvement, Parental Support and Family Education on Pupil Achievement and Adjustment: a Literature Review*, Research Report 433, London: Department for Education and Skills.

Docking, J. (1990) *Primary Schools and Parents*, London: Hodder and Stoughton.

Dyson, A. and Robson, E. (1999) *School, Family, Community: Mapping School Inclusion in the UK*, Leicester: Youth Work Press.

Ecclestone, K. and Hayes, D. (2009) *The Dangerous Rise of Therapeutic Education*, London: Routledge.

Edwards, A. and Warin, J. (1999) 'Parental involvement in raising the achievement of primary school pupils: why bother?', *Oxford Review of Education*, 25: 325–41.

Feiler, A., Andrews, J., Greenhough, P., Hughes, M., Johnson, D., Scanlan, M. and Yee, W. C. (2007) *Improving Primary Literacy: Linking Home and School*, London: Routledge.

Filer, A. and Pollard, A. (2000) *The Social World of Pupil Assessment in Primary School*, London: Continuum.

Greenhough, P., Hughes, M., Andrews, J., Goldstein, H., McNess, E., Osborn, M., Pollard, A., Stinchcombe, V. and Yee, W. C. (2007) 'What effect does involving parents in knowledge exchange activities during transfer from Key Stage 2 to Key Stage 3 have on children's attainment and learning dispositions?', paper presented at the BERA conference, London, September 2007. Available at www.leeds.ac.uk/educol/documents/169930.doc.

Heath, S. B. (1983) *Ways with Words: Language, Life and Work in Communities and Classrooms*, Cambridge: Cambridge University Press.

Hughes, M. and Greenhough, P. (2006) 'Boxes, bags and videotapes: enhancing home–school communication through knowledge exchange activities', *Educational Review*, 58: 471–89.

Hughes, M. and Greenhough, P. (2007) '"We do it a different way at my school!" mathematics homework as a site for tension and conflict', in A. Watson and P. Winbourne (eds) *New Directions for Situated Cognition in Mathematics Education*, New York: Springer, pp. 129–52.

Hughes, M., Wikeley, F. and Nash, T. (1994) *Parents and their Children's Schools*, Oxford: Blackwell.

Lam, M. and Pollard, A. (2006) 'A conceptual framework for understanding children as agents in the transition from home to kindergarten', *Early Years*, 26: 123–41.

Lareau, A. (2000) *Home Advantage: Social Class and Parental Intervention in Elementary Education* (2nd edn), Lanham: Rowman & Littlefield.

Lave, J. and Wenger, E. (1991) *Situated Learning: Legitimate Peripheral Participation*, Cambridge: Cambridge University Press.

Pollard, A. (1996) *The Social World of Children's Learning*, London: Cassell.

Pollard, A. and Filer, A. (1999) *The Social World of Pupil Career in Primary School*, London: Cassell.

Star, S. L. and Griesemer, J. (1989) 'Institutional ecology, "translations" and boundary objects: amateurs and professionals in Berkeley's museum of vertebrate zoology, 1907–1939', *Social Studies of Science*, 19: 387–420.

Street, B., Baker, D. and Tomlin, A. (2005) *Navigating Numeracies: Home/School Numeracy Practices*, Dordrecht: Springer.

Vincent, C. (1996) *Parents and Teachers: Power and Participation*, London: Falmer.

Wenger, E. (1998) *Communities of Practice: Learning, Meaning and Identity*, Cambridge: Cambridge University Press.

Winter, J., Andrews, J., Greenhough, P., Hughes, M., Salway, L. and Yee, W. C. (2009) *Improving Primary Mathematics: Linking Home and School*, London: Routledge.

3   Transgression for transition?

White urban middle-class families
making and managing 'against the
grain' school choices

David James and Phoebe Beedell

Introduction

As the editors of this volume point out in the introduction, there is a contemporary belief amongst policy makers and many educational professionals that the
concept of *transition* may be highly significant in issues of social inclusion and
exclusion. There is also a belief that enabling people to *manage transitions more
effectively* is itself a possible and worthwhile policy objective with implications
for achieving greater social justice. With these beliefs in mind, this chapter draws
upon a study of middle-class school choices at a pivotal transition, namely that
from primary to secondary schooling. Both this and the subsequent period of
secondary schooling were highly managed processes. As well as revealing the
nature of a particular kind of 'transition management', the data and analysis
lead us to question the idea that such practices do anything to promote equality:
indeed, they may do the very opposite.

We begin the chapter with a sketch of the features of the study that are most
relevant to this discussion. We then set out several important concepts of *transition* that appear helpful to understanding the social practices of families as
they anticipate, make, manage and live with 'against the grain' school choices.
Finally, we focus upon the nature and extent of the *management* of the transition,
comparing this to other research-based insights on parenting. We show that even
counter-intuitive school choices appear to bring advantages to middle-class children, and suggest that these may be at the expense of other school pupils.

The project to which we refer was funded by the Economic and Social Research
Council (Award reference RES-148-25-0023) as part of their Identities and Social
Action programme. Entitled Identity, Educational Choice and the White Urban
Middle Classes, the research focused on 125 white middle-class families sending
their children to urban, socially diverse comprehensives with average or below-
average league-table positions.[1] In most cases, other options were available to the
families – though these other options would often have required actions such as
buying and selling houses, renting a new address or paying for private schooling.
As well as looking at motivations and orientations, the study examined how identities gave shape to – and were shaped by – dilemmas of educational choice, and
how class and ethnic differences were handled. The study covered a 30-month
period and was based in London and two other cities, 'Riverton' in the south-

west and 'Norton' in the north-east of England. The schools attended were more ethnically mixed in London than in Riverton or Norton. Families were identified through a mixture of responses to an advertisement in the national press, identification by head teachers and 'snowballing'. Interviews took place in the homes of the families. For parents these covered their own biography and educational background, the process of choosing a secondary school, and their experiences of primary and secondary schools. For children, interviews included looking at the part they had played in choices of school, current and past experiences of schooling, and their attitudes to social and ethnic diversity.

Amongst the many conclusions of the study, we found that counter-intuitive school choice was for the most part perceived and experienced as a risky strategy. It was often motivated by ideas about ethical behaviour, but there was more evidence of an individualised 'investment' orientation than there was of being driven by a sense of community or the common good. Family history was important too, with some parents reacting specifically to their own educational past. The transition and subsequent schooling was highly monitored, and it often appeared to yield its own form of social advantage.

The meaning of transition

It is worth considering established uses of the term *transition*. Aside from its technical uses in specific fields (such as physics, music and architecture), there are two meanings that are worth noting. The first is a concept used by psychologists interested in how people cope with trauma and major change, and by those bringing psychological concepts to bear on organisational problems. We might call this an *individualist* concept of transition. For some, the 'transition cycle' is nothing less than a survival mechanism inside each individual:

> Just as the fight and flight response has evolved to equip us to cope with danger, the transition cycle enables humans to adapt to trauma and change. Both are powerful survival mechanisms. They operate spontaneously and are available to everyone from presidents to refugees. But they can go badly wrong in modern societies. Possibly the most important feature of transition psychology is that it explains the mechanism by which individuals make radical changes of values and attitudes most appropriate to a new environment i.e. personal transformation. So transition awareness and transition management skills are fundamental issues for leaders who seek to transform organisations and societies. Because transitions are an individual process, leaders can facilitate or impede personal transformation but not demand it ... Greater awareness of transitions may be a key to personal and national survival in an era of unprecedented change.
>
> (Williams 1999)

A second and rather different use of the term refers to whole nation-states that were formerly parts of the Soviet Union, formerly communist, or less 'developed'. The journal, *Economics of Transition*, published on behalf of the European Bank for Reconstruction and Development, has a particular interest in the 'transition economies of Central and Eastern Europe and the CIS, China and Vietnam, as well as enlightening studies of reform and institutional change in other emerging market environments, including India and Latin America'.[2] Here, transition appears to denote a particular kind of upward trajectory characterised by progress, economic development and new opportunities to make profit.

To many, these are powerful and attractive ideas. However, both the *individualist* and the *economic development* conceptions of transition are of limited use in relation to educational policy and practice, and we would argue that *sociological* conceptions offer more promise. There are several contenders. They include the interactionist notion of transitions, articulated by Denzin (2001) as *epiphanies*. These are turning points in a person's life, but importantly they are moments when both the social and the personal are in focus, sometimes described as the intersection of the public and the private worlds, or public and private troubles. Along with other aspects of Denzin's work, there is a clear link here to C. Wright Mills (1959). Fuller, citing Elder *et al.* (2003), points out that Mills' call for a sociological imagination, which looks for the connections between biography and social structures, was important in the development of lifecourse theory and is helpful when looking at mid-life transitions (Fuller 2007).

A different concept of transition comes from the work of Raymond Boudon, who distinguished some time ago between primary and secondary effects of social class. Primary effects include the different academic abilities of children whereas secondary effects include the kinds of choices made by people in different social class groupings at key transition points in their educational careers (Boudon 1974). Boudon's particular focus was on how people weigh up the costs and benefits to them of pursuing particular routes or pathways, and how (contrary to crude versions of human capital or rational action models) such calculations will not have the same meaning and currency in different social groups. This insight has since become built-in to a whole range of studies and is part of the most elaborate rational choice modelling, where the factors at a key moment of school transition are expressed in a mathematical equation containing values for 'expected utility', 'educational benefit', 'anticipated social status decline', 'investment risk' and so forth (see Pietsch and Stubbe 2007).

Boudon is sometimes contrasted with Bourdieu, with the latter being positioned, inaccurately in our view, as 'culturally determinist'. Yet in rejecting crude notions of rational action, and in trying to understand differential stakes and positions, they wrestle in different ways with the same problem. For Bourdieu, the habitus frames strategy: it provides a sense of reality, of possibilities and limits, within which decisions for action are taken. In their turn, these actions confirm or develop fields – in other words, they affect the space for subsequent actions or choices of other people.

Paton *et al.* (2008) illustrate the importance of 'networks of intimacy' in the processes of making decisions (and non-decisions) around education and employment transitions. Networks of intimacy often include several family members and other key individuals. Our fieldwork was slightly more focused on parents and children, but just as illustrative of the significance of family habitus, whether we were exploring parents' own past experiences of schooling, or listening to young people talking about their day to day experiences. For example, there were often particular 'family stories', where parents and children would independently refer to the same events or episodes in their accounts of school choice and schooling.

A further theme in recent discussion is the idea that in the last decade or so, key transitions have become more difficult or complex. Fuller provides a summary of the main reasons that a theory of reflexive modernity may be helpful in understanding the increase in mature student participation in higher educa-tion, including the decline of certain traditions, a heightened sense of risk and a greater perception of identity as something to be 'made' (Fuller 2007: 222). Yet not all those studying transitions would support this view. Although writing specifically about the school to work transition, Vickerstaff (2003) makes the point that it is too simplistic to characterise transitions of the 1950s and 1960s as smooth and unproblematic, and contemporary transitions as full of 'uncer-tainties, fluctuations, discontinuities, reversals and seesaws' (EGRIS 2001, cited in Vickerstaff 2003: 275). In other words, it would appear easy to overstate the individualisation thesis of the rise and presumed ubiquity of a reflexive project of the self – themes that are usually set out with reference to Beck (1992) and Giddens (1991). Undoubtedly, there are shifts in the context for choice-making with regard to participation in education or training, linked to policy, and these can change horizons for action at certain stages in people's lives (see Patton *et al.* 2008: 22–3). Nevertheless, most choices are also highly framed by social struc-tures and positionings. Du Bois-Reymond, for example, suggests that 'choice biographies' are themselves unequally distributed (du Bois-Reymond 1998).

Although the research project did not set out to develop a specific theorisation of transition, it is helpful to look at some of the project data for what it suggests about transitions and their management. We found tools from the social theory of Bourdieu particularly helpful for this purpose. We now turn to the different types of transition that run through our data on 'against the grain' secondary school choice.

Types of transition in school choice

Broadly speaking, there were four concepts of transition apparent in the data and analysis of the project. The first, and perhaps most predictable, was the pivotal movement of children between primary and secondary schools. This transition had the potential to produce a great deal of anxiety and was seen by all our partici-pants as 'high stakes', having major and continuing ramifications. The perceived quality of secondary schools is a major dynamic in the housing market and is often, at least for the more occupationally and geographically mobile, a major consideration in choices about where to live. Estate agents regularly incorpo-rate information about schools in the details they provide to prospective buyers. Of the many marketised aspects of educational provision, this one is surely the most developed in policy and practice. Secondary school league tables do not only function to create pressure for so-called improvement in standards: they also seem (and in some hands, purport) to offer a set of information on which parents and children can make 'good', informed choices. The assumption here is that unchosen schools will either improve or wither away. In other words, schools themselves are seen as dynamic players with a great deal of choice in how well they do, and are widely perceived as having a trajectory (they are 'on the up' or 'coasting', or worse). The end of primary schooling is also a point at which a significant minority of children who have been in the state sector enter private secondary schools.

Secondly, there were profound experiences of transition in the lives of many of the parents we interviewed, between generations and in terms of social class namely transitions in family 'position', both historical and immediate. Families, or key relationships in families, have a *habitus*. That is, they have a set of collective dispositions that generate a sense of place and a sense of reality. Families 'carry' certain key narratives and experiences as shared property and these are used as reference points for decisions and/or the interpretation of consequences of actions. For example, a surprisingly high 59 per cent of the parents in our sample had been to either private or selective state (usually grammar) schools and these school backgrounds of parents remained very important in contemporary choices. Several of the more established middle-class parents made school choices that were a conscious reaction to the perceived narrowness, socially and/or academically, of their own schooling. On the other hand, particularly amongst the 'first generation' middle-class families, the choice of an ordinary state school sometimes reflected a wish to reproduce in microcosm the trajectories of the parents, with a desire on the part of parents that their children should have to compete in ordinary circumstances and should experience something of the same climb they had themselves made as part of their own upward mobility.

Thirdly, geographical transitions were often important. Nearly 70 per cent of the parents we interviewed were 'incomers' to the area or city where they now lived. This high level of geographical mobility was accompanied by a remarkably high rate of qualifications held, with 83 per cent qualified to degree level and over a quarter with postgraduate qualifications. There were other important senses of place too in people's commentary on the relationship between housing, house purchase and school catchment, or where a child's journey to school involved 'transitions' such as crossing borders that had high social significance. Even in a small city, different areas had a particular social meaning and school choices were sometimes framed by more and less acceptable journeys or destinations.

Fourthly, our analysis highlights transitions in *identity*, at least in the sense of *identifications*. Psycho-socially, the self can be understood as defined or redefined in relation to a 'generalised other' through a variety of possible mechanisms. For some middle-class white families 'the other' is the white working class, and there is a contrasting positive identification with black and minority ethnic groups. Thus, white working-class children were sometimes derided as 'chavs' or 'trash' whilst the white middle-class family was seen as having an ethnic identity that was distinguished by its cosmopolitan acceptance and tolerance of ethnic diversity and even its anti-racism. It is therefore meaningful to speak of different notions of 'whiteness' and a perceived transition of ethnicity. We have documented and discussed this tendency and its probable effects, showing how some white middle-class families saw themselves as 'a darker shade of pale' (see Reay *et al.* 2007).

The managing of transition

Arguably, the ideal-typical consumer in neo-liberal times makes informed choices having considered the relevant information about products or services. This holds whether they are buying a car, buying toothpaste or selecting a secondary school. In England and in some other places, a marketised view of educational choice has become the keystone of much educational policy, with the percentage of high GCSE passes taken as the proxy for the 'quality' of any given school. One of the reasons for the prevalence of this view is that many middle-class parents – literally and metaphorically – 'buy into' the marketised ideal. Beyond the small percentage who pay for private education, many more seek out schools with high A*–C league-table positions and the social composition that often comes with it. Many see the choice of such schools as maximising the chances that their own children will do relatively well – or at least see the league-table position as proof of the school's capabilities.

On the whole, the parents in our study did not share in this mainstream perspective. Rather, there was a degree of recognition and sometimes a confidence that conventional outcomes can be relied upon to take care of themselves when it comes to young people from relatively supportive, comfortable, middle-class homes who have already shown themselves to be 'clever' or 'bright'. These parents are concerned as much (sometimes more) with schooling as a socialising opportunity to acquire certain ethical qualities and the capacity to deal with a 'tough' world, to be able to 'relate' to a wide range of people, and to 'wise up'. Our interviews cover this ground extensively, and parents listed all kinds of characteristics that they thought could be nurtured in a socially mixed school. Similarly, several parents spoke in terms we might summarise as a 'school of hard knocks' approach. One of these referred to the '[drug] dealers at the gates' of her son's school and presented this as a positive feature insofar as he had to learn to cope with it and having done so would be equipped to cope with any challenging situation in life.

Such concerns are anchored in normative or value-based perspectives, but also in specific experiences. In many families, there were moral objections to the purchase of privilege. In some, parents cited examples of other young people known to them who represented what they did not want their own children to become. A particularly clear example of this was the Smiths, one of whom taught in a university. They expressed dismay at how many of the students they taught, who had been highly successful in academic terms, were nevertheless 'clueless' about so many things. The Smiths did not want their own children to turn out the same way. In some families, parents' personal experiences of 'narrow' schooling were a key 'push' factor in the choice of school. In others, the desire for the young person to 'stand out' was important. Rather than becoming 'invisible' in amongst a group of higher achieving pupils, as they might in some schools, an averagely performing school was expected by some parents to provide a context in which their son or daughter would do well and be noticed for doing well.

These kinds of engagement with the educational world break with the mainstream established patterns of the most privileged, though they may have much in common with longer-established choices of 'alternative' schooling, such as Steiner schools. It is clearly not an example of the illusory defying of social gravity, the attempt to unilaterally escape from the multilateral markers of social position which Bourdieu (1984: 370) termed a 'dream of social flying'. Rather, it is based on a more or less sociological reading of educational processes. The parents take a hands-on approach to constructing a total schooling experience that is designed to lead to much more than academic credentials. Whilst it is quite abstract, the Bourdieusian concept of social capital appears to be helpful in grasping what they are doing. For Bourdieu, social capital is 'the product of investment strategies, individual or collective, consciously or unconsciously aimed at establishing or reproducing social relationships that are directly useable in the short or long term' (Bourdieu 1997: 52). As with Coleman, social capital here is about networks, connections, who you know, who owes you a favour, and so forth. However, there the parallel ends, and Bourdieu is referring to something more dynamic, that is *worked at* and is *generative of* and *responsive to* conditions of social inequality.

It is worth unpacking this idea a little more. Everyone has social capital, but it manifests itself in class-specific forms. Like economic and cultural capital, it works to reproduce class relations. Bourdieu talks of 'endowments' of capital that students bring into educational settings. There is also 'conversion' between capitals (Apple 2004; Grenfell and James 1998). The clearest example of this is where economic capital is used to purchase highly specialised forms of secondary education that offer small class-sizes, historically-embedded expectations and a clear position in the *field* of possible schools. Thus, wealth becomes converted into cultural capital, including a high probability of high-grade A levels, a certain kind of confidence and self-regard, and a dramatically increased chance of entry into the most prestigious universities. In turn, the institution at which the degree is completed can carry high cultural capital and this has a high chance of reconversion into high earnings (economic capital) via employment that offers the sort of returns that can be used to purchase a similar advantage in the next generation. At each stage, the individual embodies something of the position of the particular institution in the *field*, and this stays with them, 'rubs off' on them, marked by signs as wide-ranging as linguistic style, manners, friends and acquaintances, ways of thinking, tastes, leisure pursuits, appearance and, of course, educational credentials. Social capital (like economic and cultural capital) is one form taken by the 'currency' of inequality. It is always in relation to a *field* of positions.

Having made the choice of an averagely – or below averagely – performing state secondary school for their children, many parents in our study surprised us with the high levels of monitoring, intervention and control that they brought to bear once secondary schooling was under way. We acknowledge that they *may* have acted in similar ways had they chosen high-performing schools, but would argue that this is unlikely. Altogether, 61 (25 per cent) of the parents in our families were or had been a school governor – and in London this rose to 30 per cent. A high proportion of these were or had been chairs of governing bodies. There were also many other 'insider' contacts and relationships with schools too, such as friendships with particular teachers or heads, or other connections through work, and some evidence that such contacts were 'used'.

Some aspects of transition management are illustrated well by the Smith family mentioned earlier in connection with a dislike for privilege. The Smiths lived in a substantial four-bedroom house in Riverton and towards the end of her primary schooling, their daughter had been desperate to go to a nearby private secondary school along with her three close friends from the primary school. Whilst they did value academic success, the Smiths were against forms of schooling that they considered would simply reproduce social advantage. Our interviews with Angela Smith also made it clear that she and her husband saw comparisons of schools that used figures on GCSE attainment as virtually meaningless. Like many others in our sample, these parents had strong values about education providing (a) social mixing and (b) opportunities to become 'streetwise'. They also had the wish to realise this vision: in the run-up to the transition, they put considerable direct effort into orchestrating and broadening the range of children with whom their daughter came into contact, including helping with the running of a youth group that contained some of the children going to Meadowood, the chosen school.

Several months after the transition, we asked Sadie how she was getting on in her secondary school:

Sadie:	Well, I met people and I became friendly with them but it took ages, really, really ages to get settled in.
Interviewer:	Do you remember how you were feeling?
Sadie:	I was getting slightly bullied at the time
Interviewer:	Were you?
Sadie:	Yes, being called 'posh', 'keener' that kind of stuff, that kind of unsettled me and we [i.e. her parents] had to go to school about it and stuff.
Interviewer:	So did your mum or dad have a word with the teachers?
Sadie:	Yes, and I went with them.
Interviewer:	Good. Do you feel that's been resolved now?
Sadie:	Yes, but then the person started up again, so we filled in some bullying forms and it got sorted out.
Interviewer:	Good, so you're a bit happier about that now? It's never easy that kind of thing, is it? So aside from that experience, the bullying stuff and that kind of thing, do you feel like you belong, you fit into the school?
Sadie:	Yes, I don't want to leave.
Interviewer:	You don't want to leave, you like it. What if I said I had a word with your mum and dad – and this isn't true, this is just pretend, OK?
Sadie:	OK.
Interviewer:	What if I said I had a word with your mum and dad, and I had a word with the head teachers and there's a place for you tomorrow at Hawthorne's (the nearby private secondary school attended by

Sadie's closest friends from primary school) and you can go there, what would you say?

Sadie: Yes.

Interviewer: You would want to?

Sadie: Yes, but I've just settled in and my friends have changed, the people who went there, I probably have changed too and I'd lose touch with all the other friends. And, me and all my friends made a pact not to change schools unless we were forced and had to move away to a different country.

Interviewer: That's nice, this is your current friends?

Sadie: Yes.

Interviewer: You said 'we're staying here, all together'?

Sadie: Yes.

Sadie's level of commitment to the school is impressive. It seems important to note that she is, in a sense, more *thoroughly* committed than her parents to the particular school: their commitment is to the school as a vehicle for certain forms of socialisation, and if it doesn't work out, they talk of having 'options'. These include, as a last resort, 'going against their principles' and moving to a smaller house so as to be able to afford private education.

Her mother Angela's account of the bullying episode brings to light another important aspect. The bullying had started a few weeks after Sadie began at Meadowood, and Sadie had not wanted her parents to get involved in dealing with it. Angela said 'it really reminded me of all my experience of working with women going through domestic violence, of how they turned in on themselves, all those feelings of lack of self confidence, lack of respect for yourself, believing what's been said about you'. The resolution came in two stages. Firstly, as in Sadie's account, Sadie and her parents met with the head of year, out of school hours, and the perpetrators were confronted the next day. But secondly, after there was some resumption of the problem, Angela drew upon a different resource:

She did get a learning mentor for a little bit which just gave her that bit of extra security at school – a different adult who she really likes, but that happened because I'm friends with one of the assistant head teachers, and she's always wanting to know how it's going from our point of view. I fed back and he sorted it out, whereas the head of year was supposed to have done something about it and he never got round to doing it. And it was only because I had that route in to push, otherwise I'd have had to go back, see him again, make another appointment ... that's one of those middle-class privileges, really, in lots of ways that you get in that environment, it shouldn't be like that, I shouldn't have been relying on that.

(Angela, second interview)

The assistant head, who was a friend and was 'always wanting to know how it's going from our point of view', is not an isolated feature across our study. Similar episodes, and sometimes a similar self-awareness and mild guilt about privileged access to school personnel or systems, appeared in several of our interviews. But, one of the likely reasons that it was possible for these parents to micro-manage the transition and subsequent school experience, was that schools were, for their part, highly responsive to parental intervention. They appeared especially keen to 'hang on' to white middle-class pupils. We have no data on how deliberate all the many instances of this actually were, but we are clear about the tendency for schools to divert certain resources to the children in our study. Nearly all were in 'Gifted and Talented' schemes, which attract extra resources for the school to cater for those children with the 'ability to excel', and in one school an entire A level subject was kept open for one student so as to dissuade them from leaving to go elsewhere for post-16 courses. Many head teachers put time and effort into trying to persuade middle-class parents to choose their school, or to stay if they were thinking of leaving. Clearly, they think that the school is better off as a whole if it contains more middle-class pupils. It would seem, then, that schools also operate with a 'sociological' appreciation of which kinds of children are most likely to help them rise in the league tables.

Who has the means to manage transition?

If there is such a thing as 'managing transition', it follows that some people will be better at it (or better placed) than others. The idea that people can be assisted to this end is an attractive one in policy terms, not least because it appears to be a sensitive and caring policy response to the news that market arrangements may exacerbate inequalities. In a marketised system, this problem can be portrayed as one of individual resources and responsibility, or rather the lack of them. If there is general agreement about the signifiers of a good secondary school, as well as plentiful information that is in the public domain, then it is possible to make 'bad' choices. This in turn means that people can be seen as individually responsible for such choices, opening up two possibilities – they can be blamed, or helped. Thus, offering help to people so that they can better 'manage transitions' may not be quite as innocent and benign as it first appears, and it may be understood as an instance of long-standing themes in policy responses around social inclusion/ exclusion (see Levitas 2005).

A further problem here is the positive halo around the concept of 'choice' itself. Greater choice, accompanied by more information, is often presented as an incontrovertible 'good' in government policy, as a self-evident proxy for freedom, or as proof that one lives in a democracy. However, a more subtle concept of choice is necessary, not least because in the case of schools, the information that dominates perceptions of quality is league-table position based on higher grade GCSE examination results. Families like the Smiths do indeed value academic success, but they are *committed* to a particular vision of 'the good', or 'good socialisation' which is in some conflict with dominant assumptions about how educational success is to be secured. Commitments are not the same as preferences and have a stronger bearing on practice, partly because they are the *felt* as well as the *thought* aspects of social life, to do with habitus and the psychic dimension of social class (see Reay 2005). The significance of strong commitments is illustrated in many of the families in our study. In the case of the Smiths, we would point to commitments that are strong enough to override the loss of Sadie's friendships with the move to secondary school and to cope with the bullying episode. Sadie's answer to our 'magic wand' question, about suddenly being able to attend her original school of choice, can also be taken to illustrate the strength of a particular commitment. (For further discussion of the distinction between commitments and preferences, see Archer 2000 and Sayer 2005.)

Like the British middle-class young women in the study by Walkerdine *et al.* (2001), these families shared a view that high academic achievement and performance were 'the norm'. For example, the expectation of university entry was almost universal amongst our interviewees, parents and young people alike. However, our data also show that in the case of parents making 'against the grain' choices of secondary school, a great deal of thought, time and effort was being put in to other aspects and dimensions of the young person's experiences, capacities and trajectory. This, in turn, leads us to the 'reflexive project of the self' that some writers have attributed to neo-liberalism (or simply to the conditions of post-modernity or high modernity – see, for example, Giddens 1991 and Elliott 2001).

We would predict that, in general, most parents are concerned, and many are engaged, with the detail of schooling. Yet many of the parents we studied went much further than this, and the manner of their engagement could justifiably be termed *parental managerialism*. The term managerialism usually refers to beliefs and practices in workplaces and organisations. It is 'underpinned by an ideology which assumes that all aspects of organisational life can and should be controlled. In other words, that ambiguity can and should be radically reduced or eliminated' (Wallace and Hoyle 2005: 9). Like managerialism in the workplace, this parental managerialism is premised on a belief that all the important variables are controllable and within reach. It is a reflexive project of the self of the child, and it necessitates a great deal of deliberate activity.

In their study of parenting, Walkerdine and Lucey (1989) showed how middle-class mothers tended to turn everyday interactions into explicit learning opportunities, and to give elaborate explanations to children for imposed restrictions, whilst working-class mothers tended to be non-interventionist and to give clearer boundaries with less justification. Lareau's work (e.g. 2003) also outlined processes of 'concerted cultivation' amongst middle-class parents in the USA. The parental managerialism we have found appears to be the extension beyond the early years, and beyond the home, of similar sets of practices. There are similarities with Reay's earlier analysis of parental engagements with schools and how the success or productivity of these encounters differed for mothers with different resources of cultural capital (e.g. Reay 1998). There are strong resonances too with a study of parental voice which showed that whilst there were similarities across all parents, one group who were highly involved with schools had a particular habitus in relation to education which included a 'responsibility to monitor children's achievement and the school provision' (Vincent and Martin 2002: 125).

We would argue that a person's capacity to 'manage transition' is in large part a question of cultural and social capital. In order to be effective when it is taken outside the home, parental managerialism is likely to depend on contacts and connections that go beyond a standard relationship to the school as an organisation. As we have seen, governorship and other contacts with schools were quite common across our sample, and schools were highly responsive to parental concerns. One of our interviews with a young person in London illustrates more of the nature of this type and level of parental engagement:

> My mum is like a big complainer if anything doesn't go right at school she is like first there talking to the head teacher. She's good friends with him now. In Year 7 she managed to get an English teacher sort of sacked, she is a bit like that; she is a bit of a tyrant. She'll like, if I come back and they haven't marked my book for a while, then she will be 'OK I am going to go and tell the school' because she wants me to have the best education I can and whereas I would rather just think, oh, let's wait for someone else to do it, she is the one to do it. She is really involved with the school, she is standing for governor. Yeah she really, like, feels strongly about trying to get me to do the best ... and also she really wants to try and get more middle-class people to go to Copeland School. And she has drawn up, like made a little committee, and this year when people were being shown around the school as a middle-class parent she tried to like get other middle-class parents to send their kids to Copeland.
>
> (Ella Harding)

There was a great deal of this parental managerialism visible in our data. In addition, there were frequent instances of high intervention, advocacy and marketing of the sort described by Ella Harding.

Conclusion

Our analysis of 'against the grain' secondary school choice amongst white middle-class families illustrates a high level of parental management of primary to secondary school transition and of subsequent schooling. However, we also suggest that it is too simplistic to see such transitions solely or primarily as being about the skills or capacities of individuals to make good choices. In a nutshell, what some would regard as 'bad' choices turned out very well indeed for the families we studied, whether one is looking at qualifications attained, university entrance, or the qualities and characteristics that were attributed to schooling. This turns attention to more fundamental questions about structures of inequality and the actions and processes that constitute them.

The study puts a large question mark against the idea that, for all its possible benefits, enabling people to better manage primary to secondary school transitions is an efficient route to greater social justice. The idea of managing transitions is itself based on an inadequate model of social inequality, one which locates the causes in individual deficits of attitude or information, or perceptions of (ir)responsibility. This is entirely in keeping with neo-liberal political thinking and with the perennial individualist thrust in Western cultures (see e.g. Geertz 1979; James 2003), and is also indicative of what Mike Savage has described about the assumed normality of white middle-class lifestyles in contemporary policy (Savage 2003). The linked idea of 'responsibilisation' (see for example Dwyer 1998) continues to be a popular idea in some policy circles.

However, the difficulty is that there is more at stake than the properties of individuals. Horizons for action are collectively generated, experienced and deeply felt, and far from being neutral and technical matters, educational processes are themselves shot through with differential social valuing. There is a deep-rooted, intimate and largely mutually confirming relationship between social class and educational opportunity and attainment, yet it would seem that the habitual policy responses to the effects of this continue to misrecognise the nature of the relationship. In schools, this gives us such things as ever increasing pressure to raise the proportion of pupils gaining 5 or more 'good' passes at GCSE, accompanied by a remarkable shift in terminology, where a 'satisfactory' result in inspections of quality can be relabelled as 'coasting' and therefore become newly problematic. In universities, it gives us a focus on 'widening participation students', where information and attitudes are seen as the barriers to participation presumed to afflict working-class young people.

We share with Brantlinger a wish to point out that because educational processes and credentials are recognised as positional goods, and must be understood relationally, one cannot really view any choice-making or other intervention in splendid isolation. As she puts it:

> As high tracks are created to accommodate the preferences of affluent parents, low-income children are relegated to low tracks ... the middle class determines the nature of public education for their children and, simultaneously, even if inadvertently, for children of other classes.
>
> (Brantlinger 2003: 59)

Like the notion of choice itself, the idea of working on the management of transitions to promote greater equality fails to take proper account of the above points. There is convincing empirical evidence from a German study that the primary to secondary transition actually *deepens* prior inequalities (Pietsch and Stubbe 2007). The point to be taken from this is that the passage between one setting and another is not just a 'transition' to be 'managed': It is *itself* a site for social practices that generate and underline difference. One person's transition is, simultaneously and subsequently, a generative part of the context for another person's transition.

Notes

1   The 'headline' measure in such league tables is the percentage of pupils gaining five or more A* to C passes at GCSE. At the time of the fieldwork, the national average figures were 58.5 per cent (for 2006) and 56.5 per cent (for 2005). Such figures are widely used by politicians and policy makers as a proxy for 'standards' or 'quality' of secondary schools.

2   See publisher's web pages, e.g. http://www.blackwellpublishing.com/journal. asp?ref=0967-0750 (accessed December 2008).

Bibliography

Apple, M. W. (2004) *Ideology and Curriculum* (3rd edn), London: RoutledgeFalmer.

Archer, M. S. (2000) *Being Human*, Cambridge: Cambridge University Press.

Beck, U. (1992) *The Risk Society*, London: Sage.

Boudon, R. (1974) *Education, Opportunity and Social Inequality*, New York: Wiley.

Bourdieu, P. (1984) *Distinction: a Social Critique of the Judgement of Taste*, London: Routledge.

—— (1997) 'The forms of capital' in A. H Halsey, H. Lauder, P. Brown and A. S. Wells (eds) *Education, Culture Economy and Society*, Oxford: Oxford University Press.

Brantlinger, E. (2003) *Dividing Classes: How the Middle Class Negotiates and Rationalizes School Advantage*, London: RoutledgeFalmer.

Denzin, N. (2001) *Interpretive Interactionism* (2nd edn) London: Sage Publications.

Du Bois-Reymond, M. (1998) '"I don't want to commit myself yet": young people's life concepts', *Journal of Youth Studies*, 1: 63–79.

Dwyer, P. (1998) 'Conditional citizens? Welfare rights and responsibilities in the late 1990s', *Critical Social Policy*, 18: 493–517.

Elder, G. H., Kirkpatrick Johnson, M., and Crosnoe, R. (2003) 'The emergence of and development of life course theory', in J. Mortimore and M. Shanahan (eds) *Handbook of the Life Course*, New York: Kluwer Academic Publishers.

Elliott, A. (2001) *Concepts of the Self*, Cambridge: Polity Press.

Fuller, A. (2007) 'Mid-life "transitions" to higher education: developing a multi-level explanation of increasing participation', *Studies in the Education of Adults*, 39: 217–35.

Geertz, C. (1979) 'From the native's point of view: on the nature of anthropological understanding', in P. Rabinow and W. M. Sullivan (eds) *Interpretive Social Science*, Berkeley: University of California Press.

Giddens, A. (1991) *Modernity and Self-identity*, Cambridge: Polity.

Grenfell, M. and James, D. (1998) *Bourdieu and Education: Acts of Practical Theory*, London: Falmer.

James, D. (2003) 'The love puddle: a simple story and some difficult questions', *Educational Action Research*, 13: 111–17.

Lareau, A. (2003) *Unequal Childhoods: Class, Race and Family Life*, Berkeley, CA: University of California Press.

Levitas, R. (2005) *The Inclusive Society? Social Exclusion and New Labour*, Basingstoke: Palgrave Macmillan.

Mills, C. W. (1959) *The Sociological Imagination*, New York: Oxford University Press.

Paton, K., Fuller, A. and Heath, S. (2008) 'Educational and career decision-making: challenging the context of choice', paper presented at Illuminating the Hidden World of Vocational Learning and Post-School Transitions Conference, Institute of Education, University of London, February 2008.

Pietsch, M. and Stubbe, T. C. (2007) 'Inequality in the transition from primary to secondary school: school choices and educational disparities in Germany', *European Educational Research Journal*, 6: 424–45.

Reay, D. (1998) *Class Work: Mothers' Involvement in their Children's Primary Schooling*, London: University College Press.

—— (2005) 'Beyond consciousness? The psychic landscape of social class', *Sociology*, 39: 911–28.

Reay, D., Hollingworth, S., Williams, K., Crozier, G., Jamieson, F., James, D., Beedell, P. (2007) '"A darker shade of pale?" Whiteness, the middle classes and multi-ethnic inner city schooling', *Sociology*, 41; 1041–60.

Savage, M. (2003) 'A new class paradigm', *British Journal of Sociology of Education*, 23: 535–41.

Sayer, A. (2005) *The Moral Significance of Class*, Cambridge: Cambridge University Press.

Vickerstaff, S. (2003) 'Apprenticeship in the "golden age": were youth transitions really smooth and unproblematic back then?', *Work, Employment and Society*, 17: 269–87.

Vincent, C. and Martin, J. (2002) 'Class, culture and agency: researching parental voice', *Discourse: Studies in the Cultural Politics of Education*, 23: 108–27.

Walkerdine, V. and Lucey, H. (1989) *Democracy in the Kitchen*, London: Virago.

Walkerdine, V., Lucey, H. and Melody, J. (2001) *Growing up Girls: Psychosocial Explorations of Gender and Class*, London: Palgrave.

Wallace, M. and Hoyle, E. (2005) 'Towards effective management of a reformed teaching profession', paper presented to ESRC Teaching and Learning Research Programme thematic seminar series Changing Teacher Roles, Identities and Professionalism, King's College London, July 2005.

Williams, D. (1999) 'Human responses to change', *Futures*, 31: 609–16.

4 Reading and writing the self as a college student

Fluidity and ambivalence across contexts

Candice Satchwell and Roz Ivanič

Introduction

In this chapter, we contribute to the nuancing of the notion of 'transition' through the lens of the literacy practices of students on courses in colleges of further education. We first briefly describe the Literacies for Learning in Further Education project on which the chapter draws. We then introduce the concept of 'literacy practices' as part of people's lives in and out of college, focusing particularly on the ways in which identities are inscribed in literacy practices, and on the role of identification in people's participation in them. In particular, we show how literacy practices can be analysed into constituents, each of which can be configured in infinite ways. A change in the configuration of any one of these constituents changes the nature of the practice and may change the extent to which a person will identify with the roles and subject positions held out by the practice.

In the main part of the paper, we use this heuristic to explain two types of transition we encountered in our data. The research did not set out to throw light on institutional transitions, but focused firstly on the daily informal transitions between college and non-college activities, and secondly on subtle transitions over time for individuals as they attended college courses. Firstly, we compare two students on the same Catering and Hospitality course, one of whom made connections as he negotiated the daily transitions between his college work and his part-time work and hence identified with the literacy practices on the course, and one of whom did so to a lesser degree. Secondly, we compare two moments in one student's life, showing – through the lens of researching her literacy practices – how she made the transition from not identifying with the roles, positions and practices on her course to identifying with them strongly a year later.

The Literacies for Learning in Further Education project[1]

The Literacies for Learning in Further Education (LfLFE) project aimed to identify literacy practices that enable students to succeed in learning across the curriculum. One of its major objectives has been to uncover actual and potential overlaps and connections between the reading and writing students do in their everyday lives for their own purposes and the literacy demands of their courses.

Further education colleges are a core part of the education service in the UK. Traditionally they provided occupational qualifications for school-leavers, and the bulk of their full-time students are still 16–19. However, over the years, the scope of what they provide and the profile of their students have changed significantly. Most UK colleges now provide educational opportunities from basic education through to higher education, as do community colleges and two-year colleges in Canada and the US. They also provide both academic and occupational qualifications. The age range of students can vary from 14 to the elderly.

Young people go to college for a variety of reasons, for example because they want to leave school, because they need to retake exams failed at school, because they do not want to go to university or do not have the right qualifications to go, or because they want to take 'vocational' subjects or qualifications not offered at school. Older people go to college, for example, to train or retrain in a different trade, to study in a local setting to increase their qualifications, having left school without them, or to expand their horizons and to enhance the quality of their lives on a personal level. For these reasons, the students at FE colleges are widely diverse, of differing ages, backgrounds and abilities. The likelihood is that the students have not opted for an academic course of study in their lives up to this point, although many mature students embark on academic careers through the college route.

To illustrate, in our research, a typical class of students taking an introductory course in hospitality and catering included a majority of young people straight from school with low level qualifications; two slightly older students who had taken higher level qualifications in academic subjects in school, but then switched to a more practical subject area; one mature student from Nigeria who had a degree in biology; and a mature student from Hong Kong. In terms of literacy, these students had widely varying experiences, expectations and levels of capability, but they were all expected to undertake the same course content, using the same teaching materials and the same assessment tools. As with many of the courses we researched, there was a focus on practical work, but also a substantial weight given to recording, in written form, the practical experiences gained, and learning – through classroom instruction – about theory underpinning practice in the vocation for which they were training.

The project was a collaboration between the University of Stirling, Lancaster University and four further education colleges and ran from January 2004 to June 2007. Six university-based researchers worked with 16 college lecturers to research their own courses and students. More than a hundred students took part in researching 32 units of study across eleven curriculum areas. Childcare was studied in common across all four colleges and the other areas ranged from A level social sciences to National Vocational Qualifications (NVQs) in Painting and Decorating.

Staff and students themselves tended to talk about literacy in terms of what students *can't* do, rather than in terms of what they *can* do. This is a manifestation of the deficit discourse of literacy that is prevalent in FE. This discourse is rooted in an autonomous model of literacy as a set of singular and transferable cognitive technical skills that can be taught, measured and tested against pre-specified standards. This discourse results in students routinely being given 'diagnostic' and 'screening' tests for literacy to determine their literacy 'level'. This way of viewing literacy is situated within a view of learning as the acquisition of knowledge and skills through direct instruction, rather than learning through participation.

However, when the project introduced to FE practitioners and students a broader view of literacy from a social practices perspective, as described in the next section, the project found that students engage in a multiplicity and abundance of literacy practices in their everyday lives, compared with the very specific sets of practices that are valued within the context of college. They engage not only in vernacular literacy practices – that is, those which arise from their own interests and concerns – but also in a wide range of bureaucratic, more formal literacy practices which are demanded by the practicalities of their lives (see Fowler and Edwards 2005; Smith 2005).

We found that the reading and writing students do on their college courses tend to be relatively restricted, with a particular focus on assessment. These 'pedagogic literacy practices' included, for example, making notes from textbooks or teacher-produced PowerPoint presentations, reading printed handouts, compiling specified information from the Internet, and specific 'assessment literacy practices', which included writing reports or essays, answering short written questions, and completing logs and portfolios as evidence of learning. Looking at courses through the lens of their literacy practices has also revealed that the demands on lower level courses are in many respects greater than those on higher level courses, and that there is often a tension between vocational and academic goals within the same course, the former involving, for example, reading and writing associated with simulations of work tasks, and the latter usually involving writing essays and reading for factual learning (see Edwards and Smith 2005; Satchwell and Ivanič 2007).

The final year of the research was devoted to developing, implementing and evaluating small changes in practice based on the understandings reached about vernacular and pedagogic literacies. Through the close analysis of these changes, the project found that aspects of the literacy practices from students' everyday lives, for example their collaborative nature, could be harnessed as resources for learning. It identified a list of 'aspects' of literacy practices, as represented in the framework which we discuss in the next section. The research has contributed to social scientific understanding by refining the concept of literacy practices, by reconceptualising 'transfer' and 'border crossing', and by demonstrating how the semiotic (meaning making) aspects of learning are integral to the cognitive and the practical. (For further details about the research project as a whole see Pardoe and Ivanič 2007; Ivanič *et al.* 2007; 2009; and for a discussion of the project methodology see Mannion and Ivanič 2007.)

The concept of 'literacy practices'

The LfLFE project made a unique contribution to the work of the Teaching and Learning Research Programme by studying learning through the lens of the literacy practices that mediate it. Rather than focusing on literacy as the 'target' of education, the project focused on literacy as a tool, a resource through which learning and teaching are accomplished. Within the project, literacy was not conceptualised as an autonomous value-free attribute lying within the individual – a set of singular and transferable cognitive technical skills that can be taught, measured and tested at a level of competence against pre-specified standards. Instead, the project worked with a social view of literacy, as developed within the New Literacy Studies (Street 1984; Barton 2007; Barton and Hamilton 1998; Baynham 1995). In a social view of literacy, reading and writing are not viewed as decontextualised 'skills' but as 'practices' embedded in their social contexts. A 'literacy practice' is a culturally recognisable way of utilising written language: a social practice that entails reading and/or writing something. This is an 'ecological' view, in which literacy practices vary from one context to another according to the purposes they serve, according to the meanings and values attached to them, and according to other aspects of their social context. This view leads the researcher to focus on the social, affective, technological and practical differences between, for example, the reading and writing involved in finding and booking a holiday for the family, and those involved in preparing for a history exam (Barton et al. 2000). A view of literacy, as adopted in FE, as a set of skills that can be tested, would not recognise the differences implicit in the comparison between these two practices. The LfLFE project used an ethnographic methodology to investigate in more detail the literacy practices in which further education students were engaged both on their courses and elsewhere in their lives.

Following work by Dell Hymes (1962) in anthropology and sociolinguistics, Theo van Leeuwen (1993) in semiotics, James Gee (1992) in relation to discourses, and others, any social practice can be seen as composed of a number of elements. Literacy practices when seen as social practices also comprise such elements, identified by Hamilton (2000) as participants, settings, artefacts and activities. The LfLFE project findings went further in elaborating these basic elements into a more detailed list of aspects of any literacy practice. The list of aspects was arrived at through examining the differences between literacy practices in and out of college, as part of the curriculum and as part of everyday life, and how each practice was viewed by participants (or partial or non-participants) in that literacy practice in relation to themselves. The list of aspects emerged as common factors that allowed for comparison among practices in the data. For the purposes of this chapter, we are focusing on the following eleven aspects of a literacy practice identified during the project: participants, audience, purpose, text-type, artefact, medium, mode, content, activity, place, and time/duration. Of these, six are aspects of any social practice – participants, purpose, artefact, activity, place, and time/duration – and can be mapped onto theoretical representations of the structure of any social practice or of social action, such as the Activity Theory triangle. The others, audience, text-type, medium, mode, and content are specific to communicative practices (spoken, written and visual), and we have found it useful to specify them when analysing and comparing the literacy practices which are the focus of the LfLFE project.[2] In this chapter we pay particular attention to two additional aspects – roles and subject positions inscribed in a practice, and values associated with a practice – and highlight their special significance. Figures 4.1 and 4.2 take these aspects of literacy practices as their starting point.

We would argue that any social practice, which has a communicative element, is constituted by at least these eleven aspects. However, the aspects are realised differently in different practices. Each aspect can be configured in an infinite number of ways. So, taking for example the text-type aspect, in the literacy practice of reading and writing in order to choose and book a family holiday, some of the text-types to be read are likely to be non-linear web pages, whereas in the literacy practice of preparing for a history exam many of the text-types to be read are likely to be relatively linear textbook paragraphs. Web pages and textbook paragraphs are different configurations of the 'text-type' aspect of literacy practices. In turn, there are infinite combinations of such configurations leading to the rich multiplicity of potential literacy practices. Hence, a change in how an element is configured changes the nature of the practice.

Further, we argue that participation in any one literacy practice can vary according to the experience of an individual in relation to that literacy practice. This goes some way to explaining how different people experience and react to literacy practices differently. In our research, these differences were related to the literacy practices in which the people engaged elsewhere in their lives. We illustrate this idea further below.

Characteristics of students' everyday literacy practices

Before examining specific pedagogic literacy practices, we set out our findings with regard to the characteristics of the literacy practices students tended to favour in their everyday lives. Although many students had to engage in various kinds of formal reading and writing such as filling in forms or applying for a place for a child at nursery, those practices which the students involved in our research tended to choose to participate in – and we would argue, tended to identify with – had the following characteristics:

- mostly multimodal, e.g. involving speech, music, gesture, movement, colour, pictures, symbols;
- mostly multimedia, e.g. including sound, electronic and paper media;
- shared, interactive, participatory – virtual and/or real;
- non-linear, i.e. involving complex, varied reading paths;
- agentic, i.e. with the student being in charge;
- purposeful to the student;
- clear audience perceived by the student;
- generative, i.e. involving sense making and creativity;
- self-determined in terms of activity, time and place.

We attempted to superimpose these characteristics onto our list of aspects of literacy practices, as shown in Table 4.1. The central column of words lists the aspects. In order to show that each of these can be configured in many ways, we presented each aspect as a continuum from one possible configuration on the

Table 4.1 Aspects of literacy practices, and illustrative continua of configurations

	Aspects of literacy practices	
Experienced as …		*Experienced as …*
More than one	Participants	One
Clear	Audience	Ambiguous
Clear	Purpose	Ambiguous
Non-linear	Text-type	Linear
Personal	Artefact	Impersonal
Multimedia	Medium	Mostly paper
Multimodal	Mode	Monomodal
Generative	Content	Non-generative
Agentic	Activity	Imposed
Not designated	Place	Designated
Self-determined	Time/Duration	Specified

left to its opposite on the right. We used the characteristics of students' everyday literacy practices to specify the configurations or 'settings' on the left-hand side of the diagram, and identified opposite attributes to specify those on the right. The two ends of the scales are not intended to be binary opposites, but rather to indicate a continuum along which each aspect is *experienced* by an individual. For each of the aspects, we have chosen one continuum of configurations to illustrate our point. However, these continua are not the only ones possible. For example, in respect of the 'purpose' aspect of literacy practices, we have chosen to focus on the continuum from 'clear to ambiguous', but we might also add a continuum from single-purposed to multi-purposed. In principle, several continua of configurations could be added in respect of each 'aspect'.

Roles, subject positions and values

In addition to the aspects of a literacy practice listed in Table 4.1, there are also less easily defined aspects of any social practice: the roles, subject positions inscribed in it, and the values associated with it. These aspects are crucial to explaining how one person experiences a literacy practice differently from another person, and can be seen to influence, and be influenced by all the other aspects. In our view, roles, subject positions and values are not separable from the more tangible aspects of literacy practices, but should be understood as overarching aspects, inextricably intertwined with the others. For this reason, these aspects are placed at the top of the list, and in reverse shading, as in Table 4.2.

Roles and subject positions are the socially available possibilities for selfhood that are inscribed in a practice and are afforded by participation in it (Ivanič 1998, 2005, 2006). A practice holds out one or more roles: for example, the role of 'friend' or of 'student'. A practice holds out one or more subject positions: for example, being a meticulous person, being an eco-warrior, being prepared to spend

Table 4.2 Roles and subject positions, and values as aspects of literacy practices

Aspects of literacy practices		
Experienced as …		*Experienced as …*
Identified with	Roles and subject positions inscribed in the practice	Not identified with
Shared	Values associated with the practice	Not shared
More than one	Participants	One
Clear	Audience	Ambiguous
Clear	Purpose	Ambiguous
Non-linear	Text-type	Linear
Personal	Artefact	Impersonal
Multimedia	Medium	Mostly paper
Multimodal	Mode	Monomodal
Generative	Content	Non-generative
Agentic	Activity	Imposed
Not designated	Place	Designated
Self-determined	Time/Duration	Specified

a long time on writing, being a Francophile, or being authoritative. Such roles and subject positions are inscribed in literacy practices in that reading or writing in a particular way, in a particular participation structure, for a particular purpose, using particular discourses, genres, tools and technologies, in a particular place and time is associated with being a particular type of person. People will identify with the roles and subject positions inscribed in a practice to varying degrees – hence the continuum from 'identified with' to 'not identified with' which we suggest is particularly significant in explaining why students vary in their uptake of literacy practices. People may identify with the positioning inscribed in some aspects of a literacy practice and not others: for example, they may identify with the use of technology, but not with the purpose of the practice; with the collaborative participation structure, but not with the content – these aspects will be in tension with one another for identification with the practice as a whole.

'Values' can be interpreted in two ways, both as sharing values associated with a practice, and a valuing of the practice itself. Arguably, successful essay writing involves both seeing a value in writing an essay in itself, and taking on the values of academic writing – coherent argumentation, accurate spelling, punctuation, paragraphing, etc. It is possible to write an essay without either set of values in place, but it will be easier and the essay is more likely to fit the marking criteria if they are, albeit temporarily. People identify (or don't identify) with the roles and subject positions inscribed in a practice, and therefore take on (or don't take on) the values associated with that practice.

Examining roles, identities and values contributes to an understanding of how aspects of a literacy practice can be configured in different ways. In any literacy practice the participants take on roles or identities and subscribe to particular values. When writing a letter we adjust our style and content according to whom we are sending the letter to: our role can be of friend, customer, patient, etc., and our sense of identity alters accordingly, as does our value system. As a friend we may value honesty, humour, intimacy – and our writing will reflect those values; as a customer we may value quality service, attention to detail – and we will write accordingly. As an example from everyday life, and as elaborated by Gee (2003), two individuals can participate in playing a computer game, but they can experience the practice differently according to whether or not they share the values associated with the practice, or identify with the roles and subject positions inscribed in the practice. Whether or not an individual shares the values, roles and subject positions of a literacy practice will determine how far they are likely to uphold or adhere to the characteristics associated with the literacy practice.

Hence, a literacy practice affords roles and subject positions, and is imbued with values, potentially resulting in the social or discoursal construction of identity through participation in that practice. However, this depends on the extent to which individuals identify with that practice in the sense of desiring to take on the goals, values and identities associated with it (sometimes called 'affiliation'). People are largely agents in the construction of their identities through reading and writing: they read and write their 'selves' through the practices they do or don't participate in.[3]

Using the framework as a heuristic for analysing literacy practices

We now illustrate the use of the framework as a heuristic for understanding and comparing literacy practices by analysing two literacy practices: one from students' own lives and associated with outside of college, and one required for a course of study and associated with being in college.

Text messaging is a literacy practice engaged in by the vast majority of the students we interviewed as a continuous element in their lives. Figure 4.1 represents our analysis of this literacy practice as experienced by these students. The 'spaghetti' line represents this impressionistically, by linking together the points on the continua for each of the aspects of the practice. It is not intended as a precise quantitative analysis, but as a broad-brush indication of how one literacy practice looks in order to compare it with another.

We can see from this impression that – although the students do not always see the content as particularly generative in the sense that it is not always creative or interesting (some students remarked on the banality of their text messages) – they experience the practice in ways that resonate with the characteristics of their everyday literacy practices as we have listed them: clear audience and purpose, agentic, self-determined, multimodal, etc. They also identify with the practice as something that they and their friends 'own' as a preferred means of communication, and they share the values associated with sending and receiving text messages. This means that these students are most likely to be amongst those creating new registers using the affordances and constraints of the technology as described, for example, by Greenfield and Subrahmanyam (2003) in relation to chat room discourse.

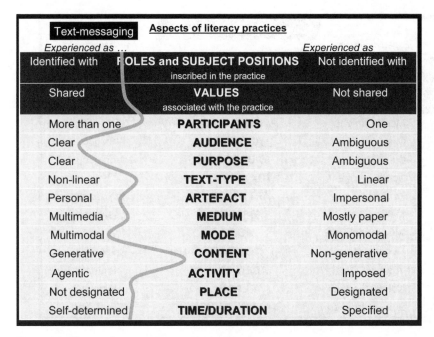

Text-messaging	**Aspects of literacy practices**	
Experienced as …		*Experienced as*
Identified with	**ROLES and SUBJECT POSITIONS** inscribed in the practice	Not identified with
Shared	**VALUES** associated with the practice	Not shared
More than one	**PARTICIPANTS**	One
Clear	**AUDIENCE**	Ambiguous
Clear	**PURPOSE**	Ambiguous
Non-linear	**TEXT-TYPE**	Linear
Personal	**ARTEFACT**	Impersonal
Multimedia	**MEDIUM**	Mostly paper
Multimodal	**MODE**	Monomodal
Generative	**CONTENT**	Non-generative
Agentic	**ACTIVITY**	Imposed
Not designated	**PLACE**	Designated
Self-determined	**TIME/DURATION**	Specified

Figure 4.1 How students experience text messaging

For the students in the LfLFE project, their roles and identities when sending a text message were clearly defined, as they were when engaging in other literacy practices of their own choosing. When in college, however, their roles and identities were less well defined, and their value systems were sometimes at odds with the requirements of the literacy practices on their courses. For example, the literacy practice of completing an NVQ logbook for these students can be represented as shown in Figure 4.2.

The process of filling in boxes already provided, on paper, using Standard English, working at a desk, individually, is likely to be experienced as almost the opposite of a literacy practice they would choose to do in their own time. Most of the students on NVQ courses found the practice of filling in their logbooks to be extremely tedious, time-consuming, boring and difficult to carry out without reference to a tutor. The fact that the practice was near impossible without help (a tutor remarked that the only reason she knew how to do it herself was through years of practice) instantly put the student in a position of powerlessness – a lack of agency in the activity and a loss of identity. The actual practice of writing in the logbook also seemed to have little to do with what they were learning – recording information after the event was a chore additional to and separate from the activity itself. Hence, the logbook seemed to have little inherent value, and the values associated with the practice, that is, ensuring that every box was ticked and signed, and every task was recorded in the right section under the right heading, were often not shared by the students.

Completing NVQ log book		
Experienced as ...		*Experienced as ...*
Identified with	**ROLES and SUBJECT POSITIONS** inscribed in the practice	Not identified with
Shared	**VALUES** associated with the practice	Not shared
More than one	**PARTICIPANTS**	One
Clear	**AUDIENCE**	Ambiguous
Clear	**PURPOSE**	Ambiguous
Non-linear	**TEXT-TYPE**	Linear
Personal	**ARTEFACT**	Impersonal
Multimedia	**MEDIUM**	Mostly paper
Multimodal	**MODE**	Monomodal
Generative	**CONTENT**	Non-generative
Agentic	**ACTIVITY**	Imposed
Not designated	**PLACE**	Designated
Self-determined	**TIME/DURATION**	Specified

Figure 4.2 How students experience completing the NVQ logbook

While many students would not share the values and identities associated with the practice of completing a logbook, this does not mean that they do not value and identify with the vocation for which they are training. For some students the identification with the future held out by the qualification was sufficient to negotiate the transition from college-based practices to work. For others, for whom the future was less clearly defined or imagined, the literacy practice of completing a logbook proved to be more of an obstacle. The case studies below illustrate this point.

The framework can be used in educational settings as a tool both for analysing students' literacy practices and for fine-tuning pedagogic practice. A key to this 'fine-tuning' is to examine the 'identities', 'subject positions' and 'writer roles' inscribed in literacy practices and to reconfigure such practices in ways with which students can identify. A change in the configuration of any one of the constituents changes the nature of the practice and may change the extent to which a person will identify with the roles and subject positions held out by the practice. The change can be effected by a tutor in an attempt to align required literacy practices more closely with those valued by students, or the change can be effected by an individual through the roles, subject positions and values they bring to a literacy practice, thereby changing their experience of that literacy practice.

Literacy theory as a heuristic for understanding identities in transition

Different people experience the same literacy practice in different ways, and the same person may experience the same literacy practice differently at different times. In this sense, identities can be in transition over time as an identity evolves, or can even vary during one day or one lesson. The following case studies illustrate the different ways in which identity can impact on the experience of literacy. In the first two examples, the individuals experience the same literacy practice in different ways, while in the third example the same literacy practices are experienced differently over time. We also illustrate ways in which deliberately altering the configuration of a literacy practice can influence participation and identification with that practice.

Negotiating the transition from education into work: Logan as agent

Logan was a student on an NVQ Catering and Hospitality course. When we met him he was on a level 2 course, which he completed and then moved up to level 3, which is generally undertaken only by students hoping to work in a managerial role. Logan agreed with his peers that filling in the logbook was boring and difficult. He said, 'The logbook is very, very hard to understand I think. Sometimes looking at it, it just bugs my head' and 'You've only got a small space to write in so you have to sit there for twenty minutes and think what am I going to write in this and how am I going to get everything that I need to show I've done into this tiny little box?' However, Logan was dedicated to a future in the catering industry:

> My mum says, oh get a job in an office or something, I just, it's not me, I'm more of a hands-on person, and I like, I like making people happy, and stuff, do you know what I mean ... I like the feeling it gives me when I see someone's happy with the meal they've got and they've got a smile on their face, and the whole restaurant's talking and there's a happy atmosphere.

'It's just not me' explains his own feelings of identity. The way he felt about the course also related to his sense of identity, and changed as time went on:

> I struggled last year, I wasn't as interested in the course as I am this year ... when I came into this year, I was put onto an NVQ level 2 course, and straight away I was more interested and it was like, right, I've got all this new stuff to learn now, and it's like well, yeah, and then this year it's got even better and I'm even more interested now. It seems like the more responsibility, or the more trust someone will put into me, the better I can work.

Logan here is articulating the importance of agency in his engagement with his learning. The point is made further when he explains the extra work he undertakes in the running of the training restaurant, taking on the role of head waiter even when he is 'just a student' and producing information sheets, menus and PowerPoint presentations to be shown in the restaurant:

If you get me into a project which I'm interested in, like I won't be bothered how much time I spend on it, I'll sit there and I'll do it until I'm happy and happy that it is correct.

This appears to be in sharp contrast to the way in which he talked about his attitude to reading and writing in an educational context:

I'm not too keen on reading, I've never, never read a book after high school, I've never picked up a book to read it.

He also complained about the drafting and re-drafting required for writing at school. Explaining why this was different from spending hours working on a PowerPoint, or a computer game which requires extensive reading to take part in it, he said:

I think it's the actual, the sitting down and having to concentrate all the time on the piece of paper and the words, that just look so plain on this piece of paper, do you know what I mean? I think it's the very, just how plain things are when you're reading and writing.

The fact that Logan is willing to spend his own time on producing texts for the training kitchen is related to his sense of identity. For this reason, even though he disliked the logbook and the activity of filling it in, he could see a purpose in completing it in that he could see how it would lead to a future career with which he identified:

Interviewer: If you went for a job interview, you wouldn't take the logbook with you, would you?
Logan: I would. I'd say this is my logbook, if you want to look through it, cos I'm going to put all my stuff in it like, all my little certificates and stuff, or I might put them into my CV but get a copy made for my logbook, cos it shows you've got like if ... just in case he asks, what was your NVQ like?

Logan was keen to distinguish himself from other candidates at an interview he could envisage in the future, all of whom would have the same NVQ qualification. A way for him to do this was to have an immaculate logbook. For Logan, the NVQ logbook is purposeful, he can perceive an audience for it – a future employer – and the artefact of the logbook itself therefore becomes much more personal to him. Because he feels more ownership of the book, he sometimes fills it in at home and spends his own time on it, rather than confining it to the college. It is still paper-based, he still finds it boring, but for him it does have characteristics that make it more in tune with students' everyday literacy practices in certain aspects. Logan values the practice of completing his NVQ logbook, although he does not identify with the paper-based, linear, black and white, uncreative aspects of the practice. He does strongly identify with the role, the subject positions and the values of being a restaurant manager for which he needs his qualification. Hence, he identifies with the purpose and future identity, but not with the literacy practice itself.

Figure 4.3 shows examples of pages from Logan's logbook, which illustrate his keenness to demonstrate his competence in ways beyond the affordances of the boxes supplied: he has filled his boxes with closely handwritten text, and has included additional information beyond. This was in spite of his feelings about his handwriting and his aversion to writing on paper:

> Say I wrote an essay fully handwritten I would be able to pick out so many different font styles in there it would be unbelievable, my handwriting it's got no fashion to it at all. Honestly.

For Logan then, his identity was securely located in the future held out by the course and its incumbent literacy practices. As a student on a Catering and Hospitality course, he was negotiating the transition from the identity of a schoolboy to the identity he envisaged for himself as working in a restaurant. He was able to engage successfully in the literacy practices required, such as filling in the logbook, as well as literacy practices beyond course requirements such as writing information sheets, because he was in control of positioning himself in relation to them. His values changed over time to fall in line with those associated with a future in the restaurant business. His sense of agency was crucial to him participating fully in the literacy practices required and ultimately contributed to his exhaustive and perfectionist approach to his logbook.

Negotiating the transition from education into work: Simon

Simon was a peer of Logan's who described himself as someone who always wants to be 'doing'. When asked how he felt about written work at school, he replied with some force, 'Well, I didn't *like* it' – as though this should be obvious. Along with Logan, and many other students on vocational courses, such as Catering and Hospitality, he did not include himself as an 'academic type'.

Yet in his spare time he read *Caterer* and *Restaurant* magazines, had recently begun reading a biography of a cook and he downloaded recipes from the Internet. He bought a book by Raymond Blanc and had cooked recipes from it for his parents. Simon was very clear that he wanted to be 'a chef, definitely', and his interests outside of college concurred with his desire. When he talked about his college work, he described being daunted by it at the beginning, but then coming to terms with it. Describing the impending transition from level 2 to level 3, he said:

Simon:	The assignments will be a bit more challenging, yeah. [...] The logbook's a lot bigger as well ...
Interviewer:	Right. Does that worry you?
Simon:	It does a bit.

Q10. What are your job roles and responsibilities when working in the Restaurant:

Job Role	Responsibilities	
Head Waiter	Taking orders, Alerting people to allergies, helping customers with Menu Making customers feel welcome →	Portion Control, giving cutlery changes, serving sweets, helping others
Waiter	lay up, take drinks orders, greeting guests, cutlery change serving courses, Silver Service →	Polishing cutlery watering custom → dealing with initial complain
Still Room	when in still it is mostly doing mis-en-place. Are pouring butlers, sweet trolley, polish plates →	make sure service gear is ready and preparing Tea and coffee
Reception	you are the first person the guests come in contact with, this means you must be Polite, Pleasent *	
Bar Person	Bottling up, being able to send the correct drinks and handling cash.	✓

* and helpful, directing people to tables. You must be able to deal with cash and take bookings. you are in charge of cash which means you have to send bills out to customers with the right amount charged.

Q6. If a visitor comes to reception and asks for directions to Hairdressing what would you do?

• I would ask a coworker to escort them to that department

• If there was nobody about to take them then I would Politly tell them I can't leave the desk and give
Q7. How do we receive and assist the following visitors? them the best directions i could.

A Salesperson Cold Calling or some-one with an appointment to see your Line Manager –
I would ask to see some identification then offer them a seat, maybe a complimentary coffee depending on how important they were
An engineer arriving to repair the freezer – then greet my line manager and tell I would show them to the piece of equipment ——— them about which is in need of maintenence then I would go get the line the visitor. ✓
manager and the chef so to give background on damaged item
Q8. Who is responsible for ensuring that guests are greeted and directed efficiently?

• Anyone who comes into contact with guests are responsible for ensuring guests are looked after, greeted and
Q9. Why is it important that these jobs are given to the appropriate people? be, but is mainly directed to the place they wish to the receptionists

• because Customer Care is the most important responsibility, Part of any business because if you can't
Q10. What services offered by your organisation (the college) are available to customers? any profit

• Speciality Evenings   • travel Shop
  i.e. valentines, any fautkes.
• Silver Service   • Bistro (small cafe type open kitchen)
• Banquet Service   • Roeburn Suite
                            (conferences). ✓

Q11. Describe the Organisations structure

The Organisational structure is a hierachy • with   it then Splits into
5 different sections including:- Admin, Beauty therapy, Retail, Catering and hairdressing. ✓
Q12. What else does the college offer that is only available to the Restaurant Customers?

• three Course Meal.   • Alchohol
• table Service   • Silver Service ✓

Figure 4.3 Pages from Logan's logbook

But then he went on to compare his feelings of apprehension to how he felt before embarking on level 2 after completing level 1 and indicated that he knew he would manage. Several times in interview he described how he had progressed, overcoming difficulties and what he describes as 'challenges', for example,

> I used to find it quite difficult to read recipes but not at all any more, it's like second nature now, I don't have any problem with that.

> I used to have quite a bad concentration really. I did used to have a bad concentration, but not so much any more because it interests me more, and when I'm interested I'll listen.

His 'interest' (in both senses of the word) in the course was evidently a factor in his success and this in itself can be seen as an influencing factor in his experience of the literacy practices on the course as well as those related to the course but in his everyday life.

Simon might be described as someone who was coping well with the demands of the course because he was dedicated to becoming a chef. He chose to attend a college a long way from his home because it had a good reputation, which meant he had a very long day travelling to and from college. He also worked long shifts at the weekend in a restaurant. It was clearly the written, 'academic' part of the course that he found difficult, but he was willing to take on these challenges in order to gain the qualification that he has set his heart on.

His relationship to his logbook is more pragmatic than Logan's, and he did not see it so much as a reflection of himself:

Simon: I don't think I'd take my logbook to an interview, no. No, never thought of taking my logbook to an interview.

Interviewer: So the logbook for you isn't necessarily the important bit. The important bit is the qualification.

Simon: Qualification, yeah, I'd just tell them how far I am into my NVQ2 or whatever.

Figure 4.4 represents the difference in the way the two young men experienced the literacy practice of completing the logbook. The literacy practice itself is the same in as far as the reading and writing required to carry it out are the same: a practice in which the written text reifies knowledge, understanding capability and learning (Barton and Hamilton 2005). However, the experience of the practice is subtly different for each. Simon's engagement in the practice is more structurally determined: he treats the practice as a task imposed by the institution. In contrast, Logan exerts agency and ownership over the task, which, we suggest, explains why his completion of the logbook is more comprehensive.

For the students on the catering course, the logbook remained the same,[4] but individual students' experiences of completing it varied within the class. While both Logan and Simon completed the logbook successfully, the actual literacy practice of filling it in became more personal and rewarding for Logan because he used

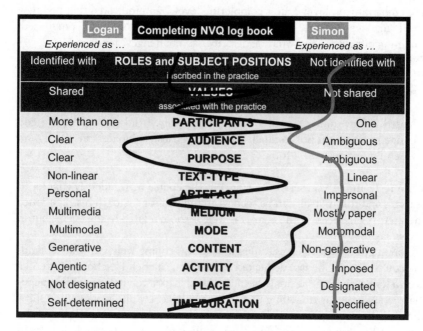

Logan	Completing NVQ log book	Simon
Experienced as ...		*Experienced as ...*
Identified with	**ROLES and SUBJECT POSITIONS** inscribed in the practice	Not identified with
Shared	**VALUES** associated with the practice	Not shared
More than one	**PARTICIPANTS**	One
Clear	**AUDIENCE**	Ambiguous
Clear	**PURPOSE**	Ambiguous
Non-linear	**TEXT-TYPE**	Linear
Personal	**ARTEFACT**	Impersonal
Multimedia	**MEDIUM**	Mostly paper
Multimodal	**MODE**	Monomodal
Generative	**CONTENT**	Non-generative
Agentic	**ACTIVITY**	Imposed
Not designated	**PLACE**	Designated
Self-determined	**TIME/DURATION**	Specified

Figure 4.4 Logan's and Simon's experiences of completing the NVQ logbook

it to represent something of his identity. This variation raises the issue of exactly what the logbook is assessing and indicates its ambiguity as an assessment tool.

The transition from non-identification to identification: Olivia

Olivia started college on a level 3 Child Care course. Despite having the requisite GCSE qualifications to enrol on the course, she struggled with the work and was advised to drop down to a level 2 course as a 'confidence-builder' (according to the tutors). She successfully completed the level 2 course during the first year of our research in the college and then moved on to take almost the identical level 3 course she started on, this time with a greatly improved outcome.

From interviews with Olivia we can see how she experienced the literacy practices required of her for the level 3 course the first time around, in 2003–4, and the second time around in 2005–6, after successfully completing the level 2 course in between. In hindsight she told us:

2003–4

Olivia: I wasn't passing my assignments and I wasn't understanding exactly what was going on. I didn't know how to make it sound more in-depth than what I was already saying cos I'm not very good at writing things down.

Interviewer:	Yeah, so how did you feel at the end of the first year then?
Olivia:	Kind of, erm, a bit angry at myself that I couldn't do it.
Interviewer:	At yourself?
Olivia:	Yeah, the fact that I wasn't, I didn't feel bright enough.

2004–5

| Interviewer: | And on the level 2 course you found yourself going into depth? |
| Olivia: | Yeah, it was really strange! The questions were a lot easier, the layout of the questions; I understood what the questions were asking me. |

2005–6

| Olivia: | Now that I've got into understanding the harder words [on level 3], I'm starting to understand what the books are telling me now. [...] The fact that I am now starting to write more and do more paper work, I'm starting to think that maybe I possibly could [be a social worker] |

Figure 4.5 represents the change in Olivia's experience of the literacy practices required of her across time, and shows how her identification with the future held out by the course (believing she could now become a social worker) and her

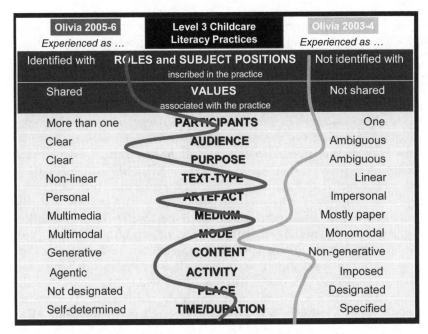

Olivia 2005-6	Level 3 Childcare	Olivia 2003-4
Experienced as ...	**Literacy Practices**	*Experienced as ...*
Identified with	**ROLES and SUBJECT POSITIONS** inscribed in the practice	Not identified with
Shared	**VALUES** associated with the practice	Not shared
More than one	**PARTICIPANTS**	One
Clear	**AUDIENCE**	Ambiguous
Clear	**PURPOSE**	Ambiguous
Non-linear	**TEXT-TYPE**	Linear
Personal	**ARTEFACT**	Impersonal
Multimedia	**MEDIUM**	Mostly paper
Multimodal	**MODE**	Monomodal
Generative	**CONTENT**	Non-generative
Agentic	**ACTIVITY**	Imposed
Not designated	**PLACE**	Designated
Self-determined	**TIME/DURATION**	Specified

Figure 4.5 Olivia's experience of literacy practices on the level 3 Child Care course

identification with the course itself (understanding the textbooks) influences her experience. Even though the courses are fundamentally the same, Olivia experiences them differently because of the difference in her self-positioning. Hence, while she felt isolated and as though she were struggling alone in 2003, she felt part of a cohesive group two years later. And while the content was the same, the fact that she could understand it better in 2005–6 meant that she found it interesting, and she considered herself to have more agency. Although the work was still mostly paper-based, she could see opportunities for incorporating other media and modes with which she was familiar in other parts of her life, and she saw relevance in her leisure reading to her course. For example, she found the novel *The Curious Incident of the Dog in the Night-time* relevant as it referred to a boy with autism, and she read newspaper articles about child abuse with renewed interest. Hence, the transition between college and her everyday life became less of an obvious shift and more of a continuum. In turn, the literacy practices she participated in at college became more resonant with the characteristics of the practices in her everyday life.

Olivia's subject position over time was transformed from an underachieving student who 'didn't feel bright enough' to a successful student who 'understand[s] what books are telling [her] now'. The process of transition has involved identification as someone who has access to an academic literacy as well as someone who has a realistic chance of a career working in an area that interests her.

Easing the transition to study: fine-tuning pedagogic literacy practices

So how did Olivia's transition in role and subject position come about? It was partly an increase in confidence, partly an acclimatisation to the requirements of college. We would also suggest that the engagement with the literacy practices in the interim level 2 course contributed significantly to those changes. Olivia's tutor – a tutor-researcher on the LfLFE project – deliberately incorporated aspects of students' everyday literacy practices into her classroom activities. Instead of conventional pedagogic practices such as individual essay writing, writing answers to questions and reading textbooks, the tasks she set involved the students in multimodal and multimedia practical activities such as designing posters, making leaflets and creating PowerPoint presentations. These were largely collaborative activities in that the class organised themselves into groups to produce posters and presentations. Crucially, also, the activities allowed for students bringing their own interests from outside college into the classroom. This was manifested in the subjects of their presentations – for example, one group's topic was film and film stars, while another's was pop music. In this sense, as well as the tutor allowing students to bring music into the classroom for part of one lesson a week, the tutor was facilitating the creation of a 'third space' in the classroom (Pahl and Rowsell 2005), where outside interests were given a place within the college environment. All of these activities clearly involved literacy, but students like Olivia managed them without difficulty. This is partly because the students are able to identify

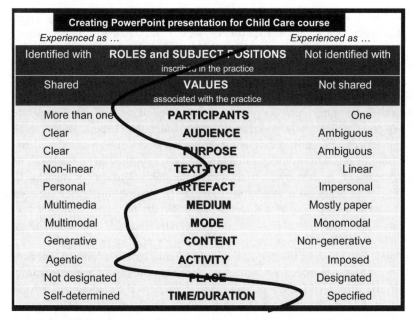

	Creating PowerPoint presentation for Child Care course	
Experienced as ...		*Experienced as ...*
Identified with	**ROLES and SUBJECT POSITIONS** inscribed in the practice	Not identified with
Shared	**VALUES** associated with the practice	Not shared
More than one	**PARTICIPANTS**	One
Clear	**AUDIENCE**	Ambiguous
Clear	**PURPOSE**	Ambiguous
Non-linear	**TEXT-TYPE**	Linear
Personal	**ARTEFACT**	Impersonal
Multimedia	**MEDIUM**	Mostly paper
Multimodal	**MODE**	Monomodal
Generative	**CONTENT**	Non-generative
Agentic	**ACTIVITY**	Imposed
Not designated	**PLACE**	Designated
Self-determined	**TIME/DURATION**	Specified

Figure 4.6 How students experienced the PowerPoint activity

with the content and the purpose of the activity, and are able to draw on the resources from their own lives. Figure 4.6 illustrates how the practice of creating a PowerPoint presentation for a childcare course draws on configurations of literacy practices in students' everyday lives, as well as having some characteristics of college-based practices.

Olivia's tutors were right to suggest that the year at level 2 would provide a confidence boost: by participating in literacy-related activities which resonated with those of her everyday life, Olivia was able to position herself positively in relation to the course and to identify herself as an able and agentic learner. Olivia's comment 'It was really strange! ... I understood what the questions were asking me', indicates the complexity of the factors involved in changing her perception of the literacy practices. We would argue that, by tapping into what Olivia was good at in her everyday life and using these skills in the production of coursework, her tutor was creating the space for Olivia to develop into someone who could recognise herself as able to study at level 3. Even though the course became more theoretical at level 3, and the literacy practices became more complex (for example, see Satchwell 2007; Ivanič and Satchwell 2007), Olivia's sense of identity altered sufficiently to take them on with ease. She no longer focused on what she couldn't do – 'I'm not very good at writing things down' – but rather on what she could – 'I'm starting to think that maybe I possibly could [be a social worker]'.

Conclusion

Our focus in this chapter has been on literacy studies as a lens through which to understand pedagogic practices. In particular, we have shown how transitions across social space and transitions across time can be investigated through attention to the literacy practices in which students are engaging. Reading and writing construct identities, and different degrees of identification with the roles and subject positions inscribed in literacy practices impact upon students' engagement and ultimately the depth of their learning. Our examples show that different students can experience a literacy practice differently, and that the same student can experience the same literacy practices differently at different stages in her development. Some students benefit from fluidity across different domains and stages of their lives, while others experience more compartmentalisation, and hence ambivalence about engaging in practices. Tutors deliberately attempting to make the reading and writing required on their courses more palatable to students can 'artificially' adjust a literacy practice. They can do this with reference to the literacy practices in which students engage most readily and adjust different aspects of the literacy practice accordingly.

The aim of the project has been to achieve fluidity between literacy practices in and out of college in order to increase identification and enhance learning. Tutors in the third phase of the project made changes to the reading and writing required on their courses by paying attention to the various aspects of the literacy practices and adjusting the configurations of one or more aspects in some way, sometimes very subtly, but thereby changing the way in which students identified with them. This was only possible, however, because the tutors understood more about their students' favoured literacy practices outside of college and were able to consider the students' construction of their identities, that is, how they perceived themselves both in the present and in the future. Overall, we found that pedagogic literacy practices can be more successfully engaged in by making the reading and writing on a course more compatible with students' sense of who they are and who they want to become.

There are therefore at least two major implications of the project. One is that it is beneficial for tutors to find out more about their students' present and projected future identities, as reflected by the literacy practices in which they currently engage, and those to which they need to aspire in order to achieve their chosen future. Another is that teachers and college staff need to pay more attention to the characteristics of students' everyday literacy practices, and to fine-tune the pedagogic literacies on their courses to achieve resonance with those practices with which the students identify. In this way, students' transitions across time and space may enrich, rather than impede, their learning.

Notes

1   The project was part of the Teaching and Learning Research Programme (TLRP) in the UK, funded by the Economic and Social Research Council (ESRC), Grant no. RES -139-25-0117. The research was conducted by a team, which included David Barton, Richard Edwards, Zoe Fowler, Greg Mannion, Kate Miller and June Smith as well as ourselves. For further details, see www.lancs.ac.uk/lflfe

2   The exact elements and number of elements on the list are not as important as the principle that there is a finite set of elements that constitute literacy practices, each of which can be configured in an infinite number of ways. We have slightly expanded or collapsed this list for different purposes in different project publications (see, for example, Pardoe and Ivanič 2007; Ivanič *et al.* 2007, 2009; Ivanič and Satchwell 2007; Ivanič 2009).

3   For further discussion of identification in relation to language and literacy practices, see Gee (2000, 2003, 2005), Wenger (1998) and, specifically referring to the LfLFE data, Ivanič (2006).

4   As part of the LfLFE project's endeavour to use an understanding of students' everyday literacy practices to inform changes in pedagogic literacy practices, the tutors on this course subsequently attempted to make the logbook more multimodal, using colour and diagrams, with more freedom to write without the confines of boxes and allowing for photographs to be included as well as writing.

Bibliography

Barton, D. (2007) *Literacy: An Introduction to the Ecology of Written Language* (2nd edn), Oxford: Blackwell.

Barton, D. and Hamilton, M. (1998) *Local Literacies: Reading and Writing in One Community*, London: Routledge.

—— (2005) 'Literacy, reification and the dynamics of social interaction', in D. Barton and K. Tusting (eds) *Beyond Communities of Practice: Language, Power and Social Context*, Cambridge: Cambridge University Press.

Barton, D., Hamilton, M. and Ivanič, R. (eds) (2000) *Situated Literacies: Reading and Writing in Context*, London: Routledge.

Baynham, M. (1995) *Literacy Practices: Investigating Literacy in Social Contexts*, London: Longman.

Edwards, R. and Smith, J. (2005) 'Swamping and spoonfeeding: literacies for learning in further education', *Journal of Vocational Education and Training*, 57: 47–60.

Fowler, Z. and Edwards, R. (2005) 'Mobility and situatedness in literacy practices: the case of further education', paper presented at the British Educational Research Association Annual Conference, University of Glamorgan, 14–17 September 2005. Available online at www.leeds.ac.uk/educol/documents/143407.doc

Gee, J. P. (1992) *The Social Mind: Language, Ideology, and Social Practice*, New York: Bergin and Garvey.

—— (2000) 'The new literacy studies: from "socially situated" to the work of the social', in D. Barton, M. Hamilton and R. Ivanič (eds) *Situated Literacies: Reading and Writing in Context*, London: Routledge.

—— (2003) *What Video Games have to Teach us about Learning and Literacy*, New York: Palgrave/Macmillan.

—— (2005) 'Semiotic social spaces and affinity spaces: from the age of mythology to today's schools', in D. Barton and K. Tusting (eds) *Beyond Communities of Practice: Language, Power and Social Context*, Cambridge: Cambridge University Press.

Greenfield and Subrahmanyam (2003) 'Characteristics of online chat', *Applied Developmental Psychology*, 24: 713–38.

Hamilton, M. (2000) 'Expanding the new literacy studies: using photographs to explore literacy as a social practice', in D. Barton, M. Hamilton and R. Ivanič (eds) *Situated Literacies: Reading and Writing in Context*, London: Routledge.

Hymes, D. (1962) 'The ethnography of communication', in T. Gladwin and W. Sturtevant (eds) *Anthropology and Human Behavior*, Washington, DC: Anthropological Society of Washington.

Ivanič, R. (1998) *Writing and Identity: the Discoursal Construction of Identity in Academic Writing*, Amsterdam: John Benjamins.

—— (2005) 'The discoursal construction of writer identity', in R. Beach, J. Green, M. Kamil and T. Shanahan (eds) *Multidisciplinary Perspectives on Literacy Research* (rev. edn), Cresskill, NJ: Hampton Press.

—— (2006) 'Language, learning and identification', in R. Kiely, P. Rea-Dickens, H. Woodfield and G. Clibbon (eds) *Language, Culture and Identity in Applied Linguistics*, London: Equinox.

—— (2009) 'Bringing literacy studies into research on learning across the curriculum', in M. Baynham and M. Prinsloo (eds) *The Future of Literacy Studies*, London: Routledge.

Ivanič, R. and Satchwell, C. (2007) 'Boundary crossings: networking and transforming literacies in research processes and college courses', *The Journal of Applied Linguistics*, 4(1): 101–24.

Ivanič, R., Edwards, R., Satchwell, C. and Smith, J. (2007) 'Possibilities for pedagogy in further education: harnessing the abundance of literacy', *British Educational Research Journal*, 33: 703–21.

Ivanič, R., Edwards, R., Barton, D., Martin-Jones, M., Fowler, Z., Hughes, B., Mannion, G., Miller, K., Satchwell, C. and Smith, J. (2009) *Improving Learning in College: Rethinking Literacies Across the Curriculum*, London: Routledge.

Mannion, G. and Ivanič, R. (2007) 'Mapping literacy practices: theory, methodology, methods', *International Journal of Qualitative Studies in Education*, 20: 15–30.

Pahl, K. and Rowsell, J. (2005) *Literacy and Education: The New Literacy Studies in the Classroom*, London: Paul Chapman.

Pardoe, S. and Ivanič, R. (2007) *Literacies for Learning in Further Education: Making Reading and Writing Practices Across the Curriculum More Useful for Learning*, DVD and accompanying booklet, Lancaster: PublicSpace Ltd and Lancaster University.

Satchwell, C. (2007) 'Creating third spaces for literacies in further education', *The Teacher Trainer*, 21(2): 11–14.

Satchwell, C. and Ivanič, R. (2007) 'The textuality of learning contexts in UK colleges', *Pedagogy, Culture and Society*, 15: 303–16.

Smith, J. (2005) 'How students' everyday literacy passions (practices) are mobilized within the further education curricula', *Journal of Vocational Education and Training*, 57: 319–34.

Street, B. (1984) *Literacy in Theory and Practice*, Cambridge: Cambridge University Press.

Van Leeuwen, T. (1993) 'Genre and field in critical discourse analysis: a synopsis', *Discourse and Society*, 4: 193–223.

Wenger, E. (1998) *Communities of Practice: Learning, Meaning and Identity*, Cambridge: Cambridge University Press.

5 Managing transitions in *Skills for Life*

Mary Hamilton

Introduction

This chapter explores learner transitions into and through the *Skills for Life* strategy that has organised the field of adult literacy, numeracy and ESOL in England (ALNE) in new ways since 2001. The analysis is framed by concepts from actor network theory and the new literacy studies that emphasise the mediating role of cultural artefacts in organising social relations. The chapter falls into three parts. The first section traces the origins of the *Skills for Life* strategy, outlining the elements of the strategy within New Labour's broader social and educational policy. Because this is a field of education that is being enclosed for the first time, it is a particularly striking example of how global forces are reshaping educational and other social policy areas. As a field that is itself in transition, it is a good site for problematising the notion of 'transition' itself. In the second section, using ethnographic and documentary evidence from recent studies, I look at how learner identities are managed within the *Skills for Life* infrastructure, particularly exploring tutor agency in the pedagogical process. In the final section the implications for our understanding of the concept of 'transitions' are considered in the light of this critical analysis.

The field of adult literacy, language and numeracy, which is the focus of this chapter, was first recognised as a policy area in the 1970s (Hamilton and Hillier 2006). It began with a 'Right to Read' campaign orchestrated by voluntary organisations and taken up by the BBC as one of the first of the media campaigns that have since become a familiar part of the social policy landscape. The campaign mobilised many volunteer teachers inspired by the social justice concerns of the time and international mass literacy campaigns. The Adult Literacy Resource Agency, a national agency for England and Wales, was set up and this became a focal point for the new field. During the subsequent 30 years, this initially unorganised domain of social action moved from the margins of educational policy into the mainstream, gradually gaining in status. Its progress has been erratic however, as it has struggled for legitimacy amidst wider shifts in national policy priorities that have constantly redefined the funding sources, goals and discourse of the emerging field.

Historical analysis of the development of adult literacy and numeracy between the 1970s and 1990s shows a fragmentary and largely informal provision that catered for a wide range of adults in settings as diverse as further education colleges, community projects, workplaces and prisons. The field was legally defined for the first time by the Further and Higher Education Act of 1992 which sets limits around what could be funded and recognised as adult basic education (see Fowler 2004; Hamilton and Hillier 2006; Coben 2006; Rosenberg 2008). From this point on it is possible to track the increasing formalisation of the field and its alignment with school achievements, vocational qualifications and international benchmarks. During this process decisions are made which determine which elements should be kept in or left out of the definitions of adult literacy and numeracy and ESOL, especially their vocational and community related aspects.

In 2001, for the first time, the government in England funded a national policy for the field – the *Skills for Life* strategy, building on the National Literacy Strategy in schools and framed by an open vision of lifelong learning. In his foreword to the *Skills for Life* strategy document, David Blunkett, then Secretary of State for Education wrote:

> A shocking 7 million adults in England cannot read and write at the level we would expect of an 11-year-old. Even more have problems with numbers. The cost to the country as a whole could be as high as £10 billion a year. The cost to people's personal lives is incalculable. [...] Despite strong roots, stretching back to the mutual learning of the nineteenth century, standards of literacy and numeracy provision have been too poor for too long. That is why, in 1998, we asked Sir Claus Moser to write his ground-breaking report, *A Fresh Start*, on literacy and numeracy in England. [...] [We] will be spending £1.5 billion over the next three years on enabling those with poor literacy and numeracy abilities to acquire the skills they need.
>
> (DfES 2001)

The strategy sets out energetically to create a specialised qualification structure and a set of professional standards to which practitioners must adhere. Core curricula defining levels and elements of knowledge in literacy, numeracy in English for Speakers of Other Languages (ESOL) and, more recently, ICT were aligned with performance in school-based subjects and calibrated to international survey league tables.

New forms of diagnostic, formative and summative assessment have defined the relevance of what students and teachers can demonstrate as subject knowledge. Key aspects of this have been the introduction of individual learning plans (ILPs) that document student progress toward curriculum goals and a national multiple-choice test that is the recognised standard of achievement. The national test is set at Level 2 of the curriculum, equivalent to GCSE. A high profile media publicity campaign targeted specific groups of potential learners identified in the strategy document, aiming to encourage reluctant adults to recognise their need for help with literacy and numeracy and to beat their 'gremlins'. Yearly participation and achievement targets were set and tied to funding, along with an inspection framework that monitors teacher performance at many levels. This has created what has been termed a 'high stakes' target culture (Goldstein 2006; Lavender *et al.* 2004).

The effect of this coordinated and rapid set of changes has been to fix the slippery and diverse pedagogical field of adult language, literacy and numeracy and make it tractable as a part of New Labour's larger social policy vision. The 'fix' can be clearly seen in the fact that the field itself has (for the time being) taken on the name of the policy: the abbreviation *Skills for Life* is currently a standard shorthand used to describe courses, tutors and learners in literacy numeracy, ESOL and ICT and the terms are used throughout publicity, training and teaching materials.

This is just the latest of many name changes signalling different constellations of subject courses and goals for the field, and the difficulty of developing positive terminology for what is often seen as a stigmatised area of provision. The inclusion of ESOL, in particular, has been a source of great instability as government policy responds to changes in refugee and migrant worker populations. The foregrounding of 'skills' signals the increasing link between literacy and vocational workplace training.

The fix aims to open unproblematic transition pathways between school and work via lifelong learning, which itself has progressively narrowed (see Field 2000; Usher and Edwards 2007). I argue in this chapter that the process of formalising these pathways also fixes the identities of those working and learning in the field through a range of interlocking processes of sorting and filtering of people and experiences. These processes affect the social relationships of teachers and learners with one another, their subjectivities and the narratives that can be told about learning in the literacy classroom. The focus of the chapter is therefore on how the transition in terms of formal progression and shaping of identity 'works' within *Skills for Life*. It takes the view that the 'successful *Skills for Life* learner' is a co-construction of the tutor, the learner and the instructional infrastructure that materialises the *Skills for Life* regime and within which tutors and learners interact.

Analytic framework

There is a growing critical literature on the notion of performativity within education that explores teachers' roles, agency and resistance to prevailing practices and discourses. Burnard and White (2008: 673–6) give a good summary of the theoretical roots of the concept of performativity. These emphasise both how identity is made through processes of repeated and routinised action and the ways in which these processes are regulated and enforced by social and/or bureaucratic norms. Ball (2001) has applied these ideas to recent educational reforms and uses Lyotard's suggestion that the extensive use of policy technologies that monitor and measure teachers' work result in a kind of 'terror' that freezes innovation and creativity, ignores or denies that which is not measurable and reaches deeply into professional identity (Ball 2003). Webb (2006) has used a Foucauldian framework to foreground performative notions of self-surveillance and microcircuits of power, showing how regimes of power are shaped and renewed in moment-by-moment interactions and how these contribute to the institutionalisation of knowledge.

To this very productive perspective I would like to bring two additional theoretical resources from Actor Network Theory (ANT) and the New Literacy Studies. Both of these approaches have resonances with the sociocultural theory which holds that identities are relational, made and shifted in the course of contentious everyday social interactions (see Holland *et al.* 2001; Bartlett 2007).

These approaches emphasise the role of *cultural artefacts* as a key to identity formation and change. Cultural artefacts mediate moment-by-moment social interactions, acting as points of contact and fixity for developing shared meanings within regimes of performativity. As Burgess (2006: 9) notes, the events within which these artefacts are embedded can be seen as 'analytical doorways into an understanding of social systems'.

ANT derives from the sociology of science and technology (see Law 1994 and Latour 2005 for clear introductions). Rather than seeing the social order as a set of structures within which individuals exert agency, ANT views it in a more fluid way as a force field within which different projects of social ordering (such as a scientific innovation or a government policy initiative) vie for influence. A project of social ordering is more or less powerful dependent on the size of the network of actants (both people and things) that gathers around it. Social projects are not stable but are constantly emerging and unravelling through everyday activities. In the creation of new social projects, a great deal is accomplished at the discoursal level of social action through which meanings are framed and shared. Such a view of social reality seems particularly apposite to the field of adult literacy given the history described above. It is possible to see the *Skills for Life* strategy as a social project in the making, one that at the time of writing this chapter had the backing of a powerful actor network – a national government and its associated agencies.

ANT uses ethnographic methodologies to analyse the trajectory of a project of social ordering, the flow and concentration of resources within this project through the *enrolment* of actors in networks. A key aspect of this methodology is to track the ways that cultural artefacts (Latour calls these 'stable mobiles') circulate through organisational structures, connecting different actors or agents and shaping specific social interactions in ways which tangle people in the very processes they also resist, a feature Michel Callon (1986) calls *interessement*. Artefacts mediate a number of key processes: *translation*, which is the realisation of equivalencies between disparate entities in order to enrol them into the social project being developed; *deletion* of features seen as insignificant to the social project. *Localising moves* involve interpreting and adapting general categories in the light of local contexts and making locally appropriate choices among a set of options. *Globalising connects*, on the other hand, align local actors with collectives synchronising individual actions with those of others.

Using the perspective of the New Literacy Studies, Barton and Hamilton (2005) identify the semiotic properties and potentialities of different classes of artefacts. They claim that written texts are a particularly powerful type of cultural artefact and that artefacts mediate the identities of all those positioned in relation to them. Thus, for example, since 'testing' is a particular social relationship, the national test of adult literacy positions not only the learner who is assessed by it, but also the teacher who prepares their students for the test, administers and marks it, fails or passes their student. The artefact affects their actions and understandings of the teaching and learning situation in new ways, some more subtle, some overt. This affects power relations (including decision-making and evaluative actions) in the educational process, the embodied physical activities in which people engage and the way time, space and language are used.

Drawing on both the New Literacy Studies and ANT, Brandt and Clinton (2000: 17) use the notion of 'sponsors' explaining that

> as a basic analytic concept, sponsors help to account for the fact that literacy practices are rarely invented or sustained by local agents alone [and enables us to ask questions about] the literacy materials in a setting. How did they get there? Who paid for them or provided them delivered them or imposed them? Who is responsible for them? How are they controlled or shared? What is the cost or obligation to the user for using them?

Cultural artefacts – including many written texts – circulate through the institutional structures and everyday activities within which tutors and students work. Tracing these trajectories can help identify the routines, origins and effects of cultural artefacts as they move from one 'sponsor' to another.

The addition of these frameworks allows me to develop a more nuanced account of how identities are constructed in the *Skills for Life* classroom that does not simply treat teachers' responses as the inauthentic performance of fabrications constructed solely for the monitoring eye (as so clearly set out in Webb 2006). I hope to show that the logic of the artefact and the practices in which it is embedded engage teachers' professional values and identity, and these are shaped by it, despite the reservations that teachers may have. These frameworks also allow me to show how both teachers' and students' identities are shaped in these interactions. In mediating the transitions of students into and through *Skills for Life* courses, teachers' professional identities are also transformed and compromised.

Analysing transition through *Skills for Life*

This section draws on a body of data that is just beginning to emerge from the *Skills for Life* era. Taken together, it offers a powerful picture of the achievements and contradictions of an ambitious policy strategy. Many of the insights are reinforced across the different studies. I begin by analysing the social project of *Skills for Life* and the processes of *enrolment, translation* and *framing* through which it has developed. I go on to explore the detail of how learner identities are managed within the *Skills for Life* strategy and the position of tutors in these processes. Using the language of ANT, I show how the globalising aims of a powerful grouping enter in the dynamics of minute-to-minute local interactions through a series of translations in which tutors are intimately implicated.

Enclosing the space of practice

As described in the introduction, *Skills for Life* has 'enclosed' the previously loose and informally organised territory of ALNE so that entry and transition are now happening within an institutional space that is strongly framed though it is itself in transition. This complicates the transition process for tutors and learners who are in a highly constrained but still unstable environment experiencing constant change (see Edwards *et al.* 2007: 164).

A fundamental aspect of the project of enclosure has been to find a definition of ALNE that is stable enough to be useful to policy. Policy actors need a baseline measurement of the extent of need which they can use to lever funding and to enable studies of progression to be carried out in order to justify the success of the policy. A suitable definition has been arrived at through designing tests, a core curriculum and measures of achievement that standardise a wide open field for the first time. International and national research and the school curriculum have been mobilised to this end. There is a tendency for such definitions, although they originate to serve the purposes of policy, to be used to organise provision and also to target and select learners who become themselves defined in terms of the measurement categories (for example, tutors will refer to a student as 'an Entry Level 3 ESOL learner').

Skills for Life is part of a wider project of international harmonisation that has its origins in the globalising ambitions of institutions like the Organisation for Economic Co-operation and Development (OECD), UNESCO and the European Union. The OECD, an international policy think-tank, has been an especially influential actor in defining adult literacy and numeracy. During the 1990s it developed a range of survey instruments, including the International Adult Literacy Survey (IALS). The aim of such surveys is to enable comparisons to be made between countries for the allocation of funding and to align systems in different countries to facilitate the movement of labour in the global economy (see OECD 1997). In Hamilton (2001), using documentary evidence, I traced the circulation of the IALS findings from their inception in the OECD through scientific, media and national policy documents and showed how they are translated into the organisation of curriculum frameworks, tests and progress records used in everyday practice. I showed how the macro links with international educational policy thinking and action could be visibly tracked to document the imprint of global forces on local events and circumstances, as advocated by Henry *et al.* (2001).

A test can redefine and fix adult identities especially by introducing the idea of levels of skill. In the UK, the results of the IALS were used as a rationale for developing the *Skills for Life* policy. The framework itself was not imported directly, but calibrated against home-grown measures that already sit more comfortably within the achievement systems of the UK education and training field. This has not been a trouble-free process (see Brooks et *al.* 2005; Moser 1999: Annex A). The national cohort studies commissioned by national government agencies over the last 50 years have been a significant resource (see Bynner and Parsons 2008 for the latest in a long series of reports). These enable what Latour calls a 'globalizing connect' (Latour 2005: 191–218): translating between international measures and frameworks already emerging in the local context.

Having calibrated literacy in this way, designing a core curriculum, standards and measures of achievement are the next steps to stabilise it. Through these, adult learners are categorised at particular levels that are also mapped to the school curriculum and achievement levels. The subject areas of literacy, numeracy and language are reduced to general statements of competency, which in turn are broken down into small elements, recorded on the ILP as SMART targets (Specific, Measurable, Achievable, Relevant and Time-related). In Hamilton (2001, 2009) I offer a more detailed description of the curriculum. This is arguably one way of viewing the subject areas involved, but not the only way. Sunderland and Wilkins (2004), for example, suggest that alternative ways of approaching language and mathematical learning include more holistic functional and task driven approaches and those starting from everyday demands which can be negotiated and translated in more collaborative and open ended ways. Therefore, for example, competences derived from grammar and punctuation could be demonstrated through writing a response to a public consultation or a wedding invitation.

Since the competences identified for adults in the current curriculum are derived from, and designed to fit seamlessly with, the school curriculum, rather than being based on research with adults, they are not necessarily aligned with the everyday practices, aspirations and diverse experiences of adult learners. In turn, the competences are tied to funding that determines what counts as a recognisable achievement thereby tugging the field into alignment with the broader goals of lifelong learning, vocational training and school-oriented education. The tight integration of audit, inspection and professional training with the curriculum framework strongly promotes the official version of what needs to be taught.

A further aspect of enclosure within *Skills for Life* has been the setting and monitoring of achievement targets for the priority groups of learners identified within the policy documents. Media publicity is geared to these groups and, on entry to programmes, they are sorted into learning levels by diagnostic and screening tests. The targets are outcomes measured as attainment of a qualification based on a national multiple-choice test, rather than participation targets. Quantitative data from policy evaluation studies (Bathmaker 2007; House of Commons Public Accounts Committee 2005) demonstrate how these targets have resulted in substantial 'mission drift' by skewing recruitment in favour of younger students already in full-time education or training and in favour of those with higher starting levels – a process in which both learners and tutors/managers exert agency of a constrained sort through the choices and decisions they make about participation.

Finally, the target groups identified in the *Skills for Life* policy (DfES 2001: paras 14–18) are all characterised by negative attributes. The following groups are listed: unemployed and low skilled, short-term workers; benefit claimants, especially lone parents; homeless and those living in disadvantaged communities; prisoners and those on probation; those with drug and alcohol problems and/or mental health issues; refugees and other non-native English speakers. The exceptions are public sector workers and the armed forces, named presumably because as employees of the government they are accessible groups to target. Research based on the national cohort studies reinforces this pattern of disadvantage.

The effect of this collocation of negative characteristics is to draw a picture of dysfunctionality that funnels disparate people into a single framework. To enter *Skills for Life* is thus to be confirmed as a member of a new underclass that is being constructed through the design and implementation of the strategy, along with other related policy initiatives (see Welshman 2006). What is seen as a positive step by government policy is, then, for the individual, predicated on accepting a state of deficit from which you will be redeemed by education. Many people do not see themselves this way and for this reason are reluctant to participate in formal literacy or numeracy learning (see Hamilton and Hillier 2006: ch. 5).

The deletion of positive characteristics in this process is especially apparent for ESOL learners who currently constitute nearly a third of *Skills for Life* learners. Many have high levels of education and qualifications in other languages and countries but these are rendered valueless as they are defined as part of the under-class based on the need to acquire proficiency in the English language and as a result of negative attitudes toward migrant groups. The effect of this is a loss of identity and social capital that is carried through into civic and working life and opportunities – literally indeed 'lost in transition'.

Living in the space of practice

What is it like to live as a tutor or learner in this newly enclosed space? How do they experience the pressures and contradictions of a high stakes assessment and monitoring culture? This section analyses how both tutors and students are enrolled in *Skills for Life* as it positions and frames them. Common themes emerge from the different data sources.

The data from learners show them to be largely positive about their experience once they come into provision – though many do not achieve qualifications and dropout is high. According to the official statistics analysed in 2003/4 (Bathmaker 2007), 60 per cent completed their course whilst 35 per cent achieved the quali-fication they were aiming for.

Tutors, on the other hand, report high levels of frustration and discomfort with their roles (see Edward *et al.* 2007; Appleby and Bathmaker 2006; Gleeson and James 2007). Working within the environment of a high stakes target culture impacts as strongly on the tutors as it does on the learners as they mediate and attempt to shield learners from the contradictions and unintended effects of the policy environment. Tutors find certain behaviour rewarded and required in order to survive financially, even if this does not coincide with what they judge to be good practice or in the interests of the learners they are serving. The tutor inter-viewed by Amy Burgess sums up her experience in this way:

> I've been a practising basic skills tutor for 15 years. I've been through all the training imaginable and I'm now at the position that what is expected of me is impossible. However you interpret directives from the 'industry' ...

and what's being thrown at us from all angles, it does not seem to meet the needs of the student, OFSTED [the inspectorate] and government funding. No matter what I do, it doesn't meet all of them at the same time.

(Burgess 2005: 11)

Two recent ESRC-funded projects provide extensive supporting data for this analysis. Exploring the effects of policy on learning and inclusion in the Learning Skills sector more generally Finlay *et al.* (2007) document the effects of continual change and the heavy demands of performativity as teachers try to navigate the 'waves of policy' (Hodgson *et al.* 2007). Interviews with further education practitioners carried out during the Transforming Learning Cultures in Further Education project show convincingly that

The shift from 'old' public management, based on municipal bureau professionalism, to 'new' public management – driven by market competition and public choice – embraces a quite different concept of public service: one that is managed, brokered and mediated by professionals in highly competitive and contested market situations. [...] Rather than occupying the position of trusted public servant, practitioners have come to be regarded as licensed deliverers of nationally produced materials, targets and provision.

(Gleeson and James 2007: 452)

In a multitude of interviews, tutors talk about the funding constraints, the lack of opportunities for meaningful professional development and training, uncertain and fractional contracts, and the proliferating paperwork demands. Qualitative data were gathered during a National Research and Development-funded *Skills for Life* learner evaluation. Interviews were carried out with managers, tutors and learners from six different sites around England in college-based, prison, probation and community settings. These show the priorities that capture tutors' attention and effort. Many staff welcomed the better coordination of provision and the new teaching resources linked to the curriculum that has resulted from the new policy. However, the materials produced within *Skills for Life* and referenced to the curriculum elements materials are inevitably designed for an 'ideal learner' seen to be someone in the age range of 16 to 25 years following a vocational course in an FE college. Tutors working with 'non-standard' learners need to adapt materials with little or no time allocated for this. Funding and contractual issues set up contradictory conditions for their work: 'part-time tutors who are paid on an hourly basis have to do the paperwork in their spare time'.

Discussions about professional development show the complexity of upskilling teachers in this field. Whilst opportunities have been increased through *Skills for Life*, the time commitment is considerable and it is still difficult for staff to access these especially if they are employed part-time or their employers are unwilling to cover their teaching. The new teaching standards also require teachers to demonstrate 'personal skills' equivalent to Level 3 and 4 in literacy and/or numeracy. They are thus subject to the same regime as the learners they teach. This requirement is a barrier to experienced volunteers who do not have the formal qualifications and cannot invest time and resources to gain them. It also affects vocational tutors who have their own subject specialisms but not the motivation to take further qualifications and are being deskilled by the insistence that they demonstrate and teach basic skills as part of their work (see Gleeson and James 2007).

Two further studies have documented the extraordinary diversity of background, aspiration and learning trajectories of learners who have to be squeezed into the standard framework offered by the policy infrastructure and to whom teachers have to respond. These studies demonstrate in detail the breadth of learner achievements outside the classroom that go largely unrecognised within learning programmes.

In a study funded by the NRDC, David Barton and colleagues carried out longitudinal case studies of learners in three different geographical sites covering a variety of formal and informal settings. They describe the ways in which learning is negotiated in sites whose primary focus may lie elsewhere – as in workplaces, homeless and rehabilitation projects. The findings emphasise the importance of recognising the unpredictable and changing circumstances of adult lives and how patterns of participation, learning goals and priorities of part-time adult students have to fit around these. The study documents the 'non-vocational' outcomes that are nonetheless significant to people in managing and developing their lives, which is the ultimate aim of basic skills provision. This project also shows that adult learners are well aware of the authority structures embedded in *Skills for Life* and a lack of control over what and how they learn is a major barrier for many people in persisting in courses (Barton et al. 2007: 135–47).

The ESRC-funded Literacies for Learning in Further Education project worked in vocational areas in four colleges, examining students' literacy practices in and out of education. Findings document the unrecognised literacy practices in which students engage outside the college setting. These are often focused on a strong leisure interest and whilst in some cases they complement and reinforce formal learning, in others, students' home-based literacy practices and those of the vocational classroom are 'so divergent that [students] are unable to bridge the gap between the two worlds' (Miller et al. 2007: 5).

Managing learner transitions

The discussion above shows that by the time the potential *Skills for Life* learner arrives in the learning programme, the transition process is well under way. They have been targeted by publicity materials or referred by others, identified as a member of a priority group. At this point, tutors become actively involved in the transition process though there are different divisions of labour in different institutions. Sometimes tutors carry out initial screening and diagnostic testing, especially in community settings. Sometimes this is done by another member of the academic or administrative staff. Tutors are allocated particular student groups and have little say over who arrives in their classrooms (Hamilton 2009).

The process of *interessement* can be well demonstrated by looking at a particular tool developed for tutors and learners to use together, one that was mentioned at the beginning of this chapter as a key aspect of *Skills for Life*. Of all the features of current provision it is the Individual Learning Plan (ILP) that links tutors and students in direct, face-to-face interaction making it a pivotal site for research (what Scollon 2001 refers to as 'a nexus of practice'). The *Skills for Life* Quality Initiative (QI), set up between 2003 and 2006 to provide advice and resources to practitioners, describes the ILP as being 'like a route map that shows where the learner is now and their planned destination in terms of their long-term goals. The role of the ILP is to plan the route that will take the learner from the starting point to the end point'. An ILP is based upon screening, initial and diagnostic assessment. It is designed to enable the learner to express their needs and aspirations for the course, and is a signed agreement with the learner on goals and targets. A completed ILP should include:

- results of assessments (initial placement and diagnostic tests);
- the learner's long-term goals – career, personal and social;
- additional support arrangements in place;
- the goals of the programme to be followed, cross-referenced to the national standards or core curriculum;
- any other goals that the learner wishes to achieve, both social and personal;
- targets and dates for meeting these;
- a programme of dated progress reviews;
- space to record achievement of targets and any developments in the ILP;
- signatures of learner and teacher.

Paperwork associated with the ILP includes termly schemes of work, session and group plans mapped to the curriculum; year planners; and student learning logs or progress sheets. These in turn generate their own explanatory paperwork: directions about how to use the different forms; prompt lists of short-term achievements (mapped to the curriculum); and 'crib sheets' of curriculum elements for the tutor to map individual targets against (see Burgess 2006).

A crucial aspect of entangling the tutor in this paperwork is the 'permissive guidance' that tutors receive. Templates, rather than ready-made forms, are offered with encouragement to practitioners to adapt and design the layout and to develop other associated documentation, procedural instructions, etc. Such guidelines are a manifestation of the soft management technologies prevalent in the EU (Ball 2008). Tutors are invited to make their own lives easier by finding ways to simplify the materials and make them less unwieldy, and to decide what will work best in their own context and experiment with it. Whilst there is flexibility in the paperwork itself, scripted training sessions induct teachers into the logic, procedures and the discourse of the newly structured field. Course notes from *Skills for Life* QI courses encourage tutors to be creative in designing an ILP fit for their own purposes:

> There is no single design for an effective ILP. Your design will depend on your learners, your programmes, the uses to which you will put your ILP and what is manageable in your organisation.

You should include as a minimum ....

You may also want to include: ....

You will need to record most of this information, but you may decide not to keep all these records in the ILP. The ILP is a working document. You may therefore decide to keep the ILP slim with skeleton records of anything that is not in current use. Many teachers and learners, however, value the easy access to a range of relevant information.

Several well-documented research studies have shown what happens in practice. Informal data collected through practitioner forums and mailing list servers (e.g. NRDC 2004) confirm the nature of tutors' work and the day-to-day difficulties of engaging with ILPs especially with ESOL learners.

Hamilton (2009) interviewed practitioners in a range of programmes, discussed the ILPs they used and analysed policy documents. Lack of time emerges as a major constraint on the use and management of the ILP, as does the dispersed nature of tutoring staff. Materials are frequently adapted and updated within providing organisations, usually by course teams or through staff development meetings, to make them easier to use, less cumbersome and more appropriate to diverse student bodies. Practitioners search for ways to retain variety but within acceptable limits, responding to the demands for audit and inspection and the advice offered by inspectors. They adjust the ILP process in order to 'hit the right buttons' and avoid financial penalties. A large amount of creativity and time are expended on this process and tutors become attached to the pro-formas they have helped produce. As part of a very public process of grading, naming and shaming, inspectors will pick out particular features of poor practice. Points of contention with inspectors described by interviewees include the need to break down targets into smaller curriculum elements, the need to review progress more frequently, to specify objectives more closely, to elicit more detailed comments from students and to involve students more fully. Practitioners reported disputes with inspectors and administrators over the ownership of the paper record. Should the student or the college keep hold of it?

Burgess (2005, 2008) carried out a detailed analysis of one teacher's practice using classroom observations and interviews. Her study focuses specifically on how the ILP organises time and space in relation to learning and learners, mapping the learners' progress through the time-bounded courses determined by funding criteria (see also Barton et al. 2007: 146). The teacher introduces an extra step in the paperwork, the student progress sheet for students to review their activities session by session and thus make it easier for them to fill in the details of their termly review (Burgess 2005: 9). Whilst enhancing the formative purpose of the ILP, this also enrols the students actively in the process of translating their achievements into the terms of the teacher's own descriptions in her sessional and termly group plan of learning activities. Burgess uses detailed discourse analysis to show how student goals and teacher comments are phrased in ways that can be recognised and easily processed by the organisation and how the pace and timing of learning become regulated to the convenience and requirements of the bureaucratic system.

Cookson *et al.* (2007) explored the fit between clients in a homeless project and the 'hard' outcomes documented through ILPs. In the fine detail possible in a single case study carried out by practitioners themselves, the report shows how key achievements valued by its clients are not recognised in the hard outcome measures used to evaluate programmes and learners but that these 'soft' outcomes reinforce the official measures and are essential for building the confidence to learn. For example, a common understanding of the goal-setting process itself cannot be assumed nor can managing a stable trajectory and participation within unpredictable life circumstances. 'Soft outcomes' highly valued by both clients and tutors included becoming less fearful, controlling angry reactions in order to intervene assertively in difficult situations, taking responsibility rather than avoiding personal tasks such as dealing with official letters, managing mental health and substance abuse issues, developing trust, the ability to function comfortably in a group and to cooperate with others. All of these can be vital steps toward educational progress. These issues are also pointed out in the study by Barton *et al.* (2007) discussed above.

Skills for Life attempts to 'fix' learner identity through a range of interlocking processes of sorting and sifting. Through the use of artefacts such as the ILP, tutors mediate these processes acting as brokers, advocates and gatekeepers. They transmit curriculum goals, organise the time and pace of learning within review periods. They manage and induct reluctant learners. They prepare students for multiple choice literacy tests and then administer the tests themselves – failing or passing students on the basis of specific testing performances, selecting and sorting both bodies and their achievements, selecting and filtering the relevant learning from the irrelevant. They do all this within the context of the high stakes audit and target culture that has been outlined above. No aspect of the tutor's formal role is outside of this. Room for manoeuvre is limited though still possible as Burgess (2005: 11) shows: the tutor in her study subverted the end-of-year report by writing her comments as messages of personal congratulation to the students.

Although the ILP is presented as a formative assessment tool for collaborative use by tutors and learners, it has significance and a trajectory that extends way beyond this function, acting as a visible channel of glocalisation processes at work (Bauman 1998) as tutors adapt the process recommended through staff development and induction to local circumstances and adjust the ILP through their experiences with auditors and inspectors. National government agencies act as the original sponsors of the ILP through the permissive guidelines they issue and the training courses they organise. ILPs are crafted and adapted locally by managers and tutors and tutors are inducted and trained in their use in-house. The actual filling in and signing of the ILP form is managed locally in various ways by administrators, managers, tutors and learners in the knowledge that they will be viewed by inspectors and assessors on professional development courses and that information from the ILPs will be collated for audit – statistical reporting to satisfy funders. The aggregated data will eventually be quoted in government documents and speeches and used to rationalise future policy action.

Transitions or funnels?

In this final section, I will consider the implications of the data presented above for our understanding of the concept of 'transitions'. Ecclestone (2007) identifies a number of elements prevalent in the literature about transition. Transition is seen as a *process* of change that involves identity, not just a shift from one location to another. It is a process of being and becoming 'somebody' and in as far as it involves navigating *institutional pathways* or systems, 'transition' is an attribute of social systems rather than the individual. Finally, it is a process that involves the imposition of the notion of *a life trajectory* assuming a unified subject and the construction of a coherent narrative. It is the process, as Stuart Hall puts it, of 'fitting our unspeakable subjectivities with the cultural and historical narratives within which our lives are lived' (Hall 1987: 44).

It should be obvious from earlier sections of this chapter how these features of transition map onto the process of becoming a *Skills for Life* learner and in particular how the cultural artefact of the ILP mediates the construction of a recognisable narrative jointly by the tutor and learner creating a new, or different, coherence to past, present and imagined future experience. In the context of *Skills for Life*, the narrative that is imposed may violate the diversity of people's experiences, aspirations and their ability to maintain fragile stabilities of their own that are not officially recognised but are nevertheless essential for mental well-being and for meaningful learning to take place.

The identification of target groups labels students at the point of recruitment and selection and in policy, research and promotional materials. Adults are sorted into levels of learning, and identified as having particular kinds of learning styles. The literacy practices and aspirations they bring into programmes are turned into subject-based curriculum elements and students are thereby inducted into the policy language. The ILP creates a coherent narrative of the individual student, translating their aspirations from literacy language or numeracy into time-defined points of progress placed in relation to the overall curriculum.

However, as well as demonstrating the micro-processes of transition, examining the experiences of adult learners' entries into formal *Skills for Life* programmes offers a challenge to the transition literature. It contests the prevalent notion of 'transition' as a positive and expansive developmental process from one known state to another. As I have documented in this chapter and elsewhere, transition in this case involves manoeuvring a hugely diverse population – in terms of life circumstances, social and educational background, motivations and abilities – into a single trajectory through a specific hierarchical framework of skills that may be a figment of the educational expert imagination. For the diversity of adult learners entering the field this presents a narrowed, standardised vision of their existing skills and aspirations. This resembles funnelling rather than flowering.

Furthermore, as I have argued above, accepting the status of a *Skills for Life* learner is to take on a traditionally stigmatised identity. This is unusual within education but is common in other social policy areas. It is more akin to states experienced by offenders, people with mental health issues or those becoming registered disabled or (in Western society) elderly. Managing entry to and through a stigmatised state throws a different light on the concept of transition and the roles of participants in the process. In particular, mobilising experiences of failure, abuse, disrespect or racism in the construction of a coherent life narrative unless balanced by positive narratives as well can be threatening and undermining to new learners. Perhaps that is why the fictional positive future is such an insistent theme in the rhetoric of *Skills for Life*. Ironically, the very policy mechanisms designed to focus resources on 'marginalised' learners also have the effect of reinforcing the view of adult education as meeting a deficit in earlier educational provision rather than designing expansive opportunities.

The point of this chapter has been to show how the identity of the *Skills for Life* learner is shaped; to identify the roles played in this process by the structural features of *Skills for Life*; and to show how tutors themselves manage this process and how tutor identities are also implicated.

To do this I have supplemented the literature on performativity with insights offered by Actor Network Theory and the New Literacy Studies to conceptualise how teachers' 'normal' motivations and desires to do right by their colleagues and their students are harnessed and co-opted by routine artefacts and the practices in which they are embedded, making effective resistance hard and using up creative energy in the effort to subvert and adapt them. This is a clear example of Callon's notion of *interessement*. Who would not be in favour of the ILP, careful diagnosis of need and transparent monitoring of progress? What else could a tutor aim for than such coherent and forward-looking provision?

I have argued that whilst the current strategy may have expanded provision and public awareness, it has done so at the expense of both tutor and learner agency in the pedagogical process, reducing the space for negotiation and decision-making. Both tutors and learners are implicated in the process of establishing a regime of practice in which subject positions are co-organised. The strategy has normalised a specific, standardised, deficit vision of the *Skills for Life* learner and has recast the professional identity of the teacher as technical expert whose job it is to apply formulaic methods of translation between learner diversity and a standardised curriculum.

Although it is possible to adapt the frameworks to alternative or more holistic approaches to teaching and learning, only very experienced and committed teachers are able to articulate a personally held vision of their work with the official discourse in order to achieve what they would see as an authentic pedagogy (see Webb 2006). As we have seen in this chapter, the funding conditions under which teachers work, their status in many cases as sessional or part-time tutors, and a lack of appropriate opportunities for professional development constrain the possibilities for such skilled adaptation.

Mature adult learners are not necessarily in transition to anywhere, but *Skills for Life* is an enactive framework that entangles learners, tutors, artefacts and routine practices to bring the impression of material transition into being and as Field (2000) and others have shown, this is part of the prevalent ideological discourse of lifelong learning. Tutors act as mediators and gatekeepers in this impression management.

Burnard and White (2008: 676–7) suggest that the constraints of performativity might be overcome by developing a different, transformative professionalism that values creativity and risk taking and works with students to visualise alternative futures. This would impact on students' learning and the transitional pathways open to them. My argument here, however, is that unless it is actively supported by policy, or until the terrorising technologies of performativity are reduced, such an alternative will be hard to put into practice in any widespread way.

As the policy moment begins to wane and government attention shifts else-where, ANT would predict a new opportunity for social ordering that will present itself to the field of adult language and literacy. *Skills for Life* will leave a legacy that *could* be reworked by a more confident professional body that hears and respects the diverse voices of student experience and can work collaboratively with them.

Bibliography

Appleby, Y. and Bathmaker, A. M. (2006) 'The new skills agenda: increased lifelong learning or new sites of inequality?', *British Educational Research Journal*, 32: 703–17.

Ball, S. J. (2001) 'Performativities and fabrication in the education economy: towards the performative society', in D. Gleeson and C. Husbands (eds) *The Performing School: Managing, Teaching and Learning in a Performance Culture*, New York: Routledge.

—— (2003) 'The teacher's soul and the terrors of performativity', *Journal of Education Policy*, 18: 215–28.

—— (2008) *The Education Debate*, Bristol: Polity Press.

Bartlett, L. (2007) 'To see and to feel: situated identities and literacy practices', *Teachers College Record*, 109: 51–69.

Barton, D. and Hamilton, M. (2005) 'Literacy, reification and the dynamics of social inter-action', in D. Barton and K. Tusting (eds) *Beyond Communities of Practice*, Cambridge: Cambridge University Press.

Barton, D., Ivanic, R., Appleby, Y., Hodge, R. and Tusting, K. (2007) *Literacy, Lives and Learning*, London: Routledge.

Bathmaker, A. M. (2007) 'The impact of *Skills for Life* on adult basic skills in England: how should we interpret trends in participation and achievement?', *International Journal of Lifelong Education*, 26: 295–313.

Bauman, Z. (1998) *Globalization: the Human Consequences*, Cambridge: Polity Press.

Brandt, D. and Clinton, K. (2000) 'Limits of the local: explaining perspectives on literacy as a social practice', *Journal of Literacy Research*, 34: 337–56.

Brooks, G., Heath, K. and Pollard, A. (2005) *Assessing Adult Literacy and Numeracy: a Review of Assessment Instruments*, London: NRDC.

Burgess, A. (2005) 'The life and times of the individual learning plan: how a text medi-ates across timescales and represents time', paper presented to the Lancaster Literacy Research Group, June 2005.

—— (2006) 'Linking the local to the global: the role of the ILP in mediating across timescales', unpublished paper, Lancaster Literacy Research Centre, March 2006.

—— (2008) 'The literacy practices of recording achievement: how a text mediates between the local and the global', *Journal of Education Policy*, 23: 49–62.

Burnard, P. and White, J. (2008) 'Creativity and performativity: counterpoints in British and Australian education', *British Educational Research Journal*, 34: 667–82.

Bynner, J. and Parsons, S. (2008) *Illuminating Disadvantage*, London: National Research and Development Centre for Adult Literacy and Numeracy.

Callon, M. (1986) 'Some elements of a sociology of translation: domestication of the scallops and the fishermen of St Brieuc Bay', in J. Law (ed.) *Power, Action and Belief: a New Sociology of Knowledge*, London: Routledge & Kegan Paul.

Coben, D. (2006) 'The social-cultural approach to adult numeracy: issues for policy and practice', in L. Tett, M. Hamilton and Y. Hillier (eds) *Adult Literacy, Numeracy and Language: Policy, Practice and Research*, Buckingham: Open University Press.

Cookson, H., Menist, C., Rices, B. and Hale, G. (2007) '*I Can': Demonstrating Soft Outcomes for Homeless and Vulnerable Learners*, London: National Research and Development Centre for Adult Literacy and Numeracy.

DfES (2001) *Skills for Life*, London: DfES.

Ecclestone, K. (2007)'Lost and Found in Transition: the Implications of "Identity", "Agency" and "Structure" for Educational Goals and Practices', keynote speech presented at the Conference of the Centre for Research on Lifelong Learning, University of Stirling, June 2007.

Edward, S., Coffield, F., Steer, R. and Gregson, M. (2007) 'Endless change in the learning and skills sector: the impact on teaching staff', *Journal of Vocational Education and Training*, 59: 155–73.

Field, J. (2000) *Lifelong Learning and the New Educational Order*, Stoke-on-Trent: Trentham Books.

Finlay, I., Edward, S., and Steer, R. (eds) (2007) 'The impact of policy on the English learning skills sector', *The Journal of Vocational Education and Training*, 59: 121–272.

Fowler, Z. (2004) 'Politically constructing adult literacy: a case study of the skills for life strategy for improving adult literacy in England 1997–2002', unpublished PhD thesis, London: University of London.

Gleeson, D. and James, D. (2007) 'The paradox of professionalism in English further education: a TLC project perspective', *Educational Review*, 59: 451–67.

Goldstein, H. (2006) 'Education for all: the globalization of learning targets', in L. Tett, M. Hamilton and Y. Hillier (eds) *Adult Literacy, Numeracy and Language: Policy, Practice and Research*, Buckingham: Open University Press.

Hall, S. (1987) 'Minimal selves', in L. Appignanesi (ed.), *Identity: the Real Me. Postmodernism and the Question of Identity* (ICA Document 6), London: ICA.

Hamilton, M. (2001) 'Privileged literacies: policy, institutional process and the life of the International Adult Literacy Survey' in *Language and Education*, 15: 178–96.

—— (2009) 'Putting words in their mouths: the alignment of identities with system goals through the use of Individual Learning Plans', *British Educational Research Journal*, 35(2): 221–42

Hamilton, M. and Hillier, Y. (2006) *Changing Faces of Adult Literacy, Language and Numeracy: a Critical History of Policy and Practice*, Stoke-on-Trent: Trentham Books.

Henry, M., Lingard, B., Rivzi, F. and Taylor, S. (2001) *The OECD: Globalisation and Education Policy*, Oxford: Pergamon.

Hodgson, A., Edward, S. and Gregson, M. (2007) 'Riding the waves of policy? The case of basic skills in adult and community learning in England', *Journal of Vocational Education and Training*, 59: 213–29.

Holland, D., Lachicotte, W., Skinner, D. and Cain, C. (2001) *Identity and Agency in Cultural Worlds*, Boston, MA: Harvard University Press.

House of Commons Public Accounts Committee – Twenty-first Report (2005) Session 2005–6. Available online at www.publications.parliament.uk/pa/cm200506/cmselect/cmpubacc/792/79202.htm

Latour, B. (2005) *Re-assembling the Social*, Oxford: Oxford University Press.

Lavender, P., Derrick, J. and Brooks, B. (2004) *Testing, Testing!*, Leicester: NIACE.

Law, J. (1994) *Organizing Modernity*, Oxford: Blackwell.

Miller, K., Smith, J., Carmichael, J. and Edwards R. (2007) 'Researching literacy for learning in the vocational curriculum', in M. Osborne, M. Houston and N. Toman (eds) *The Pedagogy of Lifelong Learning: Understanding Effective Teaching and Learning in Diverse Contexts*, London: Routledge.

Moser, C. (1999) 'A fresh start: improving literacy and numeracy', report of the working group chaired by Sir Claus Moser, London: Department for Education and Employment.

NRDC (2004) 'ILPs – Guiding the learning journey' special issue (1) of *REFLECT*, London: National Research and Development Centre for Adult Literacy and Numeracy. Available online at www.nrdc.org.uk/content.asp?CategoryID=533

OECD (1997) *Literacy Skills for the Knowledge Society*, Paris: OECD.

Rosenberg, S. (2008) *ESOL a Critical History*, Leicester: NIACE.

Scollon, R. (2001) *Mediated Discourse: the Nexus of Practice*, London: Routledge.

Sunderland, H. and Wilkins, M. (2004) 'ILPs in ESOL: theory, research and practice', *REFLECT*, 1, 8–9 October. London: National Research and Development Centre for Adult Literacy and Numeracy.

Usher, R. and Edwards, R. (2007) *Lifelong Learning: Signs, Discourses, Practices*, Dordrecht, Netherlands: Springer.

Webb, P. T. (2006) 'The choreography of accountability', *Journal of Education Policy*, 21: 201–14.

Welshman, J. (2006) *Underclass: a History of the Excluded 1880 –2000*, London/New York: Hambleton Continuum.

6 The transition from vocational education and training to higher education

A successful pathway?

Michael Hoelscher, Geoff Hayward,
Hubert Ertl and Harriet Dunbar-Goddet

Introduction

The far-reaching discourse about HE access 'is the most troublesome item in talk about HE' (Watson 2006: 93), because the research base in this area is fragmented to such a degree that almost any conclusion can be drawn from it (Gorard *et al.* 2006). Linked to this debate about HE participation, vocational education and training (VET) policy has as one of its aims increasing access to higher education via this route. However, there is little research that speaks to either the effectiveness or the efficiency of this policy, the redistributive potential of which lies not just in whether an individual participates in HE but also in which higher education institutions (HEIs) they access and which subject areas.

This chapter addresses this issue through a mainly descriptive analysis that examines where and how individuals with differing prior educational background participate in HE. First, a brief rationale for the research is presented, followed by a short introduction to the data sources employed in the analysis. Next, the distribution of students from different educational pathways over institutions and subjects is described based on an analysis of large-scale quantitative data sets. Possible reasons for these distributions are then examined using case study data. The chapter concludes with some remarks about the notion of fair access and the redistributive potential of widened access to HE.

Rationale

A central tenet of New Labour social policy is that economic efficiency and social justice run together. Employees are construed as actors striving to make themselves marketable in a more flexible labour market:

> What all this means is not that the role of Government, of the collective, of the services of the State is redundant; but changed. The rule now is not to interfere with the necessary flexibility an employer requires to operate successfully in a highly fluid changing economic market. It is to equip the employee to survive, prosper and develop in such a market, to give them the

flexibility to be able to choose a wide range of jobs and to fit family and work/ life together.

(Blair 2007)

The state's role is thereby reconceptualised primarily as ensuring adequate opportunities for individuals to develop human capital rather than, say, regulating the labour market. Such a policy vision is predicated on a belief that (1) the development of more diverse educational opportunities beyond the age of 16 will increase the participation rate of learners beyond compulsory schooling, a decisive precondition for increasing and widening participation in HE (see for instance Education and Employment Committee 2001: 33); (2) any increase in educational participation and attainment will produce both individual and social returns on investment in further education and training.

Educational participation beyond the compulsory school age has increased in the UK constantly since 1945, with a massive increase in participation in full-time provision between 1985 and 1994 (Hayward 2006; Hayward *et al.* 2004, 2005, 2006). This increase can partly be attributed to the growing availability of Level 3 vocationally oriented qualifications aimed at 16-year-olds. Such qualifications are increasingly marketed as providing a means for progressing into HE, so constituting an important component of attempts to widen participation.

UK and international research has, however, indicated that the connections made in policy discourse, between expanding post-compulsory participation via an increased vocational offer and participation in HE, are not necessarily realised in practice. For example, in the UK investigations into the educational value of some vocationally oriented qualifications, in terms of their currency for further progression, have concluded that they only offer a 'mirage of wider opportunities' (Pugsley 2004: 28; see also Wilde and Hoelscher 2007; Connor *et al.* 2006; Vickers and Bekhradnia 2007). It seems timely, therefore, to investigate whether growing participation in VET has resulted in increasing participation of people with a vocational background in HE. Given that the VET pathway is often construed as an alternative chance for those deemed 'unsuitable' for progression in the academic pathway, there is a need to assess how good an alternative it is, in terms of where, what and why graduates of the VET system study in HE.

Introduction to the data sources

Using large-scale administrative data sets, the distribution across institutions and subjects of students coming to HE via different educational pathways is explored. This analysis is supplemented by case-study work at five HEIs. The macro-level perspective of influences of student distribution across HE is thus combined with a student-level perspective on questions regarding institutional and subject choice. A detailed technical appendix for all data sets used is available on the project's website (www.tlrp.org/project%20sites/degrees/download.html). Dunbar-Goddet and Ertl (2007) outline the theoretical framework and research questions of the overall project and Dunbar-Goddet and Ertl (2008) give a detailed description and analysis of the questionnaire data.

Large-scale data sets

The Higher Education Statistics Agency undergraduate data set for 2003/4, matched with corresponding UCAS applications data sets, was used for the quantitative analysis (HESA Student Record 2003/4, copyright Higher Education Statistics Agency Limited 2007. HESA cannot accept responsibility for any inferences or conclusions derived from the data by third parties). Only English (based on postcode area), full-time, first year students under 21 that were successfully matched with the UCAS data, were analysed. The first, more pragmatic, reason for this is that only this group had all the necessary variables available. The more substantial reason is that this more homogeneous population allowed better comparability of students from different backgrounds.

Based on the available qualifications in the data set five different types of prior educational pathways were defined:

1 general academic;
2 general academic and vocational;
3 vocational;
4 foundation and access courses (FaA);
5 not level 3/not known.

Defining vocational education in the UK context is problematic (see Stasz and Wright 2004; Hayward 2006). Our definition of what constitutes a vocational qualification (e.g. VCE, ONC, OND (including BTEC and SCOTVEC equivalents), GNVQ, GSVQ, NVQ, SVQ, etc.) is essentially pragmatic, rather than conceptual. A more conceptual exploration of what constitutes vocational qualifications and what the particular characteristics of such qualifications are, as opposed to other kinds of qualifications (e.g. GCE, Highers, International Baccalaureate, HE qualifications), is essential for understanding the issues of transition between vocational and higher education. However, such a discussion goes beyond the scope of this chapter.

Case study data

The Degrees of Success project conducted two surveys with the entire intake of students in three subject areas (business studies, nursing and computing) at five HEIs for the 2006/7 academic year. One survey, the 'Transition to HE' questionnaire, asked students about their transition into higher education. Interviews with 40 students were also carried out at the five HEIs in order to gain insights into the students' rationale for choosing both HEIs and subjects, linked with the students' educational backgrounds. It is important to keep in mind that the interviews represent post-hoc rationalisations of students' decisions (for a discussion of the limitations of such data see Hall 2001).

The distribution of students over institutions and subjects

Students applying for a place in HE have to make at least two choices: which subject to study, and at which institution. Both decisions are influenced by a range of different factors, for example, their personal interests, social or ethnic background, social capital, and so on (Ball 2003; Connor 2001; Connor et al. 2004; Furlong 2005; Reay et al. 2005); prior attainment also plays a crucial role. This chapter explores the influence of one specific aspect of prior attainment: educational background.

Given the diversified nature of HE in the UK it is essential to analyse the access patterns of different groups of students regarding choice of institution (Chevalier and Conlon 2003; Urwin and Di Pietro 2005). The other aspect of choice for HE applicants is subject choice. Choice of subject is influenced by different factors, for example, gender (Universities UK and SCoP 2005: 5) and the subject chosen influences future life-chances: this decision has an important impact on earnings, on the chances of being employed (Universities UK and PricewaterhouseCoopers 2007: 5) and, as demonstrated in the student-level analysis, on accessing a particular career. The following sections analyse the distribution of students from different educational pathways across institutions and subjects.

Institutional choices

There are different classifications of HEIs. First, the distribution across the broader categories of pre- and post-'92 universities was examined. 'Other HEI' comprises mostly different kinds of colleges. The data set holds only data about students in HEIs, therefore HE students in FE are not analysed. Table 6.1 summarises the results.

In this sample, almost similar shares of students studied at pre-'92 (48.3 per cent) and post-'92 institutions (46.4 per cent). The number of students at other HEIs was quite low (5.3 per cent). However, students from different educational backgrounds were unequally distributed over the different types of institutions. Most of those with a purely academic background were found at pre-'92

Table 6.1 Institutions by educational pathways

	General academic	Academic & vocational	Vocational	Foundation & Access	Below level 3/ not known	Total
post-'92 universities	38.2%	57.7%	75.6%	71.4%	77.3%	46.4%
pre-'92 universities	58.0%	36.4%	13.5%	7.3%	16.9%	48.3%
other HEI	3.9%	5.9%	10.9%	21.3%	5.8%	5.3%

Figures are rounded in accordance with HESA's rounding methodology

Source: Higher Education Statistics Agency 2003/04

institutions (58 per cent), while the figures were much lower for all the other groups. For students with a VET background the figure was only 13.5 per cent. Conversely, VET background students were much more likely to be found in post-'92 universities.

Another way of looking at the institutions was to take into account their RAE (Research Assessment Exercise) and QAA (Quality Assurance Agency) results. On average, students with an academic prior qualification entered those institutions with much higher RAE and QAA results compared to all other groups. Those entering with a VET background only went to those universities with, on average, the lowest RAE results (Figure 6.1) and, together with those from foundation and access courses and without level 3/known qualifications, also to those institutions with significantly lower QAA results (Figure 6.2).

In summary, A-level qualifications remain the major route into the more prestigious HE institutions. Whether one uses a more traditional measure of quality, such as the distinction between pre- and post-'92 universities, or RAE and QAA results, students with a VET background are seen to be disadvantaged: taking up their studies, on average, at post-'92 universities with low RAE results. A partial explanation for this would be that learners from VET backgrounds are tracked institutionally into less prestigious HEIs. If students were acting as rational utility maximising agents, then one would expect them to apply to the most prestigious HEIs that they could.

An alternative would be that individuals act on the basis of bounded rationality, thereby tracking themselves into less prestigious institutions, through a process of individual and singular choice, in answering the question 'which is the best HEI for me'. The *Transition to HE* questionnaire aimed to shed more light on the motives underpinning institutional choice. The interviews with students then

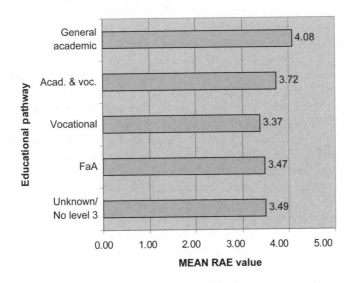

Figure 6.1 Mean RAE results of institutions by educational pathways

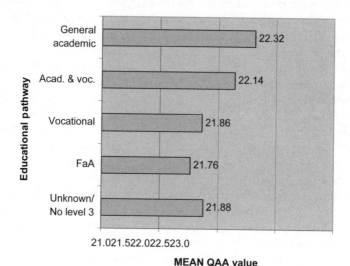

Figure 6.2 Mean QAA results of institutions by educational pathways

aimed to develop a deeper understanding of the complex and highly individual-ised process of institutional choice in which different types of students engage.

Across the sample of English institutions (a post- and a pre-'92 university and an FE college) the most common reason given for choosing an institution was its location. Around one third of students mentioned the location as the single reason for their choice to study at their university. This was valid across all educational pathways. In most cases, good location was defined as being close to home, and in some cases the financial implication of being able to live at home was explicitly mentioned. However, there were a number of other factors which defined a good location in the view of the students, including proximity to a big city, being close to family, and good travel connections.

The second most important factor of institutional choice was related to the perceived quality of the institution or the course chosen; around a quarter of students gave this as their single reason. The indicators for quality (where mentioned) varied greatly and ranged from reputation of the institution or the course and the availability of state-of-the-art facilities to the perceived high quality of staff and their teaching. Interestingly, only three students mentioned university rankings, and not a single student mentioned the RAE. The quality of research did not seem to play any role in institutional choice; in contrast, teaching quality, competence of teaching staff and student satisfaction were more frequently mentioned.

Answers that gave two or more types of reasons for the choice of an institution were very common. By far the most common combination of reasons was that of location and perceived quality (just under one fifth of answers). Considering all multiple-reason answers that included location as a factor, and adding these answers to the third of students which mentioned location as the only reason for their choice, it appeared that, for just under 60 per cent of students in the sample, the location of the HEI played an important role; a finding that is certainly in line with previous research in this area (Lischka 2003).

While the identification of single or combined reasons for institutional choice seems a reasonable way to gain an overview of the questionnaire responses, many of the interviews showed how complex decision-making processes of students in these HEIs are, and how single reasons for choices become amalgamated in real-life situations. A quote from a first year business student at a post-'92 university illustrates how personal, academic and other factors come together:

> I mean my selection process, like how I chose this university, I just kind of like looked on UCAS and found all the places that did business studies and then sort of whittled the list down by, like, oh I don't like that area, or you know this place isn't too good, or the grades are too high or too low, or something, then sort of came up with this place, mm, I mean it got rated excellent for business, so the teaching quality is really good, which is probably one of the main factors for me choosing it, I wasn't too bothered about how far away, I didn't, you know, have to be away, it's not like I hate my parents or anything.

Looking separately at the three institutions in the sample, it became clear that subtle differences in choice patterns could be identified. For instance, the importance of location (either as a single reason or in combination with other reasons) was substantially higher at the FE college (over 80 per cent of students) than at the two universities. One reason for this was that a number of students at this college indicated that they had studied there before they decided to start an HE programme: 'I have studied here for four years so I know the lecturers. It enables me to live at home with my family while I am studying'.

In contrast, reasons for choice related to quality of the institution or the course played a minor role for the students at the FE college. The same share of students (around 50 per cent) at both the pre- and post-'92 universities mentioned factors related to perceived quality either as their only reason for choosing the institution or in combination with other reasons. This finding seems surprising and might indicate that the perception of quality is a relative concept and is – in the students' perspective – not necessarily bound to 'objective' quality indicators. There seemed to be a process of 'self-limitation' at work, which led students to exclude many institutions that are located beyond perceived boundaries of physical, academic or social space. This exclusion seemed to take place early on in students' decision-making processes.

Boundaries of physical space were indicated by the emphasis on proximity to home. Academic restrictions were exercised by the grade requirements set by institutions which affected choice patterns. Some students at the post-'92 university (around 8 per cent) were the only ones to indicate that they were only offered a place at their current institution ('I found it difficult being accepted into other institutions as I did not get high A-level grades' and 'It was the best Uni I could get into when I applied'). Social reasons for choosing a particular HEI were expressed regularly, that is, linking one's own decision to that of friends: 'I also feel I can complete my course with friends in the same class, however, moving away would have [meant] meeting strangers'.

In summary, the data from the case studies indicated that there are clear limits for explaining institutional choices through rational choice models, which are *inter alia* based on the assumption of the availability and use of full information. Restrictive information strategies and other factors affecting individual choices need to be considered.

Which subjects are studied?

In a systemic perspective, different educational pathways lead not only to different kinds of institutions, but also to different subjects. This clearly makes sense, as some subjects are more vocationally oriented or HE qualifications in certain subjects are a necessary precondition for working in a specific field (such as nursing). However, there are substantial differences between wage premia/rates of return for different subjects (Blundell *et al.* 2000). The notion of fair access in HE, for those with non-traditional backgrounds, must also take into account their distribution across different subjects. Opening up access for VET students only to certain subject groups might even be regarded as a continuation of the academic/vocational divide.

An assessment of the subjects in which the different pathways are over/under-represented can be made using odds-ratios. These are calculated (Table 6.2) by comparing the likelihood of someone with a non-traditional qualification, with that of someone with an academic qualification, of being in a specific subject. Figures below one show a comparatively lower likelihood of being in that subject, figures over one show an increased chance. The reference group 'General academic' is not shown, as all figures would be one.

Extreme differences were found for 'medicine/dentistry' and 'veterinary science'. The likelihood of someone with a VET background entering these subjects was more than 25 times lower (0.04:1 = 1:25) than that for a student with traditional academic qualifications. For 'physical sciences', 'mathematical sciences', 'law', 'languages' and 'historical and philosophical studies' also, the chances were below a third of those for students with academic qualifications.

VET students were over-represented in 'engineering and technology', 'business and administrative studies', 'education' and 'combined studies' by around a factor of 1.5, in 'creative arts and design' by a factor of 2.4 and were nearly four times as likely to go into 'agriculture and related subjects' and 'computer science'. Foundation and access course students were under-represented in all but one subject ('creative arts and design'). These findings support a 'matching' hypothesis that those with vocational qualifications are more attracted to more applied subjects.

Research is unambiguous about the fact that there are different wage premia connected with degrees in different subjects (although studies vary slightly in their estimates of wage premia; see Blundell *et al.* 2000; Universities UK and PricewaterhouseCoopers 2007; Walker and Zhu 2001).There was no visibly clear pattern to the distribution of students with different prior qualifications across

Table 6.2 Odds-Ratios for non-traditional educational pathways in different subjects in comparison to general academic qualifications

	Academic & vocational	Vocational	Foundation & Access	Below level 3/not known
Medicine and dentistry	0.44	0.04	0.09	0.26
Subjects allied to medicine	1.09	0.80	0.36	1.06
Biological sciences	0.88	0.72	0.32	0.80
Veterinary science	0.70	0.03	—	0.09
Agriculture and related subjects	1.05	3.69	0.77	2.42
Physical sciences	0.65	0.27	0.23	0.42
Mathematical sciences	0.69	0.20	0.12	0.32
Computer science	2.30	3.83	0.88	2.48
Engineering and technology	0.87	1.45	0.91	1.59
Architecture, building and planning	0.89	1.11	0.45	1.15
Social studies	0.75	0.47	0.34	0.67
Law	0.83	0.33	0.27	0.50
Business and administrative studies	2.03	1.76	0.86	1.53
Mass communications and documentation	1.02	1.11	0.52	1.36
Languages	0.53	0.16	0.19	0.29
Historical and philosophical studies	0.46	0.17	0.26	0.26
Creative arts and design	1.01	2.40	7.90	1.83
Education	1.64	1.46	0.24	2.31
Combined	1.10	1.67	0.08	2.23

Source: Higher Education Statistics Agency 2003/04

more or less favourable subjects. The strong affinity to more applied subjects seemed not to result in a directly observable, unfavourable choice of subject for those from vocational backgrounds. However, as the subject groups are very broadly defined, an additional, more finely grained analysis on the differences within these groups in terms of (1) earnings and (2) matching of prior qualification and subject is missing due to data limitations. There is also a need to explore the interaction between subject choice and the HEI where that subject is studied on wage premia. This has not yet been done in the UK.

From a student-level perspective, the systemic question of the distribution of students across subjects can be regarded as an aggregate of individual decision-making processes and motivational factors. In the 'Transition to HE' questionnaire, nine items investigated the underlying motivations for studying a subject. Students were asked to express their degree of agreement with a given statement on a 5-point scale ranging from 1 ('very strongly') to 5 ('not at all'). The items represented an adapted version of those used by the Enhancing Teaching–Learning Environments in Undergraduate Courses project, in their 'Experiences of Teaching and Learning' questionnaire (Hounsell *et al.* 2005).

An exploratory factor analysis of the data generated by the nine items produced two important factors for students' subject choice, which can be thought of in terms of capturing intrinsic and extrinsic motivations for starting the subject in question. The analysis of the data with these two factors showed a high extrinsic motivation of students across the three subjects. The mean score of students for an item underlying the factor extrinsic motivation ('I want to develop knowledge and skills I can use in a career') produced mean scores of between 1.31 (business) and 1.16 (nursing), showing only minor differences between the subjects. This speaks to a high level of instrumentality amongst all students in their decision making. Such instrumentality may also reflect, for example, the fact that a nursing degree is increasingly becoming a necessity to access more senior posts in the profession.

However, it can also be seen that decision-making patterns for subject choice are highly individualised; the high standard deviations of the scores for all the items in this area are a clear indication of this. Overall, subject choice is closely bound to career prospects, a finding that seems to be valid to a similar degree for students studying at different universities, in different subjects and with different educational backgrounds. Significant differences according to subjects were found, however, in patterns of intrinsic motivation: the decision-making processes of students in computing and business seemed to be less strongly driven by intrinsic motives than those of nursing students.

Moreover, it is important to note that, when talking about students' life chances, the decision that precedes the choice of an institution or a subject is the one of whether to proceed to HE study at all, which adds to the complexity of the situation young people are facing when applying to HE. This quote from a computing student at a post-'92 university illustrates this point:

> I mean it was a tough choice to make, I mean thinking about whether or not I want to come here, be kind of out of work, not really have much money, or

just go in to work, but it kind of made me think that at the end of the day if I get this degree I should get a job with a lot more money.

The student-level investigation of decision-making processes needs to go beyond the dimensions of institution and subject choice to develop an understanding of the complex interplay between motivations and personal and social factors, an approach followed in the interviews with students with different educational backgrounds in the Degrees of Success project.

Is there a difference for subjects within different types of institutions?

The analysis of large national data sets showed that students with a VET background were under-represented in certain high-status subjects and institutions. One reason for this finding could be that the more applied subjects chosen by VET students are over-represented in post-'92 universities and other HEIs. To control this, an analysis of the interaction between the types of institutions and the subjects they offer was undertaken.

Looking only at pre- and post-'92 universities, while 'subjects allied to medicine' or 'biological sciences' were nearly equally distributed in both types of institution, there were huge differences in, for example, 'medicine and dentistry' (40 times higher proportion of students in pre- than in post-'92 HEIs) or 'education' (five times higher proportion of students in post- than in pre-'92 HEIs). No clear pattern of over- or under-representation of the high- or low-wage-premium subjects within the different HEI types was visible. Although most of the more applied subjects were over-represented in the post-'92 universities, there were exceptions like 'engineering', possibly linked to the more developed nature of this profession.

If only the subjects chosen were responsible for the differences in the distribution of pathways over the types of HEI, then one would expect the same distribution of pathways over subjects in all three types of HEI. On the contrary, the data revealed that there was a strong influence of type of institution for most subjects, even when one takes the distribution of subjects over institutions into account (Table 6.3). A-level students were much more likely to study at pre-'92 universities, even when accounting for their subjects. Students with a VET or FaA background were heavily under-represented in these institutions. For post-'92 universities the picture was reversed: A-level students were under-represented and VET and FaA students over-represented, irrespective of subject choice.

For some subjects there were no big differences between the types of institutions. The main reasons for this could be that these subjects were mainly offered at one kind of institution (medicine), or that they were dominated by one pathway (languages).

What becomes clear is that students with an academic background were much more likely to study at pre-'92 universities, even if one controls for the distribution of subjects over institutions. Their over-representation was especially visible in those subjects in which they were normally under-represented. If someone

Table 6.3 Over- and under-representation of pathways in subjects in pre-'92 universities (ratio of observed to expected distribution)

	General academic	Academic & vocational	Vocational	Foundation & Access	Below level 3/not known	% of all students studying at pre-'92 HEI
Medicine and dentistry	1.0	1.0	1.0	1.0	0.4	98.1%
Subjects allied to medicine	1.1	0.8	0.5	0.8	0.5	54.7%
Biological sciences	1.1	0.8	0.3	0.2	0.3	48.0%
Veterinary science	1.0	1.0	—	—	—	97.9%
Agriculture and related subjects	1.4	0.8	0.5	—	0.3	23.8%
Physical sciences	1.0	0.9	0.5	0.2	0.5	75.9%
Mathematical sciences	1.0	0.9	0.4	—	0.5	85.3%
Computer science	1.5	0.8	0.4	0.4	0.4	32.2%
Engineering and technology	1.2	0.8	0.4	0.2	0.5	57.1%
Architecture, building and planning	1.2	0.8	0.2	—	0.6	33.7%
Social studies	1.1	0.8	0.3	0.2	0.4	62.6%
Law	1.1	0.8	0.2	—	0.5	48.2%
Business and administrative studies	1.3	0.8	0.3	0.2	0.4	32.1%
Mass commun. and documentation	1.2	0.8	0.3	—	0.3	18.1%
Languages	1.0	0.8	0.4	0.2	0.6	71.5%
Historical and philosophical studies	1.0	0.9	0.4	0.1	0.7	75.2%
Creative arts and design	1.5	0.9	0.6	0.2	0.3	21.5%
Education	1.2	0.8	0.7	—	0.4	13.6%
Combined	1.3	1.0	—	—	—	15.3%
Ratio observed to expected % of pathways in this type of institution (taking subjects into account)	1.2	0.8	0.3	0.2	0.3	48.3%

Source: Higher Education Statistics Agency 2003/04

with an academic qualification was studying 'agriculture', 'computer science' or 'creative arts' at all, then he/she was studying at a pre-'92 institution. The under-representation of the other pathways in these institutions looked even clearer: VET students, for example, were only about one fifth as likely to study 'law' at a pre-'92 university than would be expected from their share of all law students. This means that there were independent effects of subjects and institutions. As studying at a pre-'92 HEI brings extra benefits, students with an academic background have an advantage in the labour market. This is reflected in the higher wage premium paid to those with A levels and a degree, compared to those with VET backgrounds prior to their degree courses (Purcell *et al.* 2005).

Conclusions

One explicit goal of the current widening participation agenda is to open up pathways for students from VET backgrounds into HE, connected with three different aims: first, an economic and national goal to increase overall participation in HE. Different international actors (OECD, European Union) have argued that a highly educated workforce is needed to be successful in the competitive global economy (Commission of the European Communities 2005; Keeley 2007), and UK policy is following this. Second, to widen participation to increase the share of under-represented groups in HE. Third, a notion of fair access whereby a more even distribution of students from disadvantaged backgrounds across 'higher education institutions and courses which offer the highest financial returns' (DfES 2006: 3) is achieved.

The second and third aims are deeply rooted in notions of social justice, re-articulated in New Labour policy as a concern with individual empowerment to compete successfully in a flexible and competitive labour market. Widening participation and ensuring fair access can be construed as policy mechanisms to achieve redistribution.

This chapter looked at the third aim and asked how different educational pathways lead to specific segments within HE and how this might influence the individual benefits of HE participation. At one level it seems that the policy of using vocational qualifications as a means of widening access has been successful: students with these qualifications are participating in HE. Given that such students tend to come from more disadvantaged backgrounds (Payne 2003), this strand of widening access policy seems to meet the government aspiration of enabling more young people from lower socio-economic backgrounds to enter HE, albeit in small numbers. At the system level, however, we have shown that, despite the government claim of 'parity of esteem', the traditional A-level route still opens up the best opportunities into those institutions with higher reputations. Those coming from a vocational background mostly end up in post-'92 institutions with lower RAE and QAA results. The reasons for this are likely to be a combination of tracking within a stratified HE system and individual choice.

Tracking suggests that significant institutional barriers remain, whereby VET students are funnelled into post-'92 HEIs. However, the system outcome is the aggregated result of an interaction between institutional and individual level decision-making processes. These choice processes, in terms of institutions and subjects, follow highly complex and individualised patterns. The data show that there are high degrees of self-limitation which influence applications to HE. This self-limitation affects students' perceptions of opportunities available in terms of choice of institutions and subjects. Boundaries of physical (location of HEI), academic (grade or other requirements associated with studying at a given HEI and/or a given subject) and social (perceptions and behaviour of peer groups) space have a varying degree of influence on the decision-making processes of students.

This raises questions about the redistributional logic of government policy and its effectiveness and efficiency for VET learners, who typically enter HEIs which on average provide lower income premia than pre-'92 institutions. In terms of the chosen subjects, large differences were found, but the relationship with future life chances was less clear. Given that obtaining at least some VQs at level 3, for example, through more traditional apprenticeship routes, leads to decent returns, it is questionable whether the additional investment in HE is a sensible one, given the current patterns of progression into HE via the VET pathway. Additional experience in the labour market might produce as good a return, or better, as investment in HE, a notion that was reflected in the complex decision-making rationales of some of the students interviewed about their choices. However, given a highly credentialed process of access to the labour market, at least for initial entrants, holding a degree may be necessary to access even modest first employment. For some areas, such as nursing, a degree is increasingly becoming necessary to access more senior positions.

The implications are that neither attempts to create stronger links between HE and VET programmes, nor to change perceptions of potential applicants through outreach, have resulted in evenly distributed access to HE. The policy instruments underpinning these types of initiatives are too weak to achieve the desired system outcome. Different policy instruments are needed to achieve necessary changes in both institutional and individual behaviour. If the widening participation agenda is ultimately aiming at 'equality of results' (Thomas 2001) then policy instruments need to intervene earlier in individuals' educational pathways. They need to be focused on how HEIs conceptualise their role in society, and how these translate into rationales for recruiting and selecting students.

Bibliography

Ball, S. J. (2003) *Class Strategies and the Education Market: The Middle Classes and Social Advantage*, London/New York: RoutledgeFalmer.

Blair, T. (2007) 'Our nation's future: the role of work'. Available online at www.number10. gov.uk/output/Page11405.asp. Last accessed 26 November 2007.

Blundell, R., Dearden, L., Goodman, A. and Reed, H. (2000) 'The returns to higher education in Britain: evidence from a British cohort', *The Economic Journal*, 110: F82–F99.

Chevalier, A. and Conlon, G. (2003) 'Does it pay to attend a prestigious university?', London School of Economics and Political Science working paper, London: Centre for Economics of Education.

Commission of the European Communities (2005) 'Mobilising the brainpower of Europe: enabling universities to make their full contribution to the Lisbon Strategy', communication from the Commission. COM(2005) 152 final, Brussels: EU.

Connor, H. (2001) 'Deciding for or against participation in higher education: the views of young people from lower social class backgrounds', *Higher Education Quarterly*, 55: 204–24.

Connor, H., Sinclair, E. and Banerji, N. (2006) *Progressing to Higher Education: Vocational Qualifications and Admissions*, Ormskirk: Action on Access, together with Aimhigher.

Connor, H., Tyers, C., Modood, T. and Hillage, H. (2004) *Why the Difference? A Closer Look at Higher Education Minority Ethnic Students and Graduates*, London: Institute for Employment Studies/ Department for Education and Skills (DfES).

Department for Education and Skills (DfES) (2006) *Widening Participation in Higher Education*, Darlington: DfES.

Dunbar-Goddet, H. and Ertl, H. (2007) 'Degrees of success: research on the transition from vocational education and training to higher education', working papers of the 'Degrees of Success' project, Oxford. Available online at www.tlrp.org/project%20sites/degrees/.

—— (2008) 'Investigating the learning experience of HE students with a vocational pathway: findings from a questionnaire survey', working papers of the 'Degrees of Success' Project, Oxford. Available online at http://www.tlrp.org/project%20sites/degrees/.

Education and Employment Committee (2001) *Higher Education: Access*, (fourth report), London: The Stationery Office.

Furlong, A. (2005) 'Cultural dimensions of decisions about educational participation among 14- to 19-year-olds', *Journal of Education Policy*, 20: 379–89.

Gorard, S., Smith, E., May, H., Thomas, L., Adnett, N. and Slack, K. (2006) *Review of Widening Participation Research: Addressing the Barriers to Participation in Higher Education*, York: University of York, Higher Education Academy and Institute for Access Studies.

Hall, J. (2001) *Wastage and Retention in FE and HE*, Glasgow: Scottish Council for Research in Education.

Hayward, G. (2006) *Participation, Progression and Success in Vocational Learning: a Quantitative Analysis of System Performance*, London: Learning and Skills Research Centre.

Hayward, G., Hodgson, A., Keep, E., Oancea, A., Pring, R., Spours, K. and Wilde, S. (2004) *Nuffield 14-19 Review Annual Report*, Oxford: Oxford University Department of Educational Studies.

Hayward, G., Hodgson, A., Johnson, J., Oancea, A., Pring, R., Spours, K., Wilde, S. and Wright, S. (2005). *The Nuffield Review of 14-19 Education and Training: annual report 2005–06*, Oxford: University of Oxford Department of Educational Studies.

—— (2006) *The Nuffield Review of 14-19 Education and Training: annual report 2005–06*, Oxford: University of Oxford Department of Educational Studies.

Hounsell, D., Entwistle, N., Meyer, E., Beaty, E., Tait, H., Anderson, C., Day, K. and Land, R. (2005) *Enhancing Teaching–Learning Environments in Undergraduate Courses*, London: TLRP.

Keeley, B. (2007) *Human Capital: How What you Know Shapes your Life*, Paris: OECD.

Lischka, I. (2003) *Studierwilligkeit und die Hintergründe: neue und einzelne alte Bundesländer*, Wittenberg: HoF Wittenberg.

Payne, J. (2003) Vocational Pathways at Age 16–19, research report 501, Nottingham: DfES.

Pugsley, L. (2004) *The University Challenge: Higher Education Markets and Social Stratification*, Aldershot: Ashgate.

Purcell, K., Elias, P., Davies, R. and Wilton, M. (2005) *The Class of '99: a Study of the Early Labour Market Experiences of Recent Graduates*, Nottingham: DfES.

Reay, D., David, M. and Ball, S. (2005) *Degrees of Choice: Class, Race, Gender and Higher Education*, Stoke-on-Trent: Trentham Books.

Stasz, C. and Wright, S. (2004) *Emerging Policy for Vocational Learning in England: Will It Lead to a Better System?*, London: LSRC.

Thomas, L. (2001) *Widening Participation in Post-compulsory Education*, London: Continuum.

Universities UK and PricewaterhouseCoopers (2007) *The Economic Benefits of a Degree*, research report. London: Universities UK.

Universities UK and Standing Conference of Principals (SCoP) (2005) *From the Margins to the Mainstream: Embedding Widening Participation in Higher Education (executive summary)*, London: Universities UK.

Urwin, P. and Di Pietro, G. (2005) 'The impact of research and teaching quality inputs on the employment outcomes of postgraduates', *Higher Education Quarterly*, 59: 275–95.

Vickers, P. and Bekhradnia, B. (2007) *Vocational A Levels and University Entry: is there parity of esteem?*, Higher Education Policy Institute working paper. Oxford: Higher Education Policy Institute.

Walker, I. and Zhu, Y. (2001) *The Returns to Education: Evidence from the Labour Force Surveys*, research report, London: Department for Education and Skills (DfES) and Department of Economics, University of Warwick.

Watson, D. (2006) 'New Labour and higher education', *Perspectives: Policy and Practice in Higher Education*, 10: 92–9.

Wilde, S. and Hoelscher, M. (2007) *Missed Opportunities? Non-placed Applicants in the UCAS Data*, report for UCAS, Oxford/Cheltenham: UCAS.

7 Disabled students and transitions in higher education

Elisabet Weedon and Sheila Riddell

Introduction

Within the context of the learning society and globalisation, citizens are expected to engage in learning throughout the course of their lives (Scottish Executive 2003; Field 2006), and negotiating transitions into and out of the education system is clearly of vital importance. Traditional higher education students will have experienced, according to Ecclestone *et al.* (2006), at least five transitions in their initial learning career, from first entry to school to leaving higher education. Non-traditional students, including disabled students, may experience more transitions or find the transitions harder to cope with, since they are likely to have additional barriers to contend with, including the management of complex identity issues. Over recent years, UK universities have had to think about supporting students, including facilitating successful transitions, in a much more serious way. Two decades ago, they catered for a relatively small elite group who tended to come from reasonably homogeneous (and generally socially advantaged) backgrounds. Dropout rates tended to be low since higher education students were generally not going against the grain of social expectations in completing their degree. Disabled students rarely participated in higher education because systems of additional support were not in place. Since the early 1990s, policies to widen access have achieved some degree of success and as a result most universities are now catering for a more diverse student population. Higher education institutions are also being managed much more closely (e.g. Riddell *et al.* 2007) with performance being judged against a range of benchmarks including course completion rates, employment outcomes and inclusion of non-traditional participants.

Disabled students in higher education are an important group to study for a number of reasons. First, as we discuss below, they are much more successful in managing transitions and securing future employment than the majority of disabled young people and adults. Secondly, their struggles with social identity, as well as the practical and emotional aspects of transition, may illuminate the issues faced by many higher education students, not only those who are identified as disabled. For example, a recent report on students who committed suicide noted that those with mental health difficulties were particularly at risk and that periods of transition, for example at the beginning or the end of the year, were times when this group of students were particularly vulnerable (Stanley *et al.* 2007).

This chapter draws on data from a four-year longitudinal ESCR/TLRP project (reference RES-139-25-0135) to examine the experiences of disabled students in one institution.[1] It begins by placing these experiences within the wider context of social theory relating to disability and transition. In particular, it considers:

- What are the students' experiences of transition within the institution and how do these differ by impairment and a range of other social variables?
- How does the management of transition by the institution impact on the students' experience and identity?

Research methods

The project included an initial survey of over 1,000 disabled students (Weedon and Riddell 2007), an analysis of key informant interviews and policy documents of four institutions (Riddell et al. 2007), which was followed up by three-year case studies of between eight and fourteen students in four universities. The main qualitative data used in this chapter are drawn from work in one pre-'92 institution. Fourteen students and their lecturers participated in semi-structured interviews and were observed in learning contexts over a three-year period (see Table 7.1). Case studies were written up in relation to each student, and excerpts from three of these are presented here.

The institution has a high proportion of students from independent schools (around 35 per cent) and a relatively small proportion of students from lower social class backgrounds (around 18 per cent). However, its proportion of disabled students is similar to national figures at just over 6 per cent. Of those identified as disabled, the majority fall into the category of dyslexia and the proportion of students identifying as dyslexic in this institution is higher than the national average.

Disability as a transitional status

In the welfare states of developed countries, disability has often been defined in terms of administrative categories devised by social security or social services in order to determine access to benefits and services. For example, Stone (1984) noted that disability originated as an administrative category out of a collection of separate conditions understood to be legitimate reasons for not working. Major surveys conducted within the UK and Scotland have sought to determine how many people are disabled by asking whether the individual has a long-term illness or disability which has an impact on their normal daily activities or ability to work. Surveys conducted in Scotland suggest that about 20 per cent of the population report a long-term illness or disability, a relatively high proportion compared with some other parts of the UK, particularly areas of affluence such as the south-east of England. The incidence of reporting a long-term illness or disability increases with age (see Table 7.2).

The Disability Discrimination Act 1995 operates on the assumption that a distinction may be drawn between disabled and non-disabled people to

Table 7.1 The impairments, disciplines and outcomes of the case study students

Name*	Impairment	Outcome at end of project	Discipline
Karrie	Cerebral palsy; wheelchair user	Completed with Third class honours degree	Modern Languages
Euan	Mental health	Completed with ordinary degree	Physical Sciences
Jean	Dyslexia	Completed with First class honours degree	BEd Primary
Fred	Dyslexia	Completed with a 2:2 honours degree	BA Comm. Ed.
Lesley	Multiple: mobility and hearing	Left after 3rd year due to pregnancy; returned to complete	Education: Primary
Andrew	Cerebral palsy but not in wheelchair	Completed with a 2:2 honours degree	Education: Primary
Kathryn	Diabetes	On track to complete 5 year course	Chemistry
Teresa	Epilepsy	Year out 3rd year; struggled on return and left with Dip HE	Biosciences
Anne	Dyspraxia	Completed with a 2:1 honours degree	English Lit & History
Fiona	Heart problem	Completed with a 2:1 honours degree	Zoology
Michelle	Wrist/writing problem	Completed with a Third class honours degree	History
Dave	Multiple: cystic fibrosis, epilepsy, diabetes	Withdrew after third year studies interrupted by hospitalisation, completed ordinary degree	Geosciences
Becky	Dyslexia	Completed with a 2:1 honours degree	Architecture
Mark	Dyslexia	Completed with a First class honours degree	Geography

Table 7.2 Adults with a disability or long-term illness by sex and age in 2001/2 (column percentages)

	No disability or illness	Disability	Long-term illness	Both disability and long-term illness
Men	82	7	7	4
Women	81	7	8	4
16–24	96	2	2	0
25–34	94	2	3	1
35–44	91	4	4	2
45–59	81	6	8	4
60–74	68	11	14	7
75+	55	19	18	9
Total	81	7	8	4

Source: Scottish Executive (2003)

determine who qualifies for additional support such as reasonable adjustments in the workplace and education. However, there is considerable evidence that a view of disability as a fixed social status over the lifecourse is untenable. For example, the statistics presented in Table 7.2 underline the way in which perceptions and experiences of disability differ over time. This is in line with the social model of disability as defined by Oliver (1990) and others, who regard disability as independent of impairment, in that it is a product of the social context in which an individual with impairment finds themselves. Recently, post-modern and post-structuralist writers have taken these arguments further, critiquing the taken-for-granted distinction between disabled and non-disabled people. Writers such as Corker and Shakespeare (2002) have argued that disability should be seen as the ultimate post-modern category since it is likely to be experienced so differently at various points in an individual's biography and in different environmental contexts. The implication of recent survey research and social theory is that disability should be viewed as a transitional status, which is renegotiated throughout an individual's life.

Disability and transition to adulthood

As with disability, the meaning of transition to adulthood has shifted over time. Earlier work on youth transitions tended to be based on the assumption that the young person was leaving the malleable condition of youth in order to attain the relatively stable status and identity of adulthood. The lifecourse was viewed as a series of stages which were linear, cumulative and non-reversible, with youth as the stage between childhood and adulthood, and an individual finally achieving a stable subjectivity and social being. In recent years this underlying image has been challenged by arguments about late modernity or post-modernity in which the idea of the stable subjective self is questioned (e.g. Lash and Urry 1993). The labour force of the post-modern economy is imagined as flexible, working on demand across different tasks with varying patterns of work, part-time work and unemployment, training and retraining, as production demands.

The post-modern view of transition coincided with, and was in part informed by, the global economic restructuring of the late 1970s which was driven by the massive increase in oil prices and, in many developed economies, made traditional industries such as mining and manufacturing suddenly appear to be uneconomic. One of the consequences of this economic restructuring was the loss of many male-dominated manual jobs and the virtual collapse (Bynner and Roberts 1991) of the traditional youth labour market. Up to that point, young people could leave school at the minimum leaving age and undertake five-year apprenticeships leading into relatively stable trades or, as exemplified by Willis's 'lads', a series of unskilled jobs (Bynner and Roberts 1991; Willis 1977). In 1975, 60 per cent of 16-year-olds were in full-time employment but eight years later only 18 per cent were (Riddell 1998: 190). This has, in large part, been replaced by an 'extended transition' in which young people are increasingly engaged in a period of 'training' for up to ten years after the compulsory school leaving age. For some 50 per cent of any cohort, this extended transition takes place in and through higher education while, for much of the other 50 per cent, this takes place through the ever-extending net of vocational qualifications, part training and part extended job interview. This extended transition has been formalised in law so that parents are duty-bound to provide support for any child up to the age of 25 years 'who is reasonably and appropriately undergoing instruction at an educational establishment or training for employment or for a trade, profession or vocation' (Family Law (Scotland) Act 1985, Elizabeth Chapter 37, 1(5)(b)).

While much of the public debate about such restructuring of contemporary industrial societies has focused on the transformation of the public institutions of the state and the economy, there is a parallel discourse about the transformation of self, as the 'destinations' of transitions have proved increasingly elusive. A recognition of the challenge of 'late modernity' has led to an articulation of the idea of the 'risk society' in which individuals are forced to make choices and move between different possible identities, thus negotiating a broad variety of global and personal risks (Beck 1992; Beck *et al.* 1994). Such risks are not, however, randomly distributed but are likely to adhere to class patterns with the poor attracting 'an unfortunate abundance of risks' whereas the wealthy 'can purchase safety, freedom from risk' (Beck 1992: 35). For young disabled people, risks are likely to be associated not only with social class but with other aspects of identity, in particular, impairment, and, as the case studies presented below illustrate, young disabled people in higher education do not escape these risks, despite their overall relatively privileged status.

The increasing vulnerability of young disabled people to stalled transitions and social exclusion, from which disabled young people in higher education are only partially protected, is evidenced in longitudinal studies of Glasgow special school leavers, accounting for about 1 per cent of the Glasgow school population. In the 1960s, the vast majority of special school leavers moved into full-time employment, whereas two decades later full-time post-school employment had become a relatively rare outcome (Riddell 1998). At the present time, employment and higher education remain highly unusual post-school destinations for Glasgow special school leavers, with only 4 per cent finding post-school employment compared with 26 per cent of the mainstream school population. A study of young people with learning difficulties conducted as part of the ESRC's Learning Society programme found that the majority moved into segregated courses in further education colleges (Riddell *et al.* 2001), which tended to lead away from the labour market and often involved ongoing cycles of retraining. The young people often found themselves with no other option than to stay in the parental home or live in supported accommodation or hostels, reinforcing the status of perpetual child. Very few succeeded in developing independent autonomous friendships and relationships, and had access to only very restricted forms of social capital. Even those from relatively privileged social class backgrounds failed to develop autonomous lives, suggesting that disability overrode social class in the distribution of risk.

To summarise, the revisioning of transition has particular implications for young disabled people, a group already at risk of social exclusion. On the one hand, the new view of life as a series of transitions has optimistic connotations, in that there is scope for growth and development throughout life, and immediate post-school destinations may not be as absolutely defining as was previously the case. On the other hand, the advent of the risk society means that whilst great prosperity may be available to some young people, such as the group who succeed in entering higher education institutions, others may be cast adrift with little hope of ever finding meaningful post-school activities.

Disabled young people in higher education

As noted above, disabled young people in higher education merit particular attention because their educational outcomes and life chances are markedly better than those of other disabled young people. Analysis of HESA data (Riddell *et al.* 2005) shows that disabled young people now represent just over 6 per cent of the higher education population. Since the majority are in the 18–24 age group, this is higher than might be expected in relation to the proportion of disabled people of this age in the general population, particularly since some disabled people are unlikely to get through the academic selection process (see Table 7.3).

Disabled students in higher education reflect the relative social advantage of the majority of higher education students, in particular those in the elite institutions (see Figure 7.1).

However, as noted above, in relation to the nature of their impairment, they are clearly very different from most young disabled people, with a growing proportion identifying themselves as having dyslexia (specific learning difficulties) and a very small proportion having physical or sensory impairments, mental health difficulties or personal support needs (see Table 7.3). Students with global learning difficulties are entirely absent.

Table 7.3 Categories of disability used by Higher Education Statistics Agency and percentages of undergraduates in each category in 1994/5 and 2002/3

Type of disability	1994/95	2002/03
Dyslexia	15%	49%
Blind/partially sighted	4%	3%
Deaf/hard of hearing	6%	4%
Wheelchair/mobility difficulties	6%	3%
Personal care support	0.1%	0.1%
Mental health difficulties	2%	3%
An unseen disability	53%	23%
Multiple disabilities	5%	4%
Other disability	10%	11%

Source: Higher Education Statistics Agency

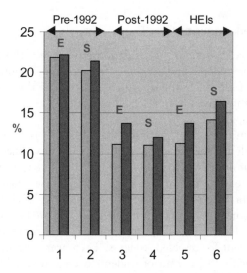

Figure 7.1 Percentage of undergraduates from social class 1 by sector, country and disability status (Source: Higher Education Statistics Agency, 2002)

Policy responses to the needs of disabled young people

As noted above, disabled students in higher education are, in general, a socially advantaged group and have a relatively high level of resource expended on them. The Disabled Students Allowance was established in 1990. It provides funds for individual students to purchase the support they need, reflecting the additional costs of living and studying which they incur. Whilst the funds available are inadequate to meet the needs of those with very significant impairments, such as those requiring 24-hour care, for the majority of students with less significant impairment, including those with dyslexia, the financial support is important, both symbolically and practically. Disabled students' support services now exist in all higher education institutions in Scotland, and these provide assessment services and emotional support, as well as pressurising academic staff to adapt their teaching and assessment practices. Since 2000, institutions have received premium funding from the Funding Councils in relation to the proportion of disabled students they educate who are in receipt of Disabled Students Allowance. This incentivises the recruitment of disabled students, and also encourages a more rigorous approach to assessment of need. The success of these policies is evidenced by the growing proportion of disabled students in higher education in the UK and their relative success in the labour market. Studies of disabled undergraduates (Riddell et al. 2005) show that they tend to be concentrated in particular disciplinary areas, for example, dyslexic students are particularly likely to study art and design subjects, and they are also less likely to obtain the highest degree awards. Whilst the dangers of social exclusion have not been removed, they have been greatly ameliorated for this group.

Case studies of disabled students

The findings provide a brief overview of the relationship between the expected outcome for this group of students and outcomes for an earlier cohort of disabled students. The issues for three of the case study students are then examined in greater depth. These three have been selected to explore the experiences of students with different impairments.

All fourteen students in our sample disclosed their disability on entry to the university; however, not all had been in contact with the Disability Office. Overall findings indicate that four out of the fourteen failed to complete their intended course, with two of these exiting with a non-Honours degree (see Euan below). Figures from the institution for the year group that entered in 2000/1 show that overall 72 per cent of all students completed their degree compared with 69.5 per cent of disabled students. The rate of non-completion was 11.9 per cent overall, compared with 16.3 per cent for disabled students. There were also differences in degree classification, with 14 per cent of students overall awarded first class Honours degrees, compared with 8.4 per cent of disabled students. Disabled students were also more likely to get a non-Honours degree than other students (12 per cent compared to a total awarded of 7.8 per cent). These figures indicate that disabled students are likely to experience greater difficulties throughout their university courses, and the nature of these difficulties is illustrated below.

Karrie

Karrie, a wheelchair user, lived in the halls of residence and had a personal assistant throughout her years of study. She believed that her parents saw themselves as working class and had not been university-educated, although she saw herself as having moved into the middle class. Her impairment meant that she had to make early contact with the institution to ensure that sufficient support was in place.

She had been well supported by her secondary school and learnt to make effective use of support such as scribes. Her language teacher had encouraged her to study Modern Languages and Karrie hoped to qualify as a teacher. Karrie identified as disabled, on the grounds that 'it's always been part of my life'.

> I actually don't mind it [being labelled disabled] to be perfectly honest. Because if you take it literally, because if you are sitting in a chair you are disabled from doing certain things. In my case walking.
>
> (Karrie, year 4)

She was aware, however, that others might have negative views:

> Well, obviously it affects the person [being in a wheelchair]. It affects people's views of you generally. If people don't know you they tend to ... assume that you are a sandwich short of a picnic ... which does hinder your socialising.
>
> (Karrie, year 2)

Partly because of the visibility of Karrie's impairment, her status as a disabled student was readily established and the institution responded with effective support, in particular ensuring that courses were delivered in accessible locations. A lecturer commented:

> Sometimes we haven't been made aware by the student or anybody else. In the case of Karrie we are fully aware and it has been really good. And in her particular case, she is really so relaxed ... she can make sure she tells me what her needs are.
>
> (Modern Languages lecturer)

One of the lecturers was perhaps more sensitive than Karrie, worrying about whether some topics might inadvertently exclude a disabled person:

> In language classes there are certain topics that are covered ... I have personally felt sometimes uneasy about dealing with certain topics such as sport ... I have been aware that Karrie could not share any of those ... she seemed OK with it.
>
> (Modern Languages lecturer)

Despite the positive features of Karrie's experience, a major constraining factor was her lack of access to social events and opportunities to build social capital. She was unable to take part in the social programme during freshers' week because getting to events in a wheelchair was too difficult. Another factor which affected her socialising was that she needed to return home every weekend:

> Yeah [I go home every weekend] because I need help with ... washing clothes and ironing ... I don't really have much choice in the matter ... I'll go for a coffee occasionally with some folk, but you know, you don't really have

> enough time to socialise properly because you're busy working at night and
> stuff ... but I know some people quite well.
>
> (Karrie, year 2)

Karrie's determination helped her make the most of the academic aspects of
her university career, although opportunities for social and emotional development, taken for granted by most students and a key part of transition to adult
life, were lacking. The difficulties, and the efforts of herself and her family to
overcome them, were particularly evident when it came to arranging her year
out in Spain. At one point she thought she might not be able to go because
of problems in finding accommodation and an assistant. Financial support was
available to pay for the assistant's accommodation, but not to cover their wages.
Finally, her father took a year out from work to accompany her, although clearly
the presence of a parent would make the experience very different from that of
most other students.

In Karrie's case, formal and informal access to teaching and learning were well
handled by the institution, but other aspects of university life, including opportunities to develop independence and to build social capital, were restricted.

Euan

Euan came from a middle-class background, studied physical sciences and entered
the university straight from school. He had mental health difficulties which had
started at secondary school with panic attacks. He had been unable to attend
school for most of the sixth year, but had instead been provided with support
from school so that he could do his exams. When he applied to the university
he decided not to disclose mental health difficulties because he did not consider
himself to be disabled and he was hoping to make a fresh start:

> I remember when I actually got the form, it said 'do you have any disability of
> any kind' and I didn't actually say anything because I thought, well, mental
> health is probably a bit of a borderline thing ... They are not going to take it
> seriously enough ... Disabled people are physically disabled.
>
> (Euan, year 2)

However, the fresh start he had hoped for did not materialise, and he had
to restart the first year three times, something which he was uneasy about
admitting:

> I don't really think about it as my first year three times because that is not
> true. I wasn't really here for the full time anyway ... everything just became
> too much for me ... the social side of it, having been at home a lot during my
> sixth year ... the new way of working as well ... my mum suspected I would
> probably fall backwards a wee bit.
>
> (Euan, year 2)

When Euan struggled during his second attempt to start his course he was advised by a contact he had made in the chaplaincy to get in touch with the disability office. He did this but was so worried about not being able to explain his case clearly that he asked his father to go with him. He was provided with help to catch up and finally settled in on his third attempt. A range of support was put in place which included a personal assistant to accompany him to lectures and study guidance support. By his second year he did not require a personal assistant but he was still using the study support.

Euan valued the support provided and came to accept that mental health difficulties were a disability, but he did not think that others would see it that way:

> I still believe that mental illnesses of all kinds ... are a disability. Not a disability in the way most people would see it. If I described myself as disabled most people would normally think 'it's a sight problem or a hearing problem' and they might not understand how the mental aspect can affect you in that way.
>
> (Euan, year 4)

He was concerned about others knowing that he had made several 'false' starts and did not want other students to see the number on his matriculation card (as this indicates year of entry). He did on one occasion mention it to another student who was supportive but this did not help him discuss it more widely. One main concern was that people would not believe him and he found it difficult to discuss this with his Director of Studies:

> My DoS is in quite a high position, he is a nice man ... but I just felt that I couldn't [discuss it with him].
>
> (Euan, year 2)

Whereas many students do not regard the process of studying as particularly problematic, Euan was forced to devote a considerable amount of time trying to work out how to study. This was a recurring theme in all the interviews and he seemed to be searching for perfection. There was a sense that this impacted on his ability to keep up with the course material. A phrase that captured this was 'but I haven't had enough time to really properly study it' (Euan, year 4). He struggled and had to resit exams.

The formal transitions from school to university and also through the university clearly presented Euan with a number of challenges, and by the end of his third year it emerged that he had failed nine out of his ten exams. This included core courses and university regulations meant that he was not allowed to progress into his final honours year. He was offered the opportunity to resit in August but felt that two months was not sufficient for him to revise for all the exams. Another option provided was for him to return a year later to resit. Provided he passed the exams he could then exit with a non-Honours degree. Euan attributed his difficulties to his grandfather's death which took place in February of his third year. He explained that he had tried to discuss his difficulties, but it seemed that further accommodations were not possible:

I went to the Disability Office and I emailed my Director of Studies saying at the time, with the exams, that I was really struggling. I just couldn't concentrate and I had just fallen too far behind ... I did actually go and see him in February ... saying I was struggling ... [then] after the exam results came out ... I went to the Disability Office and they sounded as if they did actually want to try and do something ... and they said they were going to try and get my Director of Studies down to have a discussion ... but it sounded to me that the department had basically made up their mind ... According to their rules they said I couldn't do the honours ... they said that in the past ... it wasn't such a problem but the government came in and interfered and said we don't want students doing honours years twice.

(Euan, year 4)

Euan tried to take the initiative and entered into considerable communication with the institution, and his parents had also been involved in pleading his case. The department, whilst wishing to help him, felt that no further adjustments were possible and suggested that stricter quality assurance mechanisms were a barrier to flexibility. Overall, transition into the institution had been problematic and his exit was also troubled.

Jean

Jean was a married mature student with three children who had decided to return to higher education to study a course which would allow her to find local employment. Her husband, a firefighter, worked shifts and was therefore available to help out with childcare. Because of her difficulty with spelling and structuring work, he also helped out with her written assignments. She was from a working-class background and was the only one of her siblings to attend university.

Jean was one of the last students to go through a 'fitness to practise' medical examination, which was dropped as a formal requirement by the General Teaching Council for Scotland in 2004. During the course of the examination, the doctor noticed that she had made a number of errors on the form and suggested that she might have a dyslexic-type difficulty which could be managed with reasonable adjustments on the course and in the workplace. Following appointments with the Disability Office and an educational psychologist, dyslexia was formally diagnosed and the Disabled Students Allowance awarded. However, the process was lengthy and support in the form of a laptop and software packages was not available until the second year of the course.

Jean felt that there was a real stigma attached to having reading and writing difficulties:

I come from a generation where it was looked on very badly and you were regarded as being stupid and dunce and things like that ... I didn't tell my mum for ages.

(Jean, year 2)

Throughout her time at university, she continued to have an ambivalent relationship with the concept of disability:

> I still get emails from the Disability Office to register with [a disability group]. I kind of think 'I am not disabled' ... I mean there is one argument that you know labelling it might give you more resources and yeah, it has given me extra time which I am really pleased with ... but then I kind of think well, I don't know ... we all have strands and areas of development that can be worked on.
>
> (Jean, year 3)

Despite encountering some lecturers who had little sympathy with dyslexic students, Jean felt that her university experience had been largely positive and the adjustments made, in terms of extra time in exams and access to lecture notes in advance, were adequate. However, her experience of school placement was much more difficult. The first teacher whom she confided in reacted with horror and proceeded to tell other members of staff:

> The next day I went in and she was very close to another teacher in the school, and I felt like I had been discussed, and there was kind of looks being made and things, and then that teacher, from then onwards treated me like a child, and was very, very picky.
>
> (Jean, year 3)

Because of these adverse reactions, she decided not to disclose a disability when applying for her probationary year.

Summary and conclusion

In the first part of this chapter, we reviewed recent writing on disability and transition, noting that disability must be seen as an essentially transitional status, varying between contexts and at different points in an individual's biography. We also noted major changes in the structure of the labour market over the past forty years, as jobs for young people, along with many manual jobs, have disappeared, being replaced by service sector jobs often requiring higher degrees of literacy. Transitions for all young people appear to have become more problematic, risk strewn and extended, and there is much evidence that disabled young people, particularly those who are identified as learning disabled, have become particularly vulnerable to spoiled transitions accompanied by spoiled identities.

For the minority of young disabled who succeed in entering university, there is some degree of protection from risk, but the case study students presented here exemplify some features of stalled transitions. First, it is evident that even for those disabled students who succeed academically, such as Karrie, there are difficulties in establishing social and emotional independence and building the social capital which is so crucial to a successful life after graduation. For all the students whose cases are presented here, additional input from families was crucial but might also have been experienced as disempowering. Secondly, it is evident that some students have great difficulty in accepting the identity of a disabled student, which it is necessary to do at least at a formal level in order to claim reasonable adjustments and additional resources. Finally, ambivalence around disability affects students at different points of their university career. On entering university, they are forced to make a decision about whether to disclose or not, and they are likely at this point to be unaware of the practical and social consequences of disclosing or not. At particular points of a university course, for example, when embarking on a year abroad or entering a work placement, a new set of decisions on how to deal with disclosure and organise practical support are required. Similar problems around disclosure and obtaining support are likely to arise on leaving the university and entering employment.

Overall, it appears that universities have made great progress in developing support systems for disabled students and encouraging more to disclose. For the elite, pre-'92 university attended by the students here, it was evident that the need to think more closely about student experiences at a social and emotional, as well as an academic level had come as something of a shock. Whilst routine support, such as arranging for extra time in exams, was unproblematic, dealing with more subtle aspects of negotiating transitions around disability status still required further thought. Whilst universities in many ways reflect changing social attitudes, they also have the opportunity to shape social attitudes of the future, and here their willingness to challenge some of the hidden forms of discrimination in the negotiation of transition may be particularly important.

Note

1   This research forms part of a longitudinal study 'Enhancing the learning experiences and outcomes for disabled students in higher education' funded by ESRC TLRP Phase III – reference RES-139-25-0135. It is led by Professor Mary Fuller at the University of Gloucestershire.

Bibliography

Beck, U. (1992) Risk Society: Towards a New Modernity, London: Sage.
Beck, U., Giddens, A. and Lash, S. (1994) Reflexive Modernization, Cambridge: Polity Press.
Bynner, J. and Roberts, K. (eds) (1991) Youth and Work: Transition to Employment in England and Germany, London: Anglo German Foundation.
Corker, M. and Shakespeare, T. (2002) Disability/Postmodernity: Embodying Disability Theory, London: Continuum.
Ecclestone, K., Blackmore, T., Biesta, G., Colley, H. and Hughes, M. (2006) 'Lost in transition: managing change and becoming through education and work', Nottingham: TLRP Seminar Series 'Transitions through the lifecourse', Seminar 12–13 October 2006.
Field, J. (2006) Lifelong Learning and the New Educational Order, Stoke-on-Trent: Trentham.
Lash, S. and Urry, J. (1993) Economies of Signs and Space, London: Sage.
Oliver, M. (1990) The Politics of Disablement, Basingstoke: Macmillan.

Riddell, S. (1998) 'The dynamics of transition to adulthood', in C. Robinson and L. Stalker (eds) *Growing Up with Disability*, London: Jessica Kingsley.

Riddell, S., Baron, S. and Wilson, A. (2001) *The Learning Society and People with Learning Difficulties*, Bristol: Policy Press.

Riddell, S., Tinklin, T. and Wilson, A. (2005) *Disabled Students in Higher Education*, London: Routledge.

Riddell, S., Weedon, E., Fuller, M., Healey, M., Hurst, A., Kelly, K. and Piggott, L. (2007) 'Managerialism and equalities: tensions within widening access policy and practice for disabled students in UK universities', *Higher Education*, 54: 615–28.

Scottish Executive (2003) *Life Through Learning: learning through life*. Available online at www.scotland.gov.uk/library5/lifelong/llsm-00.asp, accessed 25 March 2007.

Stanley, N., Mallon, S., Bell, J., Hilton, S. and Manthorpe, J. (2007) Summary of report: responses and prevention in student suicide: the RaPSS study. Available online at www.rapss.org.uk/, accessed 27 March 2007.

Stone, D. A. (1984) *The Disabled State*, Basingstoke: Macmillan.

Weedon, E. and Riddell, S. (2007) 'To those that have shall be given? Differing expectations of support among dyslexic students', in M. Osborne, M. Houston and N. Toman (eds) *Researching the Pedagogy of Lifelong Learning*, London: Routledge.

Willis, P. (1977) *Learning to Labour*, Farnborough: Saxon House.

8 Rethinking 'failed transitions' to higher education

Jocey Quinn

Introduction

In this chapter I will explore the concept of transition in relation to higher education (HE), drawing on a research project funded by the Joseph Rowntree Foundation about 'failed transition' amongst young working-class people who have 'dropped out' of university. I will show that a fixed concept of transition certainly informs policy and practice in HE, and that this concept is not simply inadequate, but also causes significant problems for students. Where notions of transition are inflexible and obdurate, failure follows soon behind for many young people. A 'failed transition' to HE is a mirror of multiple 'failed' transitions in the lives of working-class learners: anticipated failures, because of their supposed 'lack' of aspirations and ability, and predetermined failures because of the rigidly hierarchical education system. However, moving towards a looser definition of transition does not necessarily solve the problem. The research on 'drop out' problematises even the most flexible accounts of transition discussed in the literature and calls into question the usefulness of the concept of transition itself. My chapter will attempt to address the core questions of identity, structure and agency, which have engaged those of us involved in this debate, but will end by posing a new one. What happens when we recognise change as a permanent state of being, rather than a periodic occurrence; when flux replaces pathway as our image of life and learning?

The characteristics of transitions

Transition is integral to current conceptualisations and practices of higher education. In the UK, HE policy depicts transition to higher education as the fulfilment of a hegemonic goal. It is envisaged as natural and desirable that young people should aim to go to university. There is no comparable rite of passage that is so socially sanctioned and unquestioningly accepted as connoting both success and normality. This assumption is reified in targets such as 50 per cent of those under 30 experiencing higher education by 2010. This transition is not merely an educational one but is explicitly linked to citizenship. 'HE also brings social benefits [...] there is strong evidence that graduates are more likely to be engaged citizens' (DfES 2003a).

The emphasis has been on the pivotal moment of change, on making it to the gates and going through. Very little attention is paid to what students learn once they enter. For example, in widening participation policy documents the word most conspicuous by its absence is 'curriculum'. Emphasis instead is on 'aspiration', 'access' and 'attainment' (see Quinn 2006). So transition to HE is formulated as getting in and getting on, the student is an actor, but the terms of the transition are set by others. Transition is not postulated as a creative and interactive process and most of all it should not be turbulent and fragmented. Anything that appears to threaten this transition, such as early withdrawal, must be regulated and suppressed. Non-retention is 'setting students up to fail' and 'unacceptable' (DfES 2003b). The Higher Education Funding Council for England (HEFCE) has been tasked with 'bearing down' on those institutions that allow it to happen (DfES 2003b) and is currently doing so in a draconian fashion.

In practice, this simple pattern is highly fragmented. It is important to understand the formal mechanics of transition to HE as a historically situated practice. In an age of fragmentation and diversity, transition to HE mirrors this broader social pattern. Whilst policy depicts a common transition, what we have are many very different entries into very different institutions. The picture is becoming a familiar one, with its own aura of inevitability. Widening participation has ensured that virtually all middle-class children will go to university. Many more working-class children also enter HE than ever before, but proportionately their access has dropped since the 1960s (Reay, David and Ball 2005). When they do enter HE it is far more likely to be in a post-1992 institution or via HE in FE, and they are more likely to undertake foundation degrees than middle-class students and much less likely to enter prestigious courses such as medicine or law. The transition is also shaped by gender and race and by where you live. Fewer of those outside London will access HE, particularly if they live in disadvantaged areas (HEFCE 2005). Young women now enter in larger numbers than young men, but institutions are certainly not shaped in their image, as the curriculum and cultures of universities are still highly masculinised (Quinn 2003). Minority ethnic groups are proportionately more likely to enter than white, but only to certain institutions. In more elite universities, very few minority ethnic students will participate, and those that do will make that transition into an overwhelmingly white institution (Connor *et al.* 2004). Young, white, working-class men from disadvantaged areas are the least likely of all to enter HE and the most likely to withdraw early (NAO 2008). Transition to HE is thus highly stratified and complex. For many students the transition is incomplete and they leave early. The numbers are sufficiently high (28 per cent in some post-1992 universities) to cause the government great concern. So when we talk about transition to HE, we must ask transition by whom and to where?

The research project to which I will refer in this chapter (Quinn *et al.* 2005) concerns a particular group: young working-class people under 25, living in disadvantaged provincial areas in England, Scotland, Wales and Northern Ireland, who were the first in their family to go to university, but withdrew early. Nearly all were white and the majority were men. The universities they had attended were all post-1992 institutions with priorities for widening participation, but retention problems. All of the universities were in areas where traditional industries had virtually disappeared and the responsibility for regeneration of the locality was partly displaced onto higher education:

> It's a deprived area around here. It is below the EU-stated poverty line. Without students going to university I don't think it's going to be able to get out of that.
>
> (NUS officer, Research Jury Day)

The project was a qualitative, participative study which began with research jury days held in the 4 locations, involving a total of 120 stakeholders. The purpose of these days was to bring together a wide range of participants including students, lecturers, support staff, employers, employment agencies and representatives from the voluntary sector. The events involved invited presentations and discussions exploring perceptions of drop out and its impacts on the locality, presented to a jury of researchers. This resulted in a contextualised and localised understanding of the issue, which reconceptualised 'drop out' as a sociocultural phenomenon, rather than the individual problem of student or university (see Quinn 2004 for a full discussion). This was followed by in-depth interviews with 67 students who had withdrawn early, an international colloquium and policy seminar, interviews with careers and employment agencies and an admissions survey. The study allowed us to explore some of the meanings and implications of 'drop out' and to theorise and rethink the issue.

It is interesting to explore the findings of this study in relation to transition. The narrative of HE entry is that it signifies change – but for these students it may best signify stasis. They continued to stay in the same town, often living at home and socialising with the same groups of friends, travelling in 'packs' to university, where once they had travelled to school. Getting a job would have brought about many more changes than this transition to university study had done. In other respects, the transition was more marked for them than for their middle-class counterparts and was not the seamless progression that the policy rhetoric of 'access, aspiration and attainment' implies. They did not have funds of knowledge about the university sector, nor the confidence to negotiate it easily and bend the system to their will. Instead of feeling free to make changes in their courses and demand support from lecturers and student services, they were hesitant and embarrassed, feeling that once they had made their choices they were stuck with them and doomed to cope with them on their own. Withdrawing early appeared to be their only option, once they realised they could not progress in their studies in the way in which they needed, either for study-related reasons or because of external factors such as having to work long hours to support their degree.

In terms of the policy agenda, leaving early signifies a failed transition into university: a blocked pathway and a waste of opportunity. The young people themselves had rather different perspectives. For them, withdrawal was essentially part of an ongoing process of reassessment, of finding out what they did and didn't want to do and what they were practically able to do, given constraints such as family financial problems. Significantly, they did not want this to be the end of their engagement with university, and all but one expressed a desire to return to higher education in the future. Most asserted they had gained skills and confidence from the time they had spent there and that this experience was not a 'failed' one:

> I didn't feel like a failure ... the job I'm doing now is directly related to the course I was doing. I feel that I achieved something from it.

> I think it still set me up and prepared me for life. I didn't feel any shame.

> Before I was one of those people who didn't use to talk to many people. Now I'm really open and I have a lot of avenues. I'm quite happy now about going to university.

> I know I can make my own decisions. I was always a bit dubious about that. Now I know I can do things for myself.

> I wouldn't look at it as positive or negative. I just look at it as a learning curve.

In such statements the students deflect anticipated criticisms of their early withdrawal. They are both aware of the discursive framework of failure and shame and willing to replace this closed narrative with one of openness, learning and progress. This appears not to be a simple matter of self-justification. Most were willing to be self-critical and take responsibility for their own mistakes. Yet they were all able to envisage 'drop out' as something more than just a 'failed' transition. Instead of employing a narrative of blame of the failed university, one which is very much available to them in popular discourse, they put the period at university into the broader context of their life ahead.

With this broader vision came a different perspective on how HE might best be taken up. Ideally what they wanted were opportunities to go part-time, transfer courses, leave and return without penalty, but they had little confidence that this could actually be achieved. Essentially, they needed a flexible system to accommodate what can be conceptualised as a fluid learning self. This self was not fixed in one position and changed over time in terms of what it needed to learn and how and where it wanted to learn it. Sadly, this flexibility did not exist. In structural terms: institution and students were financially penalised for non-completion, change to part-time or other courses was not encouraged and mobility was seen as an aberration – to be feared rather than encouraged. In cultural terms, withdrawal was understood as a predictable symptom of working-class propensity to failure and the students were mostly regarded and treated accordingly by employment agencies and employers (Quinn 2004).

They knew that however they defined their experience, others would not hesitate to see failure. '*Whenever you tell anybody you are leaving they think you are just a waster.*'

Usefulness of ideas about transition, agency, identity and structure

As I have suggested, the prevalent notion of transition as a fixed turning point which takes place at a preordained time and in a certain place does not accord well with our research findings on drop out. Once the students in our study had entered university there was no transition into a qualitatively different life. There is also the question of readiness for change. Our study shows that the rhythms of the young people's learning lives do not synchronise with the set time frames offered to them. Their point of readiness for HE may lie well in the future, after they have withdrawn and reformulated their priorities and also when material conditions within the family are more able to support their study. Current norms of educational transition are temporally limited, with narrow horizons. They do not take into account the forward and backward motions of life and the closures and openings of opportunities to learn (Colley 2007) that occur because of the material dilemmas and constraints produced by economic, social and political forces:

> We can therefore see the contradictions between closures and openings as an unending and fragmenting process, which is neither linear nor simplistically circular: while one contradiction may be resolved, a new one will surface. We might more accurately depict the process, then, as a number of zigzag or spiral movements within a web of contradictions.

> (Colley 2007: 438)

However, concepts which link transition to identity, postulating transition as a process of 'becoming somebody' (see Ecclestone *et al.* 2005: 1) are equally problematic in terms of our study. They still suggest a unified humanist subject capable of being transformed by education. Authenticity is still the hallmark of this discussion, whereas it is more useful to understand the students as engaged in multiple performances. We do not see education making and shaping them into their real and perfect human form, but rather education being one of many sites where they act out certain culturally shaped roles. For example the young men in our study were involved in performances of whiteness and masculinity which drew on cultural narratives, such as nostalgia for the security and solidarity of 'lost' white jobs like pottery and mining. These cultural narratives and associated collective memories had a powerful effect on their behaviour and made it quite difficult for them to find security via education (see Quinn *et al.* 2006). Transition as a question of having a 'story to tell', as discussed in Ecclestone *et al.* (2005: 1) implies that there is an individual, meaningful narrative generated from the student themselves. In fact, students employed many interlocking narratives drawn from culture, for example, the story of the young working-class man as rebel and as family man, in order to negotiate movements into and out of university.

The linking of story and transition is also questionable, because, as Zembylas and Fendler argue, '[t]here are some stories that cannot be told, and some emotions that cannot be expressed' (2007: 328). The yoking together of the speakable with transition, inevitably leaves those with lives that are marginal and incoherent unable to make the transition to fully 'educated person'. It is no coincidence that the students in our study often felt unable to speak or to be heard: '*Nobody realised there was anything wrong and nobody asked*'.

Ecclestone *et al.* suggest that 'some transitions are never complete but have to be reworked continually' (2005: 2). Whilst I would agree that issues of class, race and gender make it more difficult for some people to claim authoritatively the final change in personal status that university education is supposed to confer, the idea that the self is constantly reworked is actually pertinent to everyone. This is a perpetual process for all of us. I would argue that we are all always lost in transition, not just in the sense of moving from one task or context to another, but as a condition of our subjectivity.

> [T]he subject is not an 'entity' or thing, or a relation between mind (interior) and body (exterior). Instead it must be understood as a series of flows, energies, movements and capacities, a series of fragments or segments capable of being linked together in ways other than those that congeal it into an identity.
>
> (Grosz 1993: 197–8)

Ecclestone (2007) has suggested that the above conception of transition is similar to others she has identified, in seeing transition as a risk that needs to be managed, with a concomitant loss for the learner in being challenged and encouraged to demonstrate autonomy. I dispute this interpretation. My vision of life as permanent flux is a celebration of risk and uncertainty, an energetic conception of subjectivity which seeks to free it from the limiting constraints of personhood.

> [T]he spiralled being who, from outside, appears to be a well-invested center, will never reach his center. The being of man is an unsettled being which all expression unsettles.
>
> (Bachelard 1994: 214)

With such a dynamic conception of transition, comes a freedom from fixating on fixed moments of change. If educational policy makers were to adopt this model, the current fetishisation of the certain time frames and activities, such as the 14–19 curriculum or widening participation for the under-25s, would make way for an emphasis on flexible, 'unsettled' and spiralling movements throughout a learning life.

Ecclestone (2007) has also raised concerns that emphasis on 'managing transitions' to university takes attention away from academic content and skills and places it on the 'personal', thus diminishing both academic subject and the individual. However, this implies that the academic subject is somehow sacrosanct and neutral, that it exists in a solid form in the same way a 'person' is seen to do. In fact the academic subject itself is a gendered, classed, raced construct. It is both a 'monolith' and a 'shape-shifter' (Quinn 2003) as it is constantly changing, but also acts to exclude what Foucault terms 'subjugated knowledges' (1980). In order to match the notion of subjectivity in a permanent state of flux and transition, we need to foster a reflexive transitional curriculum, rather than strive to protect a more fixed subject-based one. This means that our very notion of what knowledge is, how it should be ordered and exchanged must necessarily be held under question, thought and rethought all the time, and that disciplines and curricula should reflect this mutability.

So, transition rather than being a rare event is actually an everyday feature. In many respects the students in our study instinctively responded to this vision of perpetual transition and wanted to normalise multiple movements into and out of university. However, current educational systems and policies ensure that transitions are moments of crisis which must be traversed well or not at all, and a linear pathway suggests there is no going back and no opportunity to take an interesting byway. There is also another deeper factor at play: although flux may be our condition we do not necessarily welcome or accept it, and we often cling to the reassurances and defences of fixed identities and structures (see Quinn 2005 for a full discussion).

Concepts of agency have some use in understanding the process of 'drop out'. Although early withdrawal is conceived by policy makers as a symptom of failure, for the students it was often a rational decision based on circumstances that meant this was not the optimum time, place or subject to study. One could argue that they displayed a large amount of agency in taking control and leaving. Indeed this decision was usually a lonely and painful one, as they rarely turned for help to any of the available support services and only to a limited extent to their family. However, I would be wary of taking the idea of agency too far. They had employed agency, but they were still produced as helpless 'failures', with negative consequences such as poor job opportunities and limited chances to return to education. Permeating and constructing the process was a cultural narrative of 'working-class drop out', which posited early withdrawal as likely and as symptomatic of working-class lack. 'Drop out' had become a self-perpetuating narrative and this discourse was more important than individual choice or even structure. Until this narrative is challenged and replaced, social and educational structures cannot be rethought or reworked and individuals cannot be free to rewrite the script for themselves.

Problem transitions

Structures, in the sense of class, gender and ethnicity are clearly important in understanding transitions. As I have suggested, the different kinds of transitions to HE are structurally produced as well as culturally framed, and the transitions experienced by the students in our study will probably be more problematic than

o the flux of our subjectivity and to social and cultural trends then it is not
hing done and dusted, achieved and then superseded, but an opportunity
uld all be able to return to throughout life. Similarly, if the heart of knowl-
s change and challenge, when can we ever be said to know anything; rather
involved in an endless process of knowing. More and more, universities are
e site where that knowing takes place.

tinuing to position them as the prime and one-way gateway to an
ed and valuable life means that we are locked into a turnstile conception
sition.

graphy

rd, G. (1994) *The Poetics of Space*, Boston: Beacon Press.

H. (2007) 'Understanding time in learning transitions through the lifecourse',
national Studies in Sociology of Education, 17: 427–43.

H., Tyers, C., Modood, T. and Hillage, J. (2004) *Why the Difference? A Closer Look
gher Education, Minority Ethnic Students and Graduates*, London: DfES.

003a) *The Future of Higher Education*, London: DfES.

003b) *Widening Participation in Higher Education*, London: DfES.

ne, K. (2007) 'Lost and found in transition: the implications of "identity", "agency"
structure" for educational goals and practices', keynote speech presented at the
rence of the Centre for Research on Lifelong Learning, University of Stirling,
2007.

ne, K., Blackmore, T., Biesta, G., Colley, H. and Hughes, M. (2005) 'Transitions
gh the lifecourse: political, professional and academic perspectives', paper
ted at Annual TLRP/ESRC Conference, Warwick University, October 2005.

M. (1980) 'Two lectures', in C. Gordon (ed.) *Power/Knowledge: Selected Interviews
ther Writings 1972–1977*, Brighton: Harvester Press.

(1993) *Volatile Bodies: Towards a Corporeal Feminism*, Bloomington: Indiana
rsity Press.

2005) *Young Participation in Higher Education*, Bristol: HEFCE.

Audit Office (2008) *Widening Participation in Higher Education*, Report by the
roller and Auditor General HC 725 Session 2007–2008, 25 June.

d Sukhnandan, L. (1997) *Undergraduate Non-completion in Higher Education in
, Report 2*, Bristol: HEFCE.

(2003) *Powerful Subjects: Are Women Really Taking Over the University?* Stoke-
t: Trentham Books.

4) 'Understanding working class "drop out" from higher education through
cultural lens: cultural narratives and local contexts', *International Studies in
y of Education*, 14: 57–75.

5) 'Subjects and subjectivities in higher education', paper presented at annual
ace of the American Educational Research Association, Montreal, April

) 'Mass participation but no curriculum transformation' in D. Jary and R. Jones
he *Policy and Practice of Widening Participation in the Social Sciences*, Birmingham:

awy, R. and Diment, K. (2008) 'Dead end kids in dead end jobs? Reshaping
n young people in jobs without training', *Research in Post-compulsory Education*,
95.

transitions made by middle-class students to elite universities. The existence of
similar anxieties about subjects and teaching methods, shared loneliness and
need for peer support that are revealed in studies of drop out amongst students
generally (see for example Ozga and Sukhnandan 1997) may belie this emphasis
on class difference. However, research such as Reay *et al.* (2005) indicates that
notwithstanding differences related to other factors such as race, gender and
disability, many middle-class students face such educational problems with more
resources to call upon and most of all with a sense of entitlement that others will
solve these problems for them.

One of the problems of transition for the students in our study was a nagging
sense of doubt about the role and purpose of higher education. Was this a purpose-
less and drifting transition which would lead them nowhere? They mostly envisaged staying in their local area and they knew that if they did, good jobs would be
comparatively scarce, with or without a university degree. It was common knowledge that graduates were taking jobs in call centres and building sites and that
'graduateness' had lost any cachet with employers. For a goal-driven pathway and
notion of transition to work effectively, there needs to be reward at the end of it.
For these students prospects of an employment-related reward were at best hazy.
However, the students were interested in other factors, particularly in studying
subjects that stimulated them and at which they might succeed. Job prospects
were not the main motivator for withdrawing early, the desire to learn something
meaningful was the most determining factor.

Dealing with transitions

Prevalent discussions about transition to HE position working-class students as
needy, in the sense of personally inadequate and unable to cope with the rigours
of transition. In rejecting this position we should talk more of rights: the right to
enter university successfully and succeed. This is a common right of all students,
but structural disadvantage ensures that many students require support if they
are to take up this entitlement. On one level this means the provision of integrated systems of learning and personal support and advice, on a more radical
level it means changing the HE system so that flexibility becomes paramount.
Our research produced a number of pertinent recommendations which will not
in themselves solve the complex issues at play, but which can make a positive
difference to the educational experiences of students.

Institutions should not hide the fact that withdrawal is a possibility, but rather
be open about its implications. They should offer better opportunities to change
course and provide more meaningful information about individual subjects to
enable students to make well-informed choices. Personal planning of 'non-traditional pathways' into and through HE should be facilitated, which remove the
distinction between full- and part-time mode and permit less than full-time study
on all courses. Opportunities and support for students to change modes of study
from full- to part-time and vice versa should be easily available. In terms of support
there needs to be adequate financial support for students from low-income families with affordable and flexible childcare. The curriculum itself should reflect

and affirm working-class students by ensuring that working-class histories and perspectives are presented with respect rather than marginalised and ignored. If students should be thinking of leaving then universities must offer more proactive advice in terms of educational and employment options. It would be helpful to develop stronger links between administrative staff dealing with withdrawal and teaching staff and to provide training for personal tutors. It is necessary to develop pedagogy that supports the integration of all students, including learning support integrated within the curriculum. Overall, universities need to develop more holistic approaches to student support services and improve and sustain student and staff awareness of existing sources of support. In order to monitor student movement they need to ensure data on current students and those who have withdrawn is accurate.

It is essential that policy makers change both their perspectives and their practices. They should recognise the potential benefits to some students of leaving early. Student withdrawal must be placed within a lifelong learning framework, which facilitates movement out of and into higher education throughout life. In order to do this it will be necessary to review the structure of HE and move towards creating a lifelong learning framework with multiple entry and exit points and to allow longer periods of absence from HE without having to withdraw from study. This would involve removing financial penalties for HEIs and introducing payment for units studied, rather than years of registration.

Movement into higher education may always have an element of risk; indeed one could argue the riskier the better in terms of generating new perspectives and ideas. These proposals to support students in transition are designed to facilitate better lifelong learning, rather than to cushion students from challenge.

Contested aspects of transitions

The nature of the transition to higher education is materially differentiated, as I have suggested, and so too is the type of education students will receive on entry. There are vast differences in resources, locations and cultures between contemporary universities. Similarly curricular and pedagogical approaches are multiple and multiplying. Most contentious of all are questions of knowledge and the purposes of knowledge. Is the contemporary student to be an intellectual, a professional in the making, an instrument of the knowledge economy, a consumer? Is the university here to reproduce society or provide a refuge from it? In making that transition into HE is the student entering into a compact which validates them as a compliant citizen? The post-compulsory nature of HE accentuates this notion of compliance. Zembylas and Fendler (2007) have argued that 'current educational discourses make it possible for us to accept a definition of freedom that means the same thing as self governance. We have become free to be normal, and it would not be normal to act in defiance of community norms' (2007: 328). What then of the ruptured transition of 'drop out', when the unspoken pact is broken? It is possible to conceptualise the young people in our study as unruly subjects, rather than as inadequate ones. Part of this unruliness stems from non-linear understandings of what learning lives are or can

be. This they share with other young people who st[...] educational pathways, such as young people in jobs wit[...] et al. 2008). For these subjects, measurements of succ[...] patterns. Nevertheless, they cannot ultimately escape[...] when community norms are flouted:

> Because they haven't got a recognised skill or previ[...]
> to restrict their job choices and must accept the [...]
> as if 'I'm down and you're keeping me down here' [...]
> (Job Centre Plus [...]

The suggestion that 'drop out' need not be seen as [...] controversial in some quarters. Bodies such as HEFC[...] notions of retention and our calls for a more flexible [...] may take some time to register. Indeed recent decis[...] they will penalise rather than reward flexibility. Neve[...] in challenging rigid notions of successful transitions [...] that they produce negative outcomes for students an[...] needed in a postmodern society.

Conclusion

HE policy perceives transition as fixed point on [...] I have argued, what is needed is a system that f[...] into, across, out of and re-entering HE, the kind o[...] through the lifecourse. To achieve this we need to [...] sion and recognise that the concept of transitio[...] the fluidity of our learning or our lives. Transiti[...] ised, implies moving from one state, strata or loca[...] goes through a change and becomes different beco[...] is too static a viewpoint. We constantly chang[...] backwards and forwards, we do not coalesce eith[...] momentous life crisis. There is no such thing as a[...] of transition – only subjectivity and flux. This i[...] not a weakness, for 'it is better to live in a state [...] finality' (Bachelard 1994: 61). Policy makers en[...] tion, because it synchronises with their vision o[...] can be led to goals that are predefined, neat and[...] a vision of the person as an integrated, identifia[...] Subjectivity and learning are not so compliant, [...] also creativity. Higher education must have str[...] be denied, but ultimately it needs greater openn[...] the flux of our being, rather than trying to subj[...]

In arguing for the spiral not the pathway a[...] rigid conformity, we need to abandon many o[...] education and about transition. If wanting and

Co   educa   of tra

Bibli[...]

Bache[...]
Colley,[...]
    Inte[...]
Conno[...]
    at F[...]
DfES ([...]
—— (2[...]
Eccleste[...]
    and [...]
    Con[...]
    June[...]
Eccleste[...]
    thro[...]
    prese[...]
Foucaul[...]
    and [...]
Grosz, [...]
    Univ[...]
HEFCE [...]
Nationa[...]
    Com[...]
Ozga, J. [...]
    Engla[...]
Quinn, J[...]
    on-Tr[...]
—— (20[...]
    a soci[...]
    Sociol[...]
—— (20[...]
    confer[...]
    2005.[...]
—— (20[...]
    (eds), [...]
    CSAP.[...]
Quinn, J.,[...]
    debate[...]
    13: 18[...]

Quinn, J., Thomas, L., Slack, K., Casey, L., Thexton, W. and Noble, J. (2005) *From Life Crisis to Lifelong Learning: Rethinking Working Class 'Drop Out' from Higher Education*, York: York Publishing/Joseph Rowntree Foundation.

—— (2006) 'Lifting the hood: lifelong learning and young, white, provincial working-class masculinities', *British Educational Research Journal*, 32: 735–50.

Reay, D., David, M. E. and Ball, S. (2005) *Degrees of Choice: Social Class, Race and Gender in Higher Education*, Stoke-on-Trent: Trentham Books.

Zembylas, M. and Fendler, L. (2007) 'Reframing emotion in education though lenses of *parrhesia* and *care of the self*', *Studies in Philosophy and Education*, 26: 319–33.

9 Time in learning transitions through the lifecourse
A feminist perspective

Helen Colley

Introduction

As the introductory chapter in this book notes, transitions have become a major political, popular and academic concern in the UK and Europe. Factors such as the proliferation of pathways for young people, the drive to retain them in education, the increasing individualisation of social lives, and economically driven imperatives for lifelong learning have made the management of transitions – in particular, linear progression from one educational stage or institution to another – central to education policies. Transitions and their relationship to learning – both formal and informal – have also been a focus of numerous studies of young people in the sociology of education (e.g., Banks *et al.* 1992; Bates and Riseborough 1994; Hodkinson *et al.* 1996; Pollard and Filer 1999; Ball *et al.* 2000; Colley 2003; Reay *et al.* 2005). But as Ecclestone (2006) also notes, this concern takes us into difficult territory: while policy makers' understandings of transitions dominate much practice and research, they are contested strongly by critical perspectives that challenge the theoretical and methodological assumptions on which they rest.

In this chapter, I explore one underdeveloped but crucial aspect of such contestations: the theories of time which underpin different understandings of transitions and the learning associated with them. I take as my starting point the notion that sociology of education is inseparable from the social theory that informs it: all too often this relationship remains obscure, yet it influences educational research studies profoundly. As Dorothy Smith notes:

> A sociology is a systematically developed consciousness of society and social relations. The established sociology ... gives us a consciousness that looks at society, social relations, and people's lives as if we could stand outside them, ignoring the particular local places in the everyday in which we live our lives. It claims objectivity not on the basis of its capacity to speak truthfully, but in terms of its specific capacity to exclude the presence and experience of particular subjectivities. Nonetheless, of course, they are there and must be.
>
> (Smith 1987: 2)

This, then, is an attempt both to make visible the social theories of time which tacitly inform much literature on learning transitions, and to demonstrate the potential of alternative, feminist theories of time to inform radical sociological studies in this field. It will draw on the 'presence and experience of particular subjectivities' which Smith insists upon, particularly those – classed, raced and gendered – which are all too often excluded.

Whilst it is impossible to arrive at a single definition of transition which might gain consensus, it is predominantly constructed as a process of change over time – whether the change is conceptualised as being in contexts for learning or in learners' identities (or both), whether it takes place over a short or long timespan, and whatever the causes and consequences of that change may be. Almost invariably, too, studies of transition – including those that take a critical stance – attend exclusively to the nature of change, neglecting the dimension of time in which change occurs.

However, as I will argue here, without also engaging in sociological thinking about time as well as change, our understandings of transitions remain impoverished, and in ways that render social inequalities less visible. From a perspective which pays attention to differences such as gender, race and class, time can take on multiple forms apart from the linearity assumed by dominant concepts of transition. Looking at transitions through this lens can therefore help to foreground the social actions and interactions that enable and constitute learning. We need to acknowledge, however, that the study of transitions also suggests a much broader notion of 'education' than learning undertaken within formal institutions: it must also include informal and even tacit learning about who we can become and where we can locate ourselves socially and spatially.

I therefore begin by briefly reviewing diverse conceptualisations of transition from a critical perspective. I then explore competing theories of time, discussing their influence on understandings of transition, and highlighting gendered aspects of these theories. In particular, I point to the importance – and neglect – of sociological (rather than metaphysical) understandings of time in this field. I go on to illustrate the potential of a sociological perspective on time through a case study of women's transitions and learning, drawing on Mojab's (2006) work on Kurdish women in diaspora. This allows an analysis of the enactment of time in their experiences, and the impact of this upon their formal and informal learning. I conclude by pointing to the need for the sociology of education to be underpinned by a dialectical and materialist theory of time which accounts for both its objective and subjective aspects in a relational way.

Conceptualisations of transition

At both national and European policy levels, there is a concern to ensure smooth and successful progression through learning transitions, particularly in order to break cycles of social exclusion. This view is exemplified in England by policies for 'joined-up thinking' to support children's and young people's transitions, initiated by the Social Exclusion Unit's (SEU) *Bridging the Gap* (SEU 1999), and developed in the Green Paper *Every Child Matters* (Great Britain Treasury 2003), with its goals of managing transitions in order to produce health, well-being, constructive leisure activities, and educational and economic achievement. It is also at the heart of European policies, centred currently on the Lisbon Strategy to make the European Union 'the most dynamic and competitive knowledge-based economy in the world, capable of sustainable economic growth with more and better jobs and greater social cohesion' (European Parliament 2000: 11). In particular, the European Youth Pact, which formed part of the 2005 relaunch of the Lisbon Strategy (European Commission 2005), proposes specific measures for education, training and mobility to prepare young people for transition into employment. These policies have come under sustained criticism (see, for example, Colley and Hodkinson 2001; Colley 2007). Yet they continue to promote a highly teleological notion of 'progression' as a linear trajectory onward and upward, and they increasingly deflect responsibility onto the individual for learning and furthering their own career development. Failure to do so is construed as a deviant abdication of responsibility which incurs the punitive withdrawal of 'rights' – primarily the 'right' to access welfare benefits.

A second understanding emerges from educational research studies which also see transition as a movement between institutional contexts, but with a more complex 'layering' of experiences. Contextual changes may occur 'within the same time frame' or 'across time' (Lam and Pollard 2006: 124, cited in Ecclestone 2006), and also involve shifts in identity which are socially regulated. Transitions, therefore, are seen 'not only [as] the product of social institutions but are also produced by social expectations' (Ecclestone 2006: 5) in relation to institutionalised pathways and normative patterns (Elder et al. 2003). This presents a less individualised approach, and points to the ways in which institutions and practices shape the constraints and affordances that impact on transitions. It posits a more reparative rather than punitive approach in its focus on deficit rather than deviance.

A third perspective on transitions and learning resists a primary focus on institutional transitions, to consider both individual and collective transitions of a broader social and cultural nature. Antikainen et al. (1996), for example, analyse learning through life histories spanning three generations in a context of unusually rapid social and economic transformation in Finland during the twentieth century. Other studies in the sociology of education focus on the interaction of agency and structure through changes located at 'turning points' (see, for example, Banks et al. 1992; Bates and Riseborough 1994; Hodkinson and Sparkes 1997; Ball et al. 2000). Most of these reflect a general shift that has taken place in sociological thinking, from notions of the 'life cycle' to those of the 'lifecourse'.

While the life-cycle mode of analysis has been used to frame different (usually age-related) stages in ways that draw attention to the determining role of social structures and the inequalities they (re)produce, it appears less useful as life and career trajectories have become more uncertain and fragmented (Collin and Young 2000; Furlong and Cartmel 1997). However, it also risks constructing as deficient those – for example, women – whose trajectories do not fit a neatly staged model, such as that represented in Levinson's seminal work *The Seasons of a Man's Life* (Levinson et al. 1978). Lifecourse analysis emphasises the life-wide 'interrelationships of individual, family and historical time' and their complexity (Allatt and Keil 1987: 3; see also Yeandle 1987). In contrast with the life-cycle approach, it focuses more on agency than structure, more on choice rather than constraint, but Allatt and Keil argue that, in studies of women's lives:

> Paradoxically ... the life-course analysts' distinction between family and individual time helps us to recognise the systematic conflation of the two in the lives of most women.
>
> (Allatt and Keil 1987: 3)

Here we see an indication of the value of sociological attention to time in life-course transitions, to which we will return in the next section of this paper.

The fourth perspective may be termed 'life-as-transition', and is discernible mainly in critical and post-structural feminist work on the lives and transitions of women (Hughes 2002b; Colley 2006; Mojab 2006; Colley *et al.* 2007). Such perspectives

> depict transitions as something much more ephemeral and fluid, where the whole of life is a form of transition, a permanent state of 'becoming' and 'unbecoming', much of which is unconscious, contradictory and iterative. This work challenges ... notions of transition as linear, staged and explicit [...] There are also hidden or tacit transitions, where people in long-term apparently stable situations adjust to changing work or social cultures, sometimes over a long period of time.
>
> (Ecclestone 2006: 6)

Moreover, Quinn (2006) challenges the assumption, central to some conceptualisations of transition which focus on 'becoming', that there exists a unified subject who is, at a certain point or over a certain period, transformed: 'we are always lost in transition, not just in the sense of moving from one task or context to another, but as a condition of our subjectivity' (Quinn 2006: 4). This has connotations for our understanding of the relationship of time to transitions, but they have rarely been explicitly explored in the sociology of education. Indeed, as Adam (1995) has pointed out, although there is a rapidly growing literature on time, it is scarcely addressed in social theorisation of any kind. It is time, then, to turn to time itself.

Time to think about time

Thinking about time has been dominated by the dualistic binary of 'social' versus 'natural' time (Adam 1995). This dichotomy has been promoted on the one hand by subjective, idealist philosophies of time advanced by Augustine and Kant. Augustine insisted on the sequential nature of time as past, present and future, united in our minds through the interplay of memory and anticipation with present experience. In Kant's metaphysics, time is also treated in an idealist manner, viewed as an a priori element of consciousness beyond historical experience itself

– it has no external reality, but is an inevitable part of the way in which we come to know the world. On the other hand, the dichotomy is also promoted by the physical sciences, especially Newtonian physics, with their emphasis on time as a 'natural' and objective process observable in, for example, astronomy. Whilst the creation of clocks and calendars claims its legitimacy by correspondence to the natural cycles of our solar system, 'clock-time' has been deconstructed to reveal its role as a socially constructed mechanism for the regulation of bodies, exemplified by the rule of timetables and bells in schools (Foucault 1991). This dualism has proved extremely difficult to overcome, including for those who have expressly sought to challenge it, and points to the need for a social theory of time (Adam 1989) or a theory of the social form of time (Neary and Rikowski 2002), which can account for both 'natural' and 'social' aspects of time, for its absolute and its relative moments, and for the relationship between them.

Time, however, is most often viewed from a perspective that accords with 'common sense', treating it as a 'natural flow', a reality in itself that is independent of social actors. This view, epitomised in the work of Turetzky (1998), under-pins dominant models of the lifecourse and transitions and the developmental psychology which often informs them. It treats time as a triadic phenomenon: opening up the present to split the past from the future, and in doing so, allowing for ever-new becomings. In most of the literature on transitions, however, this understanding is implicit and taken for granted.

One exception to the invisibility of temporal theory can be found in the work of Biesta and Tedder (2007), originally presented within the TLRP from its project *Learning Lives* to the thematic seminar series on transitions which preceded the writing of this book. Their studies of adults' life histories and learning do explicitly broach the question of time, which is central to their analysis. Drawing substantially on the work of Emirbayer and Mische (1998), they (like Turetzky) view time as a flow, one in which human agency exists as a series of changing orientations to its triadic elements:

- iterational orientations to influences from the past;
- projective orientations to future possibilities;
- practical-evaluative orientations to engagement with the present.

Within this framework, agency is viewed as the formulation of projects for the future and the realisation of those projects in the present. Agency is motivated and intentional, seeking to bring about a future which is new and different. It is about exerting control and giving direction to one's life. It is not only how we respond to events, but also our capacity to shape that responsiveness, to reflect on our orientations to the past, present and future, and to imagine them differently. Structure is viewed as an external context which itself may also change over time, and this perspective is characterised as an 'ecological' one.

Biesta and Tedder (2007) therefore argue that we need to understand how the flow of time and different temporal contexts support particular orientations and enable possible ways of acting. Learning is presented as the missing link between agency and the lifecourse, and the relationship between them is construed as teleological.

In this respect, their approach implicitly reflects Heidegger's philosophical notion of *being-in-time*, which 'privileges the mastery, lucidity, and transparency of a self that remains essentially in control of its own destiny' (Chanter 2001a: 52). This leads to a treatment of two contrasting life stories in their article: of a middle- or upper-class man with an elite education and of a poorly educated working-class woman with a disabled child. However, these stories largely fail to consider how history – political regimes, social movements and economic conditions – has influenced their lifecourses and learning. As a result, divorced from *history*, the woman's *story* appears strongly pathologised, particularly as it is read against the narrative of the more privileged man. Although the introductory chapter to this book notes that such analyses, focused on agency, claim they do not ignore social structures, Biesta and Tedder's article shows how easily such structures can be represented as a thin backdrop that then constructs social disadvantage as deficit.

Bourdieu (1992; and in Bourdieu and Wacquant 1992) offers a general sociological critique of such a conceptualisation of time and agency through his notion of practice. He argues that it is unhelpful to imagine the intentional choices of actors as if they were indeterminate and interchangeable – economically and social unconditioned – since this ignores their individual and collective history. Action, he insists, is not a question of the voluntaristic choices of individuals, simply supported or enabled by the temporal context. For Bourdieu, practice is itself an act of temporalisation. It is constituted by habitus as it is 'adjusted to the immanent tendencies of the field', and both habitus and field are expressions of history. ('Habitus' expresses both our individual dispositions and our socially structured predispositions, whilst 'field' expresses both the structural context for our actions and our strategic agency within it.) Practice anticipates the regularities and tendencies that are immanent in our social world, the future inscribed in the immediacy of the present and implied by the past that has produced our habitus. This is a very different view from that of the 'flow of time', with the splitting of past and future in order to forge an intentional goal-directed present:

> [practical sense] reads in the present state the possible future states with which the field is pregnant. For in habitus, the past, the present and the future intersect and interpenetrate one another. Habitus may be understood as virtual 'sedimented situations' [...] lodged inside the body that wait to be reactivated.
>
> (Bourdieu and Wacquant 1992: 22)

Practice, then, engenders time in acts, rather than engendering some new future which needs only to be imagined. While at a superficial level we can say any act may create a new situation, Bourdieu argues that there is not necessarily anything *socially* new about it (see also Neary and Rikowski 2002). In fact, the immanent dynamics of field and habitus, as two modes of the existence of history, mean that our acts often routinely reproduce the established social order. In particular, the unconscious fit between habitus and field is key to the continued oppression of subordinate groups, because their position within the social relations of domination 'feels right': 'it is lodged deep inside the socialized body' (Bourdieu and Wacquant 1992: 24).

> People are 'pre-occupied' by certain future outcomes inscribed in the present
> they encounter only to the extent that their habitus sensitizes and mobilizes
> them to perceive and pursue them.
>
> (Bourdieu and Wacquant 1992: 26)

Beyond this general critique, however, there are also feminist critiques of the theoretical model of time used by Biesta and Tedder. These point to a different set of dualisms that may further problematise taken-for-granted understandings of temporality in transitions.

Time and gender

> In contemporary social science both women and most aspects of time form
> the invisible part of our understanding. Both have been consistently theo-
> rised out of existence.
>
> (Adam 1989)

Barbara Adam is one of the leading international theorists of time. She has argued that dominant theories of time promote 'the pervasive vision of the "founding fathers"' (1989: 458), in which time is linear and irreversible, and that a feminist social theory of time is needed to transcend such dualistic thinking. Analysing the temporality which structures the feminine may provide important tools for feminist theory to rethink gender inequalities (Chanter 2001a), and to disrupt 'the virile categories of mastery, domination, and self-possession' promoted by androcentric views of time (Chanter 2001b: 16).

Christina Hughes (2002a) offers a comprehensive review of the ways in which feminist research illuminates the different temporal structuring of women's lives and transitions. In particular, she shows how such research reveals 'female' time not just as a series of binaries in contrast with 'male' time, but as a pervasive and complex dualism (see Table 9.1).

It is necessary to clarify here that this heuristic categorisation of different ways of experiencing time is not intended to suggest that 'female' time represents some superior, emancipatory alternative to 'male' time. Critical and post-structural forms of feminism resist the liberal notions that feminine ways of being or knowing are essential to all women, and that gender inequalities can be overcome by privileging the feminine over the masculine. Bourdieu's approach is highly relevant here. It is through the acts and practices of gendered social relations, played out in day-to-day living and learning, that time is engendered for women – particularly through the use of their time productively, reproductively and non-productively (in employed labour, in unpaid caring and domestic work, and as part of the reserve army of flexible labour, cf. Levitas 1996). However, by pointing to the different – and often oppressive – ways in which time is structured for women by the conditions of patriarchal society, these examples of 'female' time reveal and challenge the essentialist assumption that 'male' time is universal. In doing so, we can also acknowledge that dominant concepts of 'male' time in a society which

Table 9.1 Dualisms of 'male' and 'female' time

'Male' time	'Female' time
Linear	Circular
Clock-time	Driven by others' needs
Standardised	Processual
Continuous	Broken
Disciplined	Unpredictable
Commodified	Reproductive
Employment-related	Family-related
Career	Career breaks
Patriarchal	Maternalistic
Being-in-time	Giving time
Progressive	Expressive
Measurable	Flexible
Decontextualised	Embedded
Singular	Multiple/overlapping
Unidirectional	Reversible

Source: Adapted from Hughes, 2002a

is capitalist and racist as well as patriarchal may well not hold true for men who occupy subordinate class positions or who are racialised as 'Other'. My purpose, then, is to show how feminist research highlights a gendered dualism which is not just a set of simple or simplistic binaries, but a 'network of strongly linked and continuous webs of meanings' (Hughes 2002a: 17). This dualism underpins a social ordering of time that always represents as 'other' those experiences – especially those that express the materiality of time – that do not match the dominant ideal-type of 'male' time.

From a more radical feminist perspective, then, the developmental psychology which dominates the literature on lifecourse and on transitions is deeply problematic. It presents an androcentric view, based on masculinist normative models which offer no entry point for the lives that women live:

> [A] linear, mostly chronological sequence of tasks and changes [...] which implicitly ignore the possibility of distinctiveness in women's transitional experience.
>
> (Fisher 1989: 141)

This androcentric model assumes that 'the experience of transition from one stage of life to another [is] sporadic and short-term [and] moreover, bounded by extensive periods of stability' (Hughes 2002a: 139). Yet, as Quinn (2006) has powerfully argued, women often feel that they have been in transition all their lives. As Bourdieu's notion of immanence also suggests, transition is more about the social flux and permeability of gendered past, present and future time than about any 'natural flow' of male-stream time.

We need to turn, then, to analyses of women's experiences of learning and transition in their everyday lives in order to reveal the temporality that structures their lives – socially and materially – as feminine, subordinate, and 'other'; and to understand the role of temporal structuring in broader relations of ruling (Smith 1987, 1999). Here, I illustrate the potential of the sociological and feminist understandings of time outlined above with data drawn from another life-history project exploring learning, Shahrzad Mojab's study of Kurdish women refugees in Sweden (detailed in Mojab 2006). In her work Mojab adopts a critical feminist approach rooted in historical materialism, informed by dialectics, and addressing the interpenetration of gender, race and class. Drawing on the transnational feminism of Mohanty (2002) and Smith's (1987, 1999) feminist sociology of knowledge, she attends to multiple layers of analysis, from the micro- to the macro-political levels, to foreground the universal significance the particular may have, without allowing the particular to be erased by the universal. While there is not space within the remit of this chapter to re-iterate the detailed methodology of her study, this re-interpretation of published findings from her project acts as an example of how the social practices and interactions which constitute education and learning might be approached from a sociological perspective on temporality. We must make a shift here, then, away from more abstract discussion of the influence of social theories of time on studies of learning transitions, and see how they might be put to work in the sociology of education.

Learning transitions of Kurdish women refugees in Sweden

The Kurds are the fourth largest ethnic people in the Middle East. Their homeland has been forcibly divided among four neighbouring nation-states – Iran, Iraq, Turkey and Syria – which have used violence against Kurdish demands for self-rule. The idea of a unified homeland has therefore become a national dream, and Kurdish women have been involved in one of the longest nationalist projects of the twentieth and twenty-first centuries.

Throughout this time, Kurdish women have experienced transitions through a range of political regimes – colonial powers, imperialism, local dictatorships; and oppositional struggles against them – from nationalism to socialism and communism and, more recently, political Islam. In all of these, however, their lives have been encompassed by the constant of patriarchal domination, although its function and intensity has shifted with the balance of forces within and beyond the region. Women who had grown up under the secular monarchical regime of Iran before 1979 subsequently found themselves targeted as the prime objects of Islamisation. In order to resist the rise of this powerful theocracy, some made transitions which both demanded and offered new learning. They left their homes, joined the *peshmarge* (guerrilla freedom fighters) and political parties, and engaged in armed struggle, political education and community organisation. They developed sophisticated organisational and leadership skills, and they trained as nurses, radio engineers and broadcasters, social workers, community organisers, and as feminist activists. For many, this meant also acquiring a high level of literacy skills. On a daily basis, they experienced traumatic events – continual military assaults by the Islamic regime of Iran, chemical bombing by the Ba'athist regime of Iraq, imprisonment – but also the potential of socialist and feminist ideas within the 'liberated areas' of Iranian Kurdistan. Their life histories are full of informal learning during this time, more significant by far than any formal education to which they may have had access.

Following the first Gulf War in 1991, the Kurds underwent a massive dispersal, with many taking refuge in Europe, particularly in Sweden (Mojab and Hassanpour 2004). In this transition, they bore with them traumas they had undergone, but also encountered fresh ones. Escape from imprisonment, war, forced assimilation and ethnocide brought them face to face with other, less visible forms of conflict and oppression in the West that had been so indifferent to their fate at home. Despite remaining intimately involved with the political struggles of their past, Kurdish women in diaspora saw their learning being dismissed and degraded in a number of ways. Although many want to continue and develop the careers they had built through their struggle in Kurdistan, their ambitions face numerous barriers. Their existing skills are not recognised:

Shilan: If only these people [the Swedes] knew! If only they knew who I am or was, what I have done, what I can offer them today ... [They see me] as this pathetic refugee woman who only needs their empathy. While in fact what I need is a forum, a space to tell them how, as an illiterate woman, under the condition of suppression of my government, I mobilised women for the national cause – how I taught myself to read and write in order to be able to read political literature – how I learned to manage a large community of youth, support them, give them hope in life, and inspire them for a better life in future. Here in Sweden, they think I know nothing, I have no skills, they only push me to learn the language, but what for?

All too often, 'learning' for these women is reconstructed by the Swedish system as low-level training to undertake mundane, low-skilled jobs in, for example, factory work, which can have negative effects on both their physical and their mental health. This can represent a form of traumatic violence, although less overt and therefore more difficult to survive, resist or struggle against. As one woman *peshmarge* explained:

They sent me to work in a factory. The work was heavy and repetitious. I got tired soon and could not continue, but needed the government assistance. I told them about my neck and back pain, they gave me a limited sick leave and sent me to a doctor. The pills and staying at home made me very depressed. I was totally isolated, there was not even a neighbour to talk to. I saw the doctor again, this time they put me on anti-depressant drugs, which made my situation even worse ... now I am on long-term disability. These categories have many implications for me. I am limited in what I can do, I am limited in what I can learn and most importantly I don't feel good about myself.

In addition to this, women can also be marginalised by the nationalist move-ment in exile, including the male-dominated Kurdish Federation, and by feminist groups in Sweden, in ways that limit their ability to deploy the learning developed through their experiences, and position them as subordinate:

Sahar: Kurdish political parties still look at women as an auxiliary women's group with the responsibility for cooking for festive events and for putting on their colourful cloth to represent Kurdish culture in Sweden. The ones that are more progressive have good rhetoric, but in practice they are the same. When I approached the Swedish government for funding, they referred me back to the Kurdish Federation, exactly the source that I wanted to avoid. It is difficult to build an alliance with Swedish feminist groups, they think ethnic minority women are politically incapable of developing a critical feminist platform.

On an individual level, Kurdish women may also suffer domestic violence and 'honour killings' sanctioned by this patriarchal culture. Through such experiences, Kurdish women's learning becomes not only detached from their past experiences, but also from their daily struggles in Sweden. The Swedish political agenda for 'creating new citizens' cuts against these women's learning needs and aspirations, as does state support for market relations in work and in learning. Moreover, their possibilities for feminist action become closed down, in part through government funding only for male-dominated Kurdish cultural groups, and in part through their racialised exclusion from Swedish feminist groups. Research-informed recommendations have been made to the Swedish government's Integration Board to attend to the distinct needs of Kurdish women immigrants and to provide opportunities for them to counteract the overemphasis on Islam and traditionalism in Swedish media, policy and public perceptions. These, however, have been greeted with 'a long and heavy silence' (Mojab 2006: 171). As Kurdish women's agency is constructed by policy makers as thoroughly passive, so they become isolated and alienated, with little option other than to limit their struggles – and their learning – within the confines of patriarchal nationalism.

Some Kurdish women, however, have fought to go beyond these limitations, founding a community-based Kurdish-language radio programme called *Dengi Zhinan* (Voice of Women Radio), which is now also available in Kurdistan via the Internet. Its goals are both social and educational: highlighting women's issues in Sweden; discussing possible alternatives in addressing them; raising women's consciousness, especially about their physical health, sexuality and psychological well-being; and creating solidarity among women in order to overcome feelings of isolation and loneliness.

Radio discussion is an important part of the programme time. We spread knowledge of and information on women's rights, on their responsibilities as new citizens in the Swedish society, and their role in their families. We try to engage with our listeners through radio discussions. We also try to reach out to Kurdish women through other means such as meetings and seminars on a variety of topics. This radio programme has been the only Kurdish media channel in the last five years that has addressed, from the point of view of women, questions such as equality, secularism, nationalism, human rights, democracy, integration, tradition and alternatives, and family related matters such as child-raising and children's rights locally and internationally.

(Kakabaveh 2007: 128)

Despite some fierce opposition from within the Kurdish community, this radio station continues to raise funds independently and play an important role in developing a feminist perspective and supporting women's daily learning.

We see multiple transitions in such life histories, then. What do they tell us about the nature of time, and about learning?

Time and learning in Kurdish women's transitions

Mojab (2006) traces a kind of circularity in these women's transitions and the learning associated with them. This consists of a cycle of 'closure–opening–closure' in relation to life and learning, but one that resists a mechanical interpretation of circularity and demands a more dialectical one. In some cases, we can see that from a time of *closure* – for example, living under the repressive theocratic regime in Iran – women experienced *opening* as they became involved in the nationalist struggle. At the same time they encountered continuing *closures* due to the traditionally male-dominated and limiting realm of this struggle, and in response created new *openings* as they learned to challenge sexism and to organise politically around feminist as well as nationalist demands for liberation. *Closure* of a brutal kind came with traumas such as capture, imprisonment and torture by the occupying forces, followed by a new period of *opening* as they moved into exile, and initially expanded their knowledge of feminist activism through a vast array of social movements in Sweden around human rights, anti-globalisation, anti-war and environmental action. However, these movements are themselves permeated with relations of ruling which reproduce patriarchal, racist and colonial relations, so that Kurdish women attempting to engage with them have once more encountered a further *closure* that diminishes their capacity to struggle and learn and their resilience to survive. Moreover, the Swedish state's refusal to recognise their prior learning and existing knowledge, and its insistence on 'training' them instead for low-skilled, sometimes harmful work, represents an intensification of *closure* that not only prevents further learning, but undoes learning they have already acquired. As Gorman (2007) suggests, we can distinguish three types of learning here: 'survival' learning, 'resistance' learning and 'struggle' learning; and we see how, throughout their life histories and in different social and geographical spaces, women may advance or be pushed back from one to the other. We therefore can see the contradictions between closures and openings as an unending and fragmented process, which is neither linear nor simplistically circular: while one contradiction may be resolved, a new one will surface. We might more accurately depict the process, then, as a number of zigzag or spiral movements within a web of contradictions.

It has been suggested (Tett, personal comment) that such stories do not evoke circularity so much as nomadic wandering: a metaphor proposed originally by Braidotti (1994) and adapted by Hughes (2002b) with emancipatory intent, constructing women not as mere victims of oppression, but as expressing agency and autonomy through their nomadic uprootings:

> Repeated transitions are viewed as beginnings or openings and as regular patterns in the tapestry of life. They provide for a renewal of the self that does not grieve for a lost homeland.
>
> (Hughes 2002b: 415)

However, such a meaning has been critiqued as more relevant to those who enjoy the privilege of being white and Western, while women of non-white ethnicity rarely have the option of experiencing uprooting as purely positive (Gedalof 2000, cited in Hughes 2002b). What might it mean to have been uprooted by war, to find one's possibilities for action and one's learning denied rather than renewed, in a context where one's life has been dedicated to the struggle for a homeland that is occupied, partitioned and oppressed? In the face of these questions, optimistic readings of the 'nomad' rather return us to the masculinist paradigm of time as promoted by Turetzky (1998) and Biesta and Tedder (2007), with its untroubled view of agency as a matter of the imagination of future goals and the will to implement them in the present, disembedded from the material and historical conditions in which agency must be exercised.

How might we start from these women's everyday experiences of time, transition and learning, and use them as a standpoint, a *'point d'appui'* as Smith (1987) terms it, to open up a window onto the universe of patriarchal capitalism and its relations of ruling? It may help here to think of the social engendering of time on different scales. First, at the level of *epoch*, they live in an era of imperialism, where the dominant economic and political interests of the US and its allies are now played out across the world through economic underdevelopment and military operations that can scarcely be imagined by those of us who have not endured them. This experience may demand learning that simply enables survival, but may also develop into learning ways to resist the cultural domination that has also been imposed upon the Kurdish people.

Second, transitions between specific *periods* of time can be distinguished within their life histories: monarchy, the rise of theocracy, the national liberation struggle, engagement in feminist activism, future visions of socialism and communism, and diaspora. They are inextricably interlinked with transitions through particular geographical spaces – from village or city of origin, to locations of armed struggle and liberated zones, to exile in the West. These might variously be associated with 'resistance learning' and 'struggle learning', on the fronts of both national and gender oppression. In parallel, in the West where these women have taken exile, we can trace a shift from the period in which feminism was developed through mass women's movements, to the current period in which those movements have largely disappeared, where progress towards equality in education and employment is lamentably slow, and where the rights women had won are increasingly under attack. We can also note here that these women arrived in Sweden in a period where its once-exemplary welfare regime is now being cut back in the drive for economic competitiveness, and where its education and training systems are under some strain from the pressures of migration on a relatively large scale (Mojab 2006). Each of these periods is characterised variously by relations of domination, resistance and struggle, and each might therefore offer different opportunities for or restrictions upon learning.

Third, we see at the micro-level how Kurdish women's experiences in Sweden might be seen as reconfiguring all previous times and learning, in ways that recall aspects of 'female' time depicted in Table 9.1. We have already identified the contradictory circularity of the closure–opening–closure syndrome. Mojab's (2006) findings show how their imagined futures are blocked by the needs of the Swedish government to assimilate them passively as 'new citizens'; by the needs of Swedish employers for labour supply to the low-skilled end of the labour market; by the needs of male-dominated Kurdish organisations to foreground particular cultural and religious practices which reinforce patriarchy; and by the needs of Swedish feminists to preserve their own distinctive position. Time, in her analysis, can thus be seen to be enacted as broken, discontinuous, and increasingly located within isolated, domestic settings to which women are confined: conditions that suggest a reversion to some of the conditions experienced previously under the theocracy. Learning too is interrupted, restricted, even *un*learned. From 'resistance' and 'struggle' learning, women may have to retreat into 'survival' learning at best. Both their time and their learning in Sweden are restricted to particular, low-skilled forms of productive labour, to reproductive domestic work or, in some cases, to non-productive activity and disablement that undermines their capacities further still. These fragmentations and reversals of time and learning imprint their marks on these women's bodies as well as on their minds; they entail both material and social realities; they negate or even undo learning; and they bring social and physical threats to women who continue to try to find ways to resist and struggle.

Conclusions

It is hard to see how these experiences could be explained by the agentic orientations to past influences, future possibilities and engagement with the present that Biesta and Tedder (2007) use to frame their analysis – at least, without constructing these women as hopelessly in deficit. By contrast, a more critical, feminist analysis might read these life histories by paraphrasing the terms of Marx: as women making history, but not in conditions of their own making, and only succeeding when they are able to be conscious of themselves as a gender and engage in collective struggle.

The task of putting a critical sociological understanding of time to work more thoroughly in analysing empirical data, and of extending ideas about the nature and outcomes of learning through collective struggles such as those of Kurdish women, still remains to be done. Here, it has only been possible to outline such an understanding of time, and provide an illustrative case study of the potential it might offer for the sociology of education. In doing so, while I would not claim to advance any new 'theory of time', I argue that such an analysis does help to overcome the dualisms of subjective versus objective theories of time, of 'social' versus 'natural' time, by foregrounding *both* aspects of time and viewing them in relation to each other. This enables us to understand transitions beyond the all too often asymmetric rubric of change-over-time, where change is addressed but time is not. They may then be viewed as a process of change *in* particular times, that is to say, in particular epochs, periods, or moments, and mediated by the gendered, racialised and classed practices which engender those times. One lesson we have to learn from studies like that of the Kurdish women is that we may need to devote further attention to learning associated with collective consciousness, resistance and struggle, and to the lifecourse transitions associated with that learning, if those power relations are to be challenged or overturned.

Acknowledgements

I am deeply grateful to Shahrzad Mojab for permission to draw on her work here and for her suggested improvements. My thanks are also due to Gill Crozier, Kathryn Ecclestone, Rachel Gorman, and Lyn Tett for their helpful comments on earlier versions of this chapter.

Bibliography

Adam, B. (1989) 'Feminist social theory needs time: reflections on the relation between feminist thought, social theory and time as an important parameter in social analysis', *Sociological Review*, 37: 458–73.

—— (1995) *Timewatch: The Social Analysis of Time*, Cambridge: Polity.

Allatt, P. and Keil, T. (1987) 'Introduction', in P. Allatt, T. Keil, A. Bryman and B. Bytheway (eds), *Women and the Life Cycle: Transitions and Turning Points*, Basingstoke: Macmillan.

Antikainen, A., Houtsonen, J., Kauppila, J. and Huotelin, H. (1996) *Living in a Learning Society: Life-histories, Identities and Education*, London: RoutledgeFalmer.

Ball, S. J., Maguire, M. and Macrae, S. (2000) *Choices, Pathways and Transitions Post-16: New Youth, New Economies in the Global City*, London: RoutledgeFalmer.

Banks, M., Bates, I., Breakwell, G., Bynner, J., Emler, N., Jamieson, L. and Roberts, K. (1992) *Careers and Identities*, Buckingham: Open University Press.

Bates, I. and Riseborough, G. (eds) (1994) *Youth and Inequality*, Buckingham: Open University Press.

Biesta, G. and Tedder, M. (2007) 'Agency and learning in the lifecourse: towards an ecological perspective', *Studies in the Education of Adults*, 39: 132–49.

Bourdieu, P. (1992) *The Logic of Practice*, Cambridge: Polity.

Bourdieu, P. and Wacquant, L. J. D. (1992) *An Invitation to Reflexive Sociology*, Cambridge: Polity Press.

Braidotti, R. (1994) *Nomadic Subjects: Embodiment and Sexual Difference in Contemporary Feminist Theory*, New York: Columbia University Press.

Chanter, T. (2001a) *Time, Death and the Feminine: Levinas with Heidegger*, Stanford: Stanford University Press.

—— (2001b) 'Introduction', in T. Chanter (ed.) *Feminist Interpretations of Emmanuel Levinas*, University Park: Pennsylvania State University Press.

Colley, H. (2003) *Mentoring for Social Inclusion: a Critical Approach to Nurturing Mentor Relationships*, London: RoutledgeFalmer.

—— (2006) 'From childcare practitioner to FE tutor: biography, identity and lifelong learning', in C. Leathwood and B. Francis (eds) *Gender and Lifelong Learning: Critical Feminist Engagements*, London: RoutledgeFalmer.

—— (2007) 'European policies on social inclusion and youth: continuity, change and challenge', in H. Colley, P. Boetzelen, B. Hoskins and T. Parveva (eds) *Social Inclusion for Young People: Breaking Down the Barriers*, Strasbourg: Council of Europe.

Colley, H. and Hodkinson, P. (2001) 'Problems with "Bridging the Gap": the reversal of structure and agency in addressing social exclusion', in *Critical Social Policy*, 21: 337–61.

Colley, H., Hodkinson, P. and Malcolm, J. (2003) *Informality and Formality in Learning*, London: Learning and Skills Research Centre.

Colley, H., James, D. and Diment, K. (2007) 'Unbecoming teachers: towards a more dynamic notion of professional participation', *Journal of Education Policy*, 23: 173–93.

Collin, A. and Young, R. A. (2000) *The Future of Career*, Cambridge: Cambridge University Press.

Ecclestone, K. (2006) 'The rise of transitions as a political concern: the effects of assessment on identity and agency in vocational education', working paper for the Teaching and Learning Research Programme Thematic Seminar Series on 'Transitions through the lifecourse'.

Elder, G. H., Kirkpatrick Johnson, M. and Crosnoe, R. (2003) 'The emergence and development of life course theory', in J. T. Mortimer and M. J. Shanahan (eds), *Handbook of the Life Course*, New York: Kluwer Academic/Plenum.

Emirbayer, M. and Mische, A. (1998) 'What is agency?', *American Journal of Sociology*, 103(4): 962–1023.

European Commission (2005) 'Communication from the Commission to the Council on European policies concerning youth: addressing the concerns of young people in Europe – implementing the European Youth Pact and promoting active citizenship', Brussels: Commission of the European Communities. Available online at http://ec.europa.eu/youth/whitepaper/post-launch/com_206_en.pdf (accessed 13 April 2007).

European Parliament (2000) *European Council, Lisbon: Conclusions of the Presidency*. Available online at www.europarl.eu.int/bulletins/pdf/1s2000en.pdf (accessed 13 April 2007).

Fisher, J. (1989) 'Teaching "time": women's responses to adult development', in F. Forman with C. Sowton (eds) *Taking Our Time: Feminist Perspectives on Temporality*, New York: State University of New York Press.

Foucault, M. (1991) *Discipline and Punish: the Birth of the Prison*, London: Penguin Books.

Furlong, A. and Cartmel, F. (1997) *Young People and Social Change: Individualisation and Risk in Late Modernity*, Buckingham: Open University Press.

Gedalof, I. (2000) 'Identity in transit: nomads, cyborgs and women', *The European Journal of Women's Studies*, 7: 337–54.

Gorman, R. (2007) 'The feminist standpoint and the trouble with "informal learning": a way forward for Marxist-feminist educational research', in T. Green, H. Raduntz and G. Rikowski (eds) *Marxism and Education: Renewing Dialogues*, Houndmills: Palgrave Macmillan.

Great Britain Treasury (2003) *Every Child Matters* (Green Paper, Cm.5860), London: The Stationery Office.

Hodkinson, P. and Sparkes, A. C. (1997) 'Careership: a sociological theory of career decision making', *British Journal of Sociology of Education*, 18: 29–44.

Hodkinson, P., Sparkes, A. C. and Hodkinson, H. (1996) *Triumphs and Tears: Young People, Markets and the Transition from School to Work*, London: David Fulton.

Hughes, C. (2002a) *Key Concepts in Feminist Theory and Research*, London: Sage.

—— (2002b) 'Beyond the poststructuralist-modern impasse: the woman returner as "exile" and "nomad"', *Gender and Education*, 14: 411–24.

Kakabaveh, A. (2007) 'Kurdish women in Sweden: a feminist analysis of barriers to integration and strategies to overcome them', in H. Colley, P. Boetzelen, B. Hoskins and T. Parveva (eds) *Social Inclusion for Young People: Breaking Down the Barriers*, Strasbourg: Council of Europe.

Lam, M. and Pollard, A. (2006) 'A conceptual framework for understanding children as agents in the transition from home to kindergarten', *Early Years*, 26: 123–41.

Levinson, D. J., Darrow, C. N., Klein, E. B., Levinson, M. H. and McKee, B. (1978) *The Seasons of a Man's Life*, New York: Ballantine.

Levitas, R. (1996) 'The concept of social exclusion and the new Durkheimian hegemony', *Critical Social Policy*, 16: 5–20.

Mohanty, C. T. (2002) '"Under Western eyes" revisited: feminist solidarity through anti-capitalist struggles', *Signs: Journal of Women in Culture and Society*, 28: 499–535.

Mojab, S. (2004) 'The particularity of "honour" and the universality of "killing": from early warning signs to feminist pedagogy', in S. Mojab and N. Abdo (eds) *Violence in the Name of Honour: Theoretical and Political Challenges*, Istanbul: Bilgi University Press.

—— (2006) 'War and diaspora as lifelong learning contexts for immigrant women', in C. Leathwood and B. Francis (eds) *Gender and Lifelong Learning: Critical Feminist Engagements*, London: RoutledgeFalmer.

Mojab, S. and Hassanpour, A. (2004) Kurdish diaspora, in I. Skoggard (ed.) *Encyclopedia of Diasporas*, New Haven: Human Relations Area Files.

Neary, M. and Rikowski, G. (2002) 'Time and speed in the social world of capital', in G. Crow and S. Heath (eds) *Social Conceptions of Time: Structure and Process in Work and Everyday Life*, Basingstoke: Palgrave Macmillan.

Pollard, A. and Filer, A. (1999) *The Social World of Pupil Career: Strategic Biographies through Primary School*, London: Cassell.

Quinn, J. (2006) 'Re-thinking "failed transitions" to higher education', paper presented at ESRC Teaching and Learning Research Programme Thematic Seminar Series 'Transitions through the Lifecourse', May 2006.

Reay, D., David, M. E. and Ball, S. (2005) *Degrees of Choice: Social Class, Race and Gender in Higher Education*, Stoke-on-Trent: Trentham Books.

Smith, D. E. (1987) *The Everyday World as Problematic: a Feminist Sociology*, Toronto: University of Toronto Press.

—— (1999) *Writing the Social: Critique, Theory and Investigations*, Toronto: University of Toronto Press.

Social Exclusion Unit (SEU) (1999) *Bridging the Gap: New Opportunities for 16–18 year olds*, London: The Stationery Office.

Turetzky, P. (1998) *The Problems of Philosophy: Time*, New York: Routledge.

Yeandle, S. (1987) 'Married women at midlife: past experience and present change', in P. Allatt, T. Keil, A. Bryman and B. Bytheway, *Women and the Life Cycle: Transitions and Turning Points*, Basingstoke: Macmillan.

10 Working as belonging

The management of personal and collective identities

Alan Felstead, Dan Bishop, Alison Fuller,
Nick Jewson, Lorna Unwin and
Konstantinos Kakavelakis

Introduction

In this chapter we explore the concept of transitions in terms of personal and collective identity transformation at and through work. In so doing we contribute to one of the key debates in the book about why some transitions are experienced as problematic and others are not. We do this by exploring how the notion of transition can help reveal instances of 'identity work' happening in and through participation in contrasting occupations and workplaces. We take 'identity' to refer to a perceived sense of belonging to a social entity, such as an occupation, profession or organisation. Defined in this way, identity goes beyond mere membership (i.e. 'a class in itself') to include consciousness (i.e. 'a class for itself'). This moves the notion of identity from a passive to an active sense of belonging. The research findings presented here also make use of a further distinction between 'personal' and 'collective' identities. The former refers to individuals' belief that they are seen by others and they regard themselves as members of a particular group. The latter refers to the ways in which groups themselves develop a sense of belonging, over and above individual members' own personal awareness of how they are seen.

Historically, identities have been widely regarded as rooted in the world of paid work. However, the once fixed contours of a job – such as its permanency, number of hours, regularity and location – are no longer certain (Felstead and Jewson 1999; Felstead *et al.* 2005; Fevre 2007). This has sparked the suggestion that personal meaning is now based on patterns of consumption rather than patterns of employment (Woodward 2002; Ransome 2005). Others have argued that these changes, along with the flattening of management hierarchies, have modified but not removed the link between work and identity (Rhodes and Scheeres 2004). One of the aims of the chapter, then, is to explore the ways in which employment remains a salient source of personal and collective identity formation (see also Bimrose and Brown, this volume).

All identities have to be learned, as well as actively and convincingly presented and represented to others, leading to debates about the relative significance of 'structure' and 'agency' (Ecclestone 2007; Wojecki 2007). There has been considerable interest in techniques of impression management, including ways in which 'the individual in ordinary work situations presents himself [sic] and his activity to others, the ways in which he guides and controls the impression they form of him, and the kinds of things he may not do while sustaining his performance before them' (Goffman 1959: xi). Accounts which focus on impression management, however, may underestimate the significance of the intentional interventions of organisations (though see Goffman 1961c). Another aim of this chapter, therefore, is to add to the debate by exploring how organisations themselves deliberately adopt managerial strategies that involve conscious attempts to create, sustain or change workers' identities by creating opportunities for movement or transition. The central argument is that, on the one hand, in the process of making goods and services organisations do shape the personal and collective identities of workers, but, on the other, organisations differ in the extent to which the grooming of worker identities is central to the production process itself.

A third aim of the chapter is to explore relationships between work-based personal and collective identities. Drawing on research evidence, we argue that managerial strategies, organisational forms and productive processes shape the extent and form of their alignment, or misalignment. We examine how integration, tension or distance between personal and collective identities reflects social processes embedded in the organisation of work and employment and the need for people to have the capacity to move between identities, create alignment or resist making unwanted identity transitions.

The chapter explores three case studies within contrasting economic sectors: aerobics classes within the service sector; software engineers in the 'knowledge-based economy'; and automotive workers in traditional manufacturing. The sections that follow address these cases in turn. They focus on the creation of new identities, the sustenance of existing identities and the realignment of established identities. The chapter ends by arguing that worker identities are in reflexive relation with, and need to be understood in the context of, specific production processes through which products and services are made and sold. It concludes that transitions in work roles and responsibilities require identity work, and that how people respond to new expectations reveals much about the nature of the relationship between personal and collective identities at work.

Creating new identities among aerobics instructors

In service organisations, a large part of what is sold is person-to-person interaction (e.g. Witz *et al.* 2003; Bolton 2004). Employing organisations often seek to influence the nature of those interactions and, thereby, fashion the identities of service workers. However, service workers may resist becoming 'capitulated selves', ensuring that some elements of the image they portray is of their own making (Collinson 2003). This section focuses on how these issues apply to aerobics instructors.

'Aerobics' refers to fitness training classes, in dedicated rooms equipped with music systems and full-length wall mirrors, led by an exercise to music (ETM) instructor who is visible in front of the class. Instructors direct, describe and teach movement sequences, at the same time as moving in time with the music. The instructor's voice is made audible over the music through a headset radio microphone. To be effective, then, aerobics involves 'stage management' (setting the parameters of the performance *before* it takes place) and 'stage craft' (delivering a 'good performance' *while* on stage) (Goffman 1959).

The evidence presented here draws on 15 interviews with ETM instructors, often preceded by a short period of work shadowing through participation in one of their classes. Data were also collected via 20 interviews with fitness club managers and other agencies involved in the production of ETM classes. In addition, one of the authors collected data through participant observation in other classes, aerobics conventions and ETM training courses (see Felstead *et al.* 2007).

Managing the stage

Aerobics classes typically take place in studios that are part of a larger facility. Private membership clubs attract more regulars because of the annual membership costs (used, in part, to pay for a higher specification 'servicescape'). Public leisure centres, which consumers use on a pay-as-you-go basis, tend to attract more transient users. The connections between instructors and participants are usually stronger in the former than in the latter. In private facilities, therefore, participants and instructors are more likely to develop cognitive recognition of one another; 'recognising faces and getting to know names' as one respondent put it (cf. Goffman 1961a: 15).

The timing and billing of classes also influence how instructors are required to present themselves. Management arranges timetables and allocates instructors to particular slots. Classes are advertised indicating their focus, the type of equipment used and their intensity. This gives participants the illusion of choice, while subtly constraining their options. One instructor referred to those who attend on a Monday night as 'our front row people who will like loud and fast music', those who go to classes billed as high impact aerobics as 'your fitness junkies', and those who 'like it more gentle will go to "legs, bums and tums"'. Instructors have to present images and tailor classes in line with these expectations. They use a range of tactics to trigger the 'personality switch', such as changing into workout clothes (referred to as the 'Lycra syndrome'), hearing the music and putting on the headset.

Managing stage performance

ETM instructors rely on their own stage performance. They need to appear to their audience both as a 'friend' but also as an 'expert'. One of the main roles of an instructor is to lead class participants, not only in technique but also in effort and enjoyment through active participation. As well as being seen to have fun, participants also expect an instructor to lead a class with moves in time with the music, count the class into each movement sequence by good cueing, know the routine well, and demonstrate good technique and high fitness levels. Private clubs recruit only those who invest a great deal of themselves in their work. Obtaining a regular slot often requires appearing at auditions. At these events, management respondents reported looking for 'natural smiles', 'being energetic', 'someone who enjoys what they do' and 'being there for their paying public, not just themselves'. Although instructors' involvement is mostly authentic, it is a requirement of the job. In the words of one respondent: 'It's an entertainment business'. Some instructors admitted to faking their enjoyment at times.

> There's a tiny bit of acting in it always. You can't love it 100 per cent all the time ... there's always tiny bit of acting going on because you have to ... gain the rapport of people.

Instructors can either make up their own routines ('freestyle') or follow a number of ready-made routines ('pre-choreography'). The largest producer of 'pre-choreographed' classes has seven separate programmes, delivering contrasting workouts (see Felstead *et al.* 2007). Instructors receive initial training, attend quarterly workshops and they are issued with new CDs, training videos and class plans every three months. Standardisation minimises the variability of the class content, but makes it easier and quicker for instructors to appear on stage as 'experts'. While this is helpful to novices, trying to 'pass' as instructors by 'covering' their inexperience to an audience, the same inflexibility can be frustrating for experienced instructors who would prefer to invest more of themselves in their performances (Goffman 1961a: 92). Thus, for some instructors pre-choreography conveys a 'ready-made' identity that they are happy to take on, while for others it acts as a constraint on how they wish to project themselves (Becker 1951).

Each type of 'pre-choreographed' class has its own brand image and associated emotional atmosphere that instructors are required to adopt. Instructors are expected to alter the image they convey accordingly:

> It's like putting on a performance ... you have to put a different head on, you know, like Worzel Gummidge [a children's TV character who changed heads to switch personalities] [...] One of the things that they drill into you is this playing a role, playing a character.

Instructors are reminded of the importance of these personality switches in the training videos that accompany each new release:

> If you teach a number of programmes, you may need to change costume a number of times in one day [...] *It's essential that you step into the character of each programme.* (Emphasis added)

To help instructors step into character, different styles of dress are suggested. Instructors are encouraged to 'dress in programme costume' in order 'to stand in the spirit of the programme' (company training DVD). This message is repeated again and again during initial training and via the DVDs that accompany each quarterly release. This drilled behaviour begins at the first weekend of initial training, with trainee instructors copying the outfits of their trainers and becoming, in the words of some respondents, 'clones' or 'mini-mes'. Image making also extends to the use of language and particular phrases, recommended in the notes, videos and quarterly workshops.

Some instructors relished the security of being told what music to play, what moves to do at what time, how they need to dress and what they should say. Others recognised that retaining control over music selection is a way of stamping their own personality on classes:

> My personality is so through the music and it's coming from you, isn't it? And you can project you, I think, better than you can project somebody else's programme.

However, making musical choices can be challenging and time-consuming. Others recognised the benefits of 'pre-choreographed' classes:

> Music-wise, I don't have the freedom. To a certain degree, I like it because I don't have to do the thinking.

Instructors may resist becoming 'capitulated selves' by splitting their personalities and refusing to reveal their inner feelings when at odds with the image externally portrayed. They hide their personal identities behind a projected collective identity. One instructor revealed that she never let the class know her real musical likes and dislikes:

> Those tracks I don't like I'll say, 'I love this track. This is an amazing track' [...] I don't ever say I don't like a track ... [sometimes] I don't like the music, but it looks like I really like it ... You have to act.

Another tactic was to deflect criticism of the music onto the unknown individuals who had selected it for worldwide use. In these circumstances, rather than defend the music selection and fake their interest in the chosen tracks, instructors openly joined forces with participants to criticise the choices made.

In summary, then, aerobics instructors, particularly those following pre-choreographed programmes, were subjected to a proactive and didactic training in their presentation of self to consumers. Although many had enjoyed aerobics as a hobby before taking it up as a career, instructors were drilled by their employers in the projection of an approved collective identity at work. Both those who felt constrained by these requirements, and those who happily acquiesced, recognised a gap between their personal sense of identity and the collective identities that were imputed to them by participants in classes. There was an implicit need for workers to develop the capacity to move easily between the two. For those who readily 'capitulated', the transition process was not marked by dissonance or resistance. For those whose personal identities were closely bound up in their musical and creative identities, the required shift to the standardised collective identity was approached as a conscious act of performance, such that the transition appeared authentic to managers checking for compliance and conformity to externally set standards but left the individual's personal identity or sense of self relatively untouched. The management of the software company, however, adopted a different approach.

Reinforcing pre-existing identities in a software engineering company

The aim of management in the software company was to harness the creativity and skills of software engineers by ensuring that they did not experience a gap between personal and collective identities. The software company sought to build on and sustain employees' personal feelings of 'intelligence' fostered by prior success at school and university – their pre-existing personal identities – and integrate these into a collective identity characterised by belonging to an 'intelligent, technical community'. The company directors accomplished this by designing and developing a range of employment practices and processes which supported and facilitated smooth transitions from education to work as well as in relation to career progression at work.

Recent years have seen the rise of so-called 'knowledge workers'; that is, workers who apply esoteric bodies of knowledge, acquired in formal and informal learning situations to produce intangible products. Software workers are often cited as the prime example, since they 'can trade on their skill, expertise and intellectual capital' (Leadbeater 1999: 228–9; Tam *et al.* 2002; Carmel and Eisenberg 2006). Modern software development has resulted in two labour process paradigms (Quintas 1994). In the 'formalist' paradigm, software development is regarded as an engineering discipline in which product development follows set procedures and stages. In the 'pragmatist' paradigm software development is an 'ad hoc process of "hacking" (i.e. writing code without rigorous planning and then hacking at it to remove bugs and achieve results)' (Barrett 2001: 26). Other authors (e.g. Robinson *et al.* 1998) conceptualise this dichotomy as a 'hard/soft' division, where 'hard' relates to the designing of systems with a precise function, and 'soft' to the need to make a system compatible with the 'human system' that surrounds it. As Robinson *et al.* (1998: 372) argue, however, the need to reconcile the needs of multiple stakeholders in an information technology system requires 'encouraging teams that flourish across the divisions of manager, user and developer' and an end to the 'single hero and the single voice' model in which lead designers and system architects passed down their instructions to subordinates. These paradigms have consequences for the way software engineers see themselves and the way they are treated by their employers. They also have consequences for the way in which researchers conceptualise software workers. Marks and Lockyer (2005: 148), for example, argue that software developers operating under the pragmatist paradigm can be described as professionals since 'they have an implicit set of professional codes and common beliefs, values and ceremonies' and are viewed as such by many employers. This is exhibited in the way work is organised, including opportunities to work closely with peers, and to exercise autonomy and discretion.

The case study software development company discussed here sits within the pragmatic paradigm in terms of how it treated its employees as 'professionals' (in the sense of the term used above by Marks and Lockyer) and relates closely to Robinson *et al.*'s (1998) 'soft' side of the 'hard/soft' division. It must be said, however, that the company believed it was able to respond flexibly to customer need because its product development was based on firm engineering principles. The company, established in the 1980s, developed products for a wide range of customers and had built an international reputation for being both cutting-edge and reliable. Most of its several hundred workers were located in an office in the south of England. Profits are distributed annually among the employees, with shares determined by individual performance. The company only recruited graduates with excellent academic credentials from a few top UK universities, emphasising the importance of technical intelligence over other attributes.

Data were collected through observations of everyday work and team interaction in the main office, in-depth interviews with 25 engineers, and observation of the recruitment process.

Recruiting intelligent others

Without exception, the software engineers in our case study identified themselves as 'highly intelligent' people. Many cited the chance to join an 'intelligent' community as the key reason for joining the company. Some described themselves as 'techies', in that they had been interested in computers from an early age and spent their spare time designing software for 'open source' websites.

The belief amongst the software engineers that they belonged to a highly intelligent work-based community was multi-layered. It began with company brochures for potential recruits, which highlighted the need for exceptional A levels and degrees from top universities. It was fostered at the interview stage, where applicants spent time together as a group listening to presentations emphasising the company's high standards. It was internalised by successful recruits, who drew on this aspect of their collective identities in order to cope with the pressures of problem solving for the company's high profile customers, while at the same time maintaining their belief that they could trust their equally intelligent peers and managers to provide appropriate, collegial support. Software engineers, then, were characterised by a very strong 'performance team', with high levels of capacity to maintain the definition of the situation, mutual dependence and trust (Goffman 1959: 79). Both personal and collective identities of employees were forged in and around the boundaries of this reference group.

Part of the corporate narrative that candidates heard throughout the recruitment process, promoted the company's sense of itself as a 'hothouse of talent and professionalism', whose structures were designed to counteract the possibility of boredom. Recruits, thus, were assured that their personal identities would find expression in the collective identity of the company. The main channel for achieving this objective was through the organisation of work in small teams with rotating membership. In addition, employees were encouraged to fuse professional and personal identities, gaining pleasure from intellectual challenges both within and outside the workplace. The company promoted this fusion by constructing a working environment in the main office that mimicked an Oxbridge college. It also gave careful consideration to the balance of work–life interests of employees. Thus, engineers were allowed to work flexible hours and take 'sabbaticals'. For similar reasons, a Scottish office had been established purely because, in the words of one of the directors, a small group of employees 'were very happy to stay in the company, but basically could not settle in the south-east of England'. Furthermore, the performance review system and annual profit share arrangements served the important functions of visibly and concretely rewarding expertise as well as stitching employees into the fabric of the company. Thus, material rewards followed success in fusing personal and collective identities in service of the company. The power of this self-reverential community spirit was manifested in the lack of any noticeable worker resistance. The recruitment, selection, induction and management practices employed by the company ensured a smooth and supportive transition from higher education to employment. These practices built on key aspects of the personal identity characteristic of new recruits (and existing staff) to forge and then sustain a collective workplace and occupational identity among the software engineers.

Emphasising technical intelligence

According to Barrett (2005: 3–4) exaggerated claims that software workers would become the 'future aristocrats of the labour market' have 'served to obscure much of what the people developing software actually do from day to day at work'. Interviewees in our case study spent a great deal of time applying their technical expertise to a range of diagnostic activities. These involved writing thousands of lines of computer code, testing software systems and routines, and designing new product architecture. They also had to demonstrate their technical intelligence on a daily basis with customers seeking updates and progress reports. For many, therefore, the label 'engineer' aptly described the reality of their occupational role and captured their professional identity. They were also working in a relatively stable and very successful commercial environment where employee turnover was low. In that sense, they conformed more to the Japanese model of the loyal career professional, who progresses through a highly structured internal labour market, rather than the highly mobile risk-takers. Several mentioned they had rejected offers from financial companies in the City of London, offering much larger salaries, because they preferred a job with intellectual stimulation. A company director explained this as follows:

> We're talking about a lot of propeller heads here, you see. And they want to know what the next exciting technology they're going to be working on. They don't particularly want to know that I have recently negotiated so and

so with customer X or whatever ... I think that culture comes partly because ... the company is full of engineers. It's very engineering dominated.

The majority of software workers we interviewed and observed identified themselves primarily as intelligent professionals with high levels of technical ability and, hence, were keen to call themselves 'engineers'. The sense of being 'top of the class' had been forged early in life at school and then again at university. Becoming part of an 'intelligent, technical community' at work was the next step. In Goffman's terms, the 'embracement' of software engineers was manifested in their attachment to, practice of and engagement in their work roles (1961b: 106). The company they had joined was managed by people from the same mould, whose understanding of their own personal identities enabled them to develop structures and over-arching cultural narratives designed to attract and retain engineers with a similar outlook.

In summary, then, the technical and social relations of production in the software company had created personal and collective identities that were mutually constituted and reinforcing. The highly developed strategies and practices developed by the company ensured that transitions at work, for example, between job roles and responsibilities were not experienced as problematic. The very low turnover of the engineers provided indirect evidence that moving to another company would be seen and experienced as disruptive to the strong alignment of personal and collective identities that these employees appeared to enjoy and value.

Challenging well-established identities among automotive workers

Our third sector has had to cope with contraction rather than growth. Manufacturing in the UK has lost over a million jobs since 1997. Automotive component suppliers have suffered a similar fate, with industry estimates suggesting that one fifth of business has been lost over the last decade (SMMT 2002). Our research focuses on two component suppliers. One manufactured wheels and cylinder heads which it sold to major car producers; the other supplied pressed steel parts to its sole customer. Both employed around 900 people and both experienced recent job losses as a result of heightened competition. In response, both managements were seeking to develop new hybrid categories of workers, thereby challenging well-established occupational boundaries and associated patterns of collective and personal identity. As a result, the identities of some workers were under threat and this helped explain the reluctance of some to go along with management's desire for them to make the identity transitions necessary to fulfil the hybrid job roles. Our research material is based on interviews with 40 employees located in a variety of job roles, augmented by evidence from work shadowing, observation of shop floor work processes and two focus groups with employees.

Centrality of work identities

Our respondents among automotive workers differed markedly in the extent to which they placed work and employment at the centre of their personal and collective identities. For some, work remained a key determinant of how they saw themselves and how they were seen by others. For others, employment played a minor part in their personal identities and they had little sense of a collective identity as workers. As also discussed by Bimrose and Brown (this volume), these differences had consequences for attitudes to the take-up of learning opportunities.

For a number of employees, the pursuit of learning opportunities resulted in a 'career identity', with people, projects and organisations treated as means to achieve career progress (Grey 1994). For some of these workers, curiosity about production processes had snowballed into formal courses, followed by promotion. Some were career-minded from the outset, proactively seeking development, often paying for courses and/or studying in their own time. Other respondents preferred to manage their careers by moving habitually from job to job, even employer to employer, thereby enhancing their range of learning opportunities and picking up new skills quickly. Notwithstanding the differences in their approaches, all of these interviewees perceived an actual or potential link between their personal identities and their collective identities in the workplace.

In contrast, other interviewees had weak personal and collective identities as workers and were not eager to advance their careers. In the words of one respondent: 'they don't like being told anything ... [and] they're just not interested in their jobs'. Similar observations were made by several interviewees, with one manager providing a three-way categorisation:

> [There are] two different types of individuals, those who are self-starters who want to learn and who will actively seek to learn, and others who say 'well, I've never been given any opportunities' [...] And actually there is a third level as well, people who are doing a job and have got to a point where they say 'no, I like this level, I like this job, I'm happy here, I don't want to do more'.

Eroding identity boundaries

Differences in the significance of work were reflected in workers' experience of, and reactions to, attempts by management to reconfigure job demarcations in the workplace. Identity maintenance frequently entails the policing of boundaries, which establish who belongs to the group and who does not (Goffman 1959; 1961a). In the workplace, identity boundaries are often marked by the activities that individuals carry out, which have symbolic as well as practical significance. Where such boundaries are agreed between management and employees, both parties may sanction transgressors. However, in our two case study organisations, economic pressures had prompted management to reorganise work and destabilise the agreed order. This resulted in changes to the practical and symbolic boundaries of certain jobs, representing a potential challenge to personal and collective identities of some workers as they were expected to make transitions into different job roles and take on new responsibilities through the process of crossing previously established boundaries. In both companies, management responded to heightened international competition in the component supply sector, job losses and customer demands for quality assurance with a programme of 'hybridisation' of some jobs. This entailed a widening of work roles: in one case, upwards to include managerial responsibilities; in the other, downwards to encompass 'less skilled' work tasks.

In these circumstances, a gap opened between the aims of key managerial initiatives and the identities of sections of the workforce. Continued policing and underscoring of identity boundaries by workers became increasingly unhelpful to management's plans to reorganise the boundaries between job roles. In one company, reorganisation was impeded by technicians who were disinclined to make the transition to management. In the other, it was hindered by managers who refused to 'get their hands dirty'. One manager commented:

> You have engineers who want to be managers and you have good, solid, technical people who don't want to be managers. And, of course, what we all too often need is a hybrid person [...] we have some excellent hands-on people but don't ask them to write a report. And we've got others who are excellent, yes, give them all the data and the stats and they'll write a report. But, 'I've got to get my hands dirty – that's not really my scene'.

While the above provides a management perspective on the tensions created by a clash of occupational identities, our worker interviews offered a different account. Workers with strong, and aligned, personal and collective work-based identities greeted the opportunity to move to hybrid roles with dismay. For example, one of our interviewees, a tool maker/fitter, perceived the opportunity to become one of the company's newly created 'line techs', as a move from a more to a less highly skilled job, despite the fact that the new position was associated with higher pay. He declined the job on the grounds that it undermined his occupational identity and status as a skilled man who had served a craft apprenticeship. The role of 'line tech' was open to both 'skilled' (apprenticeship-trained) and 'unskilled' (those who had not served an apprenticeship) employees, which made its status ambiguous and unappealing to the toolmaker:

> The thing is that when you learn to build the tools, that's probably the most difficult thing to do. [...] That's part of your apprenticeship anyway. [...] They call you a fire-fighter. What you do is the line goes down, you have to go out and fix it, so they can keep producing the panels. We fix the dies, the actual tools that are in the presses, and the maintenance and fix the presses. The only area that's slightly grey, it's sort of a grey area, is you've got what they call line techs. Now you've got some skilled and some unskilled, but the unskilled ones won't touch the tools. [...] So, there is a big divide between skilled and unskilled.

This narrative suggests a close linkage between personal identity, collective identity and the conduct of work tasks; in particular, the length of training required, the status of 'apprenticeship' and the customs and practices of the job. It is reminiscent of Bensman and Lilienfeld's (1991) argument that the way people make sense of the world, find their place in it and interact with others is determined by their occupation. They argue that it is the actual processes involved in practising the 'craft' that has a powerful effect on development and maintenance of occupational identity. Skilled workers and managers found themselves reluctantly experiencing greater 'role distance' from the actual work practices they were expected to undertake and drawn into 'defensive practices' (e.g. resistance to the transitions desired by senior management) in order to sustain valued personal and collective work-based identities (Goffman 1961b, 1959). This can be seen in the reluctance of some skilled workers to move away from what they knew best:

> Personally, I wanted to stay doing the job I was trained to do. I look at myself as a toolmaker and I'd like to stay as close to that role as I possibly could. [...] I wasn't really sure what the role was going to be. [...] I'd rather be a hands-on on the tools, building the jobs or fixing them and doing the job that I was trained to do.

Conclusion

Notwithstanding that some automotive workers were indifferent to or detached from work-based identities, the three case studies briefly presented here suggest that work and employment remain a powerful source of personal and collective identity formation. They also indicate that participation in the tasks, skills and practices characteristic of specific productive processes strongly influence how workers see themselves and how they are seen by others. However, we have also seen that the relationship *between* personal and collective identities varies in the different employment situations and that the nature of this relationship is revealed when workers are expected to move into new job roles or conform to standardised work practices. Thus, in the service sector, the personal identities of ETM instructors were subsumed within a strong concept of collective identity being promoted by employers and their agents. Some instructors were happy to adopt this and did not experience the identity work involved as problematic. Others preferred to adopt a transitory identity to act out the work role their employers had constructed but quickly moved out of character when the performance was finished. In the 'knowledge intensive' software company, there was evidence of a close alignment, integration and compatibility between personal identities and collective organisational identity. In the manufacturing sector, skilled workers and managers with long-established and aligned personal and collective identities found changing occupational boundaries disturbing and unwelcome, and were thus resistant to making the desired work role transitions. They were highly attached to the identities that their occupational role provided and found it difficult to give up symbols of prestige, such as 'apprentice-trained' and 'skilled worker' status, even for higher pay.

This chapter also demonstrates that the importance of identity work *for the organisation* – the time and effort spent on looking, sounding and being the part – varies markedly from sector to sector. In the service sector, there was evidence that the correct presentation of self by aerobics instructors to consumers was critical to the profitable operation of companies marketing fitness classes. In this case, management went to considerable lengths to stage manage the encounter, specifying class formats, clothing, language and demeanour to mark out the transitions the instructors were required to make. In the 'knowledge intensive' software company, the mechanisms were subtler but still evident. Management sought to build on and sustain personal feelings of being 'top of the class' experienced by ultra-bright university students prior to recruitment to the company. Once they had become employees, software engineers were given latitude in how they organised their work, were encouraged to integrate work with other life interests and to perceive themselves, via relatively seamless transition, as part of an 'intelligent, technical community' of highly motivated workers. By these means, the creative energies of software engineers were harnessed to the business aims of the company. In contrast, in our traditional manufacturing case study, senior management had far less to gain from supporting well-established personal and collective identities of skilled craft workers. Indeed, these identities were seen as more of a hindrance than a help in achieving the work reorganisation deemed necessary to market success. Key workers in the automotive plants made sense of their worlds through personal and collective identities that were embedded in status formations associated with a tradition of specialist craft skills and were, therefore, resistant to job changes which involved transitions to more generic or hybrid job roles.

In short, participation in employment continues to shape personal and collective identities, but does so in diverse ways that reflect contrasts in the organisation of work and how workers identify themselves in the processes of production. By looking for instances of how organisations seek to manage and change employees' identities (sometimes explicitly, sometimes implicitly), the nature of the relationship between personal and collective identities is revealed. Our evidence points to the need for management to recognise and think carefully about the identity work likely to be involved in transitions to new or different work roles and how this will affect different types of workers. Respondents across the three cases have indicated the continuing importance of workplace identity and the implications, positive and negative, of moves which challenge their sense of self.

Acknowledgement

This research forms part of a larger project funded under the Economic and Social Research Council's Teaching and Learning Research Programme (RES-139-25-0110A). Further details available online at http://learningaswork.cf.ac.uk

Bibliography

Barrett, R. (2001) 'Labouring under an illusion? The labour process of software development in the Australian information industry', *New Technology, Work and Employment*, 16: 18–34.

—— (2005) 'Introduction: myth and reality', in R. Barrett (2005) (ed.) *Management, Labour Process and Software Development*, London: Routledge.

Becker, H. S. (1951) 'The professional dance musician and his audience', *American Journal of Sociology*, 57: 136–44.

Bensman, J. and Lilienfeld, R. (1991) *Craft and Consciousness: Occupational Technique and the Development of World Images*, New York: Aldine de Gruyter.

Bolton, S. C. (2004) 'Conceptual confusions: emotion work as skilled work', in C. Warhurst, I. Grugulis and E. Keep (eds) *The Skills That Matter*, Basingstoke: Palgrave Macmillan.

Carmel, E. and Eisenberg, J. (2006) 'Narratives that software nations tell themselves: an exploration and taxonomy', *Communications of the Association for Information Systems*, 17: 851–72.

Collinson, D. L. (2003) 'Identities and insecurities: selves at work', *Organization*, 10: 527–47.

Ecclestone, K. (2007) 'Editorial: an identity crisis? Using concepts of "identity", "agency" and "structure" in the education of adults', *Studies in the Education of Adults*, 39: 121–31.

Felstead, A. and Jewson, N. (eds) (1999) *Global Trends in Flexible Labour*, Basingstoke: Macmillan.

Felstead, A., Jewson, N. and Walters, S. (2005) *Changing Places of Work*, Basingstoke: Palgrave Macmillan.

Felstead, A., Fuller, A., Jewson, N., Kakavelakis, K. and Unwin, L. (2007) 'Grooving to the same tunes? Learning, training and productive systems in the aerobics studio', *Work, Employment and Society*, 21: 189–208.

Fevre, R. (2007) 'Employment insecurity and social theory: the power of nightmares', *Work, Employment and Society*, 21: 517–35.

Goffman, E. (1959) *The Presentation of Self in Everyday Life*, London: Penguin.

—— (1961a) *Stigma: Notes on the Management of Spoiled Identity*, London: Penguin.

—— (1961b) *Encounters: Two Studies in the Sociology of Interaction*, Indianapolis: Bobbs-Merrill Co.

—— (1961c) *Asylums*, Garden City, NY: Doubleday Anchor Book.

Grey, C. (1994) 'Career as a project of the self and labour process discipline', *Sociology*, 28: 479–97.

Leadbeater, C. (1999) *Living on Thin Air: the New Economy*, London: Viking.

Marks, A. and Lockyer, C. (2005) 'Professional identity in software work: evidence from Scotland', in R. Barrett (ed.) *Management, Labour Process and Software Development*, London: Routledge.

Quintas, P. (1994) 'Programmes innovation? Trajectories of change in software development', *Information Technology and People*, 7: 25–47.

Ransome, P. (2005) *Work, Consumption and Culture: Affluence and Social Change in the Twenty-first Century*, London: Sage.

Rhodes, C. and Scheeres, H. (2004) 'Developing people in organizations: working (on) identity', *Studies in Continuing Education*, 26: 175–93.

Robinson, H., Hall, P., Hovenden, F. and Rachel, J. (1998) 'Postmodern software development', *The Computer Journal*, 41: 363–75.

SMMT (Society of Motor Manufacturers and Traders) (2002) *Survey on the Growth Perspectives of the European Automotive Supplier Industry*, London: SMMT.

Tam, Y. M., Korczynski, M. and Frenkel, S. J. (2002) 'Organisational and occupational commitment: knowledge workers in large corporations', *Journal of Management Studies*, 39: 775–801.

Witz, A., Warhurst, C. and Nickson, D. (2003) 'The labour aesthetics and the aesthetics of organization' *Organization*, 10: 33–54.

Wojecki, A. (2007) 'What's identity got to do with it, anyway? Constructing adult learner identities in the workplace', *Studies in the Education of Adults*, 39: 168–82.

Woodward, K (2002) *Understanding Identity*, London: Arnold.

11 Adults learning in and through the workplace

Karen Evans and Edmund Waite

Introduction

The concept of learner 'trajectories', as exemplified by the research of Gorard *et al.* (e.g. 1998, 2001; Gorard and Rees 2002), represents an important attempt to theorize learning episodes through the lifecourse by aggregating individual experiences into sets of typologies. From their analysis of 1,104 education and training histories in post-war industrial South Wales, Gorard *et al.* identified eleven lifetime learning trajectories, five of which were highlighted as being particularly salient: 'non-participant', 'delayed', 'transitional', 'lifetime', 'immature'. Employing logistic regression, Gorard and Rees argued that such trajectories were predictable from such key determinants as 'age', 'place', 'gender', 'parents', 'religion' and 'school' with the result that the 'trajectory an individual takes can be accurately predicted on the basis of characteristics that are known by the time an individual reaches school-leaving age' (Gorard and Rees 2002: 64). Though representing an important theoretical advance in conceptualizing a diverse range of learning experiences and highlighting some key social parameters and constraints that shape these experiences, Gorard *et al.*'s approach is also, by the authors' own admission, highly determinative in nature and allocates a minimal role for individual agency over the lifecourse.[1] Furthermore, in an attempt to predict the determinants of workplace learning, Gorard, Rees and Fevre (1999: 15) noted the complexities involved in doing this 'especially with regard to differing views of its role'. Their conclusions underlined the importance of knowing more about the factors that influence such trajectories.

Models of adult learning that heavily emphasize structural determinants rooted in the individual's early life become increasingly challenging in light of the contemporary features of a diversified, post-industrial economy, dramatic advances in communications technology, globalization and shifting patterns in family, class, ethnicity and gender. The 'reflexivity' of 'high' or 'post-modernity' outlined by theorists such as Anthony Giddens (1990) and Ulrich Beck (1992) in which individuals, groups and social institutions routinely engage in self-examination and change in response to incoming flows of information (which in turn feeds back on the original source of knowledge) signals the dangers in over-reliance on the 'predictive determinants' of an individual's life. As highlighted by Richard Edwards 'reflexivity signifies the increased options available and the necessity of decision making, even as the implications of those decisions become less certain. Previously structured choices and opportunities are no longer held to be as determining of biographies as was previously the case' (Edwards 1998: 377).

This chapter seeks to highlight the difficulty of typologizing pathways of adult learning, based on structural determinants, and explore some of the complex range of factors that underpin these challenges, in relation to individuals who have taken part in literacy, numeracy and ESOL (English for Speakers of Other Languages) provision in the workplace. Since the launch of the national 'Skills for Life' strategy in 2001, the UK government has invested heavily in a drive to improve literacy, numeracy and ESOL provision, an important dimension of which has been the funding (largely through learning and skills councils) of 'Skills for Life' workplace courses. Such provision includes discrete literacy, numeracy and ESOL courses in the workplace, literacy embedded in IT courses, literacy embedded in vocational and job-specific training as well as learndirect 'Skills for Life' courses undertaken in online learning centres in the workplace. The Leitch Review of Skills (2006) and the subsequent 'Train to Gain' national initiative, which sets challenging new targets for improving the attainment of literacy and numeracy skills by 2020, has further developed UK policy emphasis on the significance of 'Skills for Life' workplace learning. Our data is drawn from the 'Adult Basic Skills and Workplace Learning' project, a five-year longitudinal study (2003–8) that aims to assess the effects on individuals and on organizations of engagement in workplace literacy, numeracy and ESOL programmes. A scarcity of evidence on the impact of workplace basic skills provision (Ananiadou *et al.* 2003) formed the background and underlying motivation for the establishment of the project. In this chapter we report some of the patterns that have been identified in the data on employees' participation in literacy and related programmes, and then focus in detail on the shifting 'learning orientations' of eight learners from five organizations, highlighting the significance of the workplace in providing a 'social ecology' of learning that incorporates sustained interactions between individual choices and motivations and wider structural opportunities and constraints.

Exploring life and work transitions of adult employees engaged in workplace learning

The concept of trajectories is typically used in work on transitions of young adults into the labour market, providing ideal-type segmented routes that can be used to understand a variety of personal histories (Evans and Heinz 1994). In adult life, routes diverge, experiences diversify still further and multiplicities of new contingencies come into play (termed individualization by Beck and Giddens). In researching adults' life and work experiences, initial career trajectories take on historical significance. Respondents can be asked to reflect on their experiences, looking back on influences and events. In this way 'types' can be checked against individual interpretations of where people think they are coming from, are going to and how they make sense of their experiences.

In this chapter we discuss the relationships between adult employees' individual behaviours in relation to learning (which we see as manifestations of their learning and career orientations) and the opportunities afforded to them through their workplaces. In previous work, Evans and Heinz (1993, 1994) identified 'transition behaviours' as patterns of activity that young people adopt in attempting to realize their personal interests and occupational goals through the various occupational and educational opportunity structures available to them. Transition is a process that starts, for young adults, with educational achievement, occupational 'choice' (however restricted), applying for and taking up jobs as well as establishing independent personal and family lives. These processes continue in adult life with activities undertaken with the aims of maintaining employment, changing employment, balancing work and family life, and finding personal fulfilment. They may be considered transitional where they involve changes in the adult's orientations to learning and career. Behaviours in relation to learning are the patterns of activity that people adopt in relation to learning opportunities available to them, in this case workplace programmes involving the development of 'adult basic skills' and varying degrees of opportunity to learn through new workplace and life experiences. These do not indicate enduring personal attributes, such as personal flexibility, rigidity, etc., but they do indicate complex sets of adults' motivations, beliefs and attitudes towards learning and their own capabilities to achieve in and through learning. These we term 'orientations to learning'. These orientations can change according to specific experiences of success or failure, opportunities or setbacks at any stage. Orientations towards work and career, similarly, comprise complex sets of motivations, beliefs and attitudes rooted in actual life experiences.

The employment of this framework allows us to elucidate experiences that are transitional for the adult employee in the sense of changing their learning or work/career orientations and allows us to compare these with what actually happens in their work and personal lives after engagement in new learning (i.e. the career events that ensue).

The project has undertaken structured interviews with 564 employees in 55 organizations from a variety of sectors (including transport, food manufacturing, engineering, health and local government) as well as structured interviews with the relevant managers and tutors at the selected sites. Each learner is also assessed early on in the course using an assessment tool that has been designed by NFER (National Foundation for Educational Research) for the project and which is especially designed to take account of small changes in literacy development. Follow-up structured interviews and literacy assessments have been undertaken in order to trace developments in literacy levels and working practices over time. In addition, two phases of in-depth interviews have been undertaken with a sub-sample of 66 learners from 10 sites as well as with their relevant managers and tutors.

Participation in workplace Skills for Life programmes: the potential for workplace courses to respond to shifting attitudes to learning

A total of 564 learners were interviewed at Phase 1, almost two-thirds of whom were male with an average age of just over 40. Almost all of these individuals were in permanent full-time employment at the time of the interview. The

Table 11.1 Highest qualification obtained (%)

	Learners	Non-ESOL learners	UK working age population, 2001
None	46	44	27
Level 1	11	16	12
Level 2	18	23	16
Level 1 or 2 (includes those where unclear which)	36	48	
Level 3	11	6	16
Level 4	6	2	
Level 5	1	0	29

NB: numbers in column 1 do not sum to 100

average length of employment with the current employer was almost eight years. ESOL learners represented a sizeable 35 per cent of the full sample whereas the current UK workforce is made up of only 3 per cent of employees who do not speak English as their first language. Of particular significance for the topic of this chapter is that 54 per cent of the learners had left full-time education with no qualifications; 14 per cent were qualified to Level 3 or above when they left full-time education; 23 per cent acquired further qualifications after leaving formal education; and 3 per cent acquired further qualifications at Level 3 or above after leaving full-time education.

Both structured and in-depth interviews have indicated a wide range of factors behind learners' engagement in workplace courses, beyond merely the wish to develop job-specific skills. Nearly all engagement was on a voluntary basis. Figure 11.1 provides data on the two most important outcomes that learners wanted or expected from their course at Time 1. This is then compared with the two most important outcomes that learners actually felt they achieved from the course. It is noticeable that the generic motivation of 'learning new skills' was most commonly cited (by 51 per cent of learners), and the outcome of the course surpassed such expectations. As many as 35 per cent of learners cited the improvement of work performance as a factor and rather fewer listed this as an actual outcome. This is consistent with findings from the in-depth studies which have highlighted a whole range of factors for engagement in such courses; from 'curiosity' to wanting to make up for missed earlier educational opportunities; from wanting specific help with job-relevant skills to wider career aims; from a desire to help children with schoolwork to wanting self-improvement and personal development (Evans *et al.* 2008). Also noteworthy is the ranking of 'increase chances of promotion' and 'increase chances for jobs' as 18 per cent and 24 per cent respectively, all of which suggest that for the majority of learners the motivations for learning are not tied narrowly to wishes for advancement at work, or an aspirational career trajectory.

Shifting perceptions of benefits were highlighted by the follow-up survey (Time 2), which showed that only a quarter of respondents identified the same benefits as they had when first asked, prior to taking the course (Time 1).

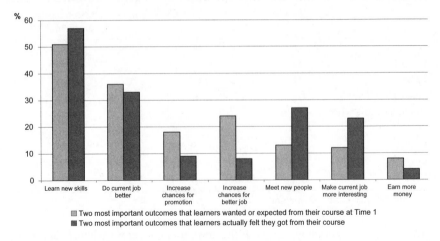

Figure 11.1 Most important expected and actual benefits from the course

Table 11.2 provides data on the outcome of the course, on an item-by-item basis, which is highly indicative of the significance of attitudinal outcomes.

The relatively large number of learners in our sample with few or no qualifications is indicative of the potential of 'Skills for Life' workplace courses to engage learners who have not benefited from other forms of educational provision. Through the employment of in-depth interviews, we are in a position to explore in detail individual attitudes to learning. The in-depth interviews have allowed us to explore the potential advantages and disadvantages of learning in the workplace rather than a college. Just under half the learners referred to the relative convenience and accessibility of workplace learning in so far as it fitted in more smoothly with their lives at work and home. For example, one ESOL learner at a bakery told us: 'workplace is better for us because we are here. [...] Because when you go home you've got to see children and you've got to cook and that ... and then people don't bother.' An employee of an engineering factory told us 'you're already here [...] which is the beauty of things. I used to go to the college, I'd be working [...] look at my watch, got to go in a minute got to go in a minute.'

The benefit of learning with colleagues in a familiar setting was also frequently cited as an advantage of workplace learning during the course of in-depth interviews. A bus driver mentioned that he preferred undertaking a course in the workplace, 'because at least its in familiar settings as opposed to I've got to find a room, J49 and Fred Bloggs will be in there waiting for you'. Similarly, an employee of an engineering company told us that he preferred 'learning at work because you're working with the people you're learning with ... they can have the chats, and ... conversations and ... discuss it amongst yourselves if they're struggling with anything'. In relation to this issue, three learners mentioned explicitly that learning with people of the same age was an advantage of workplace provision.

Several employees told us they thought that learning in the workplace was more

Table 11. 2 Outcomes of course (item-by-item basis)

Increased confidence at work	66%
Developed new skills	61%
Increased confidence outside work	59%
Met new people	58%
Affected how current job is done*	45%
Helped with use of computers outside work	33%
Helped with use of computers at work	27%
Made work more interesting	25%
Increased chances for promotion	11%
Increased chances of a better job	10%
Helped earn more money	2%

* 40% elaborated: all reported positive impact

Whether or not a course increased confidence at work was highly (and positively) related to whether a learner also thought it had helped them to do their current job better/had affected how they did the job.

'relaxed' and less intimidating than learning in a college. For example, a care worker for a local authority told us 'you're more relaxed but I think if you're going to college, it's like back to school again'. A bus driver told us 'I think you're a lot more relaxed in your workplace. [...] It's not all taken as serious as it would be in college'.

In terms of the disadvantages of workplace learning, three employees (two from a bakery and one from a transport company) made a point of mentioning that the pressure of complying with shift work had interfered with their course. Only four employees (one employee of a bakery and three care workers) stated that they preferred the idea of learning in a college rather than the workplace. Two of them (one employee of a bakery and a care worker) mentioned that they preferred to separate studying from the workplace whilst another wished to undertake a longer course and felt this was only possible in a college. The fourth individual, who undertook a management role in a residential care home, was concerned about incurring negative perceptions from her fellow employees which was possibly related to her relatively low literacy skills.

Transitions through the lifecourse: perspectives from individual case studies

In-depth interviews with 66 learners, together with follow-up in-depth interviews with the majority of these learners have allowed detailed case histories to be developed. Eight of these cases, drawn from five of the ten companies selected for detailed analysis, have been selected here to exemplify some of the diversity of individual experiences of learning over the lifecourse. No claims are made about the representativeness of these cases, given the complexity of factors involved. However, our research design allows us to 'benchmark' all of our cases against the patterns and regularities found in the wider samples (see Table 11.4).

The eight selected cases are as follows:

- Bill Williams[2] (b. 1961) has been working at Coopers (most recently as a 'seasoning technician') since leaving school. He was brought up by his mother who worked as a cook at a primary school and managed to gain a few lower-grade CSEs despite an indifferent school education. He has previously studied the Greek language at evening college in the local town, having visited Greece on holiday, but found it difficult to combine attendance on a formal course with work. Bill has completed learndirect (online learning) literacy and numeracy courses at the company's learning centre which, until recently, has been registered as an official learndirect centre.[3]
- Victoria Appiah (b. 1950) works as a receptionist at Southern Transport Systems (STS). Victoria came to England from Ghana, where her education had been interrupted as a result of her parents' transient lifestyle. She has spent much of her adult life in England, bringing up her children as a single parent. Workplace courses at STS allowed her to gain a GCSE in English followed by Maths and ICT. She has subsequently undertaken a one-year course in 'creative writing' at a London college despite the difficulties of attending a college after work.
- Trevor Woodford (b. 1982) left school at 16 with no qualifications. He undertook a variety of casual jobs before becoming a caretaker at the London Borough of Thorpton where he embarked on a 'communications course' for 3 hours a week over a 5-week period. He has subsequently taken on a supervisory role as caretaker and he plans to become a 'housing officer'.
- Melanie Taylor (b. 1968) has been working at Brightland Bakeries since she left school at the age of 16. She had previously studied Sociology and Criminology (both at Level 2) at a centre for lifelong learning. Melanie undertook Level 2 literacy and numeracy qualifications at the Brightland Bakeries' learning centre. She was subsequently promoted to the position of 'hygiene coordinator' and she currently supervises approximately 20 people.
- Tracy Beaumont (b. 1968) works on the shop floor of Coopers food factory as a 'Quality Assessor'. Previous jobs include working as a machinist in a clothes factory and as care assistant in a psychiatric hospital. She left school at the age of 16 without any qualifications and has not previously engaged in adult education. Tracy has undertaken a variety of learndirect literacy and numeracy courses at the company's learning centre.
- Kathleen Croft (b. 1956) had a disrupted education as a result of arriving in the UK at the age of 7 from the West Indies. Until recently taking voluntary severance, she worked at Southern Transport Systems as a support manager. She undertook an English course at STS which culminated in her gaining a GCSE English B grade. She is currently combining looking after her children with undertaking a computer course and plans to return to work when her children are older.
- Mike Philips (b. 1953) has been working at HLN Manufacturing (a large engineering company specializing in the manufacture of parts for cars) for the past 30 years, most recently as a forklift driver. He left school at 15 with no qualifications. He was one of eight learners that took part in a 'Skills for

Life' course that ran from May 2005 to July 2005, consisting of 1 hour 30 minute sessions for 10 weeks. The course was set up by three Union Learning Representatives (ULRs) in the company (with the support of the management) who approached the local college. He has subsequently proceeded to undertake two computer courses at Level 1 and Level 2 at the company's new learning centre (established by the company's ULRs).

- Bennie Thomas (b. 1945) was brought up in the West Indies and he came to the UK at age 19. Brought up by a mother who had no formal education and a father who showed no interest in his children's education and suffered from alcohol addiction, Bennie suffered from extreme educational disadvantage and left school at 15 with no qualifications. He has been working at STS for over 40 years and currently undertakes the role of 'ticket machine engineer'. Bennie's supervisor encouraged him to undertake English and Maths courses so as to cope with the increasing paperwork in the workplace. Bennie proceeded to embark on over 100 hours' literacy and 50 hours' numeracy courses over a three-year period at one of the company's learning centres.

Orientations to learning

The cases illustrate adults' complex sets of motivations, beliefs and attitudes towards learning, and towards their own capabilities to achieve in and through learning. They show how these learning orientations are rooted in prior educational experiences. They also show how these orientations can shift over time, how they influence engagement with workplace activities and how shifts in orientation can be supported through learning opportunities offered in and through the workplace.

The influence of early educational experiences on learning orientations

As in the case of the broader sample of employees who have been interviewed, the majority of these individuals spoke about their early educational experience in largely negative terms. Victoria felt she had suffered from her parents' uprooted lifestyle and her parents' lack of concern for her education, describing herself as her 'mum's handbag'. Similarly Kathleen Croft revealed that 'I was a bit of a day dreamer and ... when I first came to this country, I was totally overwhelmed with everything, and I think I just sort of went into myself. [...] I'm definitely a late bloomer, late starter in life'. In addition to having to cope with lack of parental support, Bennie's experience at his local school in the West Indies was marred by an insufficient number of text books and the school relied heavily on corporal punishment: 'I didn't learn anything, it just wasn't a school, it was just somewhere we go. And whether you go or not it doesn't matter'.

By his own admission, Trevor's education suffered from his lack of application at school in London: 'I suppose when I was a kid I was always the clown of the class'. Melanie felt that her confidence was adversely affected by the school environment: 'Well, I was really shy and I use to think that if they ever got me to do anything it just made me worse, that didn't help my confidence, that just made me feel worse because they embarrassed me and it just made me not want to do it more. I was really, really quiet.' Similarly Tracy mentioned that her school education had adversely affected her confidence: 'I would love to go to college but I think that's what really puts me off ... I just think well, school was that bad, it would be the same you know what I mean?' The above-mentioned advantages of workplace learning in being both accessible, convenient and (most importantly) less loaded with intimidating associations had been particularly important in allowing Tracy to engage in this form of provision.

Despite these educational disadvantages, the learners spoke of a shifting attitude to learning over the lifecourse which entailed varying efforts to overcome or negotiate with these legacies. As Trevor explained, 'when I was a kid I was always the clown of the class [...] Now I'm more grown up I can actually sit there and, like, learn something, whereas before I was too, I suppose too active'. Bill Williams similarly commented on the significance of a shifting attitude to learning which had led him to embark on the course: 'At school you have to go. I was only 16 when I left school. I'm 43 now. I just got older and dafter, some people say wiser. [...] You start to realize now that these things are worth teaching at school, you try to instil in to your child they're not just teaching you these things to make life boring, they're teaching you because you need them in the future.'

Kathleen commented both on her alteration in attitude towards learning over time as well as the significance of inter-generational changes: 'because my generation was different, my mum didn't believe in us doing homework. We were just there to cook and clean'. She is consequently keen to adopt a more involved approach with her own children (aged 8 and 11 in 2004): 'it's because I know what I went through so I'm making sure that they've got the opportunity to do their homework'. Similarly Bennie sought to encourage his six children (five of whom have now gone on to university and moved away from home) to take advantage of the educational opportunities that were denied to him: 'because I pushed them to make sure they get what I didn't get'. Victoria had similarly sought to instil in her children the educational opportunities that had been denied to her and had sought to engage in learning herself although family responsibilities had until now prevented her from taking up this opportunity: 'I've always had this edge of wanting to learn. But er–, working and having children is another issue'.

Despite his indifferent school education, Mike Philips made a point of encouraging his own children to study seriously at school and they (and his wife) had subsequently gone on to study at university: 'there was only me in our house, that had got no qualifications or certificates or anything. I mean even our dog had got a pedigree, so I thought it's time to catch up'.

The effect of workplace courses on learning orientations

The individuals' involvement in workplace courses had an important effect in consolidating and expanding these shifting learning trajectories. One important dimension of this process (which is also evident in the quantitative data in Table 11.5) was an increased boost in confidence which also led to a broadening of horizons and willingness to take on more educational challenges.

For example, Trevor Woodford experienced a motivational boost as a result of attending the course, revealing that the course gave him 'more confidence to go for it'. Trevor's confidence has been boosted by evidence of what he has accomplished and this has facilitated his efforts to gain promotion in the workplace: 'Maybe I thought I had it there before but now I've actually done it on a course as well and seen better. [...] I'm writing letters and speaking on the phone, its just given me a bit more confidence in that way.'

Melanie had already undertaken courses at adult colleges, but appreciated the workplace courses as a means of further alleviating the legacy of school experience: 'Doing the courses at work ... it sort of made you feel that going back to the classroom wasn't as daunting as you think it would be. Do you know what I mean? I suppose I thought they'd treat you like a child but they didn't. I didn't like school.' The process of alleviating her fears had allowed Melanie to take on more challenge: 'I think it was always probably like a bit of fear factor with me but then once I started doing it and I found it weren't that bad and now it's like now, I just like it now, I like learning new things all the time.'

Victoria emphasized her growth in self-confidence as the most significant personal outcome and describes the freedom from previous constraints in passionate terms: 'You know, I wish I could describe it stronger than what I'm saying, it's like you've been caged and set free. That's how I feel.' Such a sentiment prompted Victoria to embark on a year-long creative writing course after the completion of the workplace courses at STS.

During her employment at STS, Kathleen mentioned that the course had given her more 'impetus, to go further and do more, that's really made me feel right, you can do this and try and do something else. It has encouraged me to move on. [...] Even yesterday I bought a course book to see what else is out there, what else is available for me to study.' Although she subsequently took voluntary severance, Kathleen drew upon her experience of studying as an important resource for developing her future career (once her children had grown up): 'I'm not going to bury myself here, I'm thinking well what can I branch out and do.'

Tracy reported that the courses have had some effect in improving confidence. However her confidence is still low despite having completed the literacy Level 2 test: 'But I'm still not there you know what I mean just cos I've got it [i.e. the Literacy L2]. I still haven't got the confidence'. She still feels that she struggles with reading, especially in public situations: 'it's like if you go in a meeting and you read things I panic, I panic, you know what I mean I'm really like conscious about it. [...] Because like a lot of people take the mickey because you can't read, and now I'm really self-conscious of it'. Tracy's case is an example both of the potential advantages of workplace learning (her fear of formal learning means that she would not have engaged with other forms of educational provision) as well as the limits that exist in addressing deep-seated anxieties in some individuals.

Several individuals also mentioned that courses inspired them to encourage their family and friends to embark on learning. Mike expressed great enthusiasm about the skills he had gained from the computer course and revealed that he encouraged his fellow employees to take up learning opportunities.

Although Bennie was unable to take an active role in assisting his elder children with their homework, he is now able, as a result of the course, to be actively involved in his youngest son's schoolwork. He set aside a room which he uses as a study for both himself and his 14-year-old son 'now I'm preparing a room, I'm doing it up properly for [...] my son and I, to actually do our study there. [...] I've already told my son ... his name is Alex, I said this room will be Alex and Bennie room, it's true so all his work he will do there, his paper work, I will show him how to file it and everything. [...] So it [the course] helped me a lot you know.'

Orientation to careers and career development

In upholding the importance of literacy and numeracy skills for economic advancement, Skills for Life discourse assumes a particular career trajectory for those individuals who are involved in workplace programmes; that of enhanced performance at work and increased potential for promotion at work. Yet, data from structured and in-depth interviews with learners and managers suggests that participation in such programmes is motivated, on an individual and organizational level, by a far wider range of factors than merely the wish to improve performance at work. Moreover, involvement in such courses, in the majority of cases, does not relate to what may be described as an 'aspirational' career trajectory.

It is noticeable that of the eight learners mentioned above, three learners (Bill, Tracy and Mike) were motivated to learn by factors that were entirely unrelated to the workplace. Bill's main experience of literacy in the workplace is through recording faults in machinery. However, he feels that his literacy skills have not impeded him in the workplace since he can 'muddle through': 'I only put flavour on crisps ... they give you the flash title "seasoning technician" but all I do is put a bit of dust on some slices that I fry on a table'. Bill's main reason for signing up for the courses was that he was 'just curious. [...] I mean I left school with no qualifications to speak of, CSE things, which are probably in museums now'. The literacy courses have helped him with writing letters and have improved his capacity to help his child with homework but have not impacted substantially on the workplace 'you have sheets to fill in every day, but there's very little writing involved, it doesn't matter if it's grammatically correct or not'. Bill is planning to stay with his current company in more or less the same job: 'I've only got 16 years to go until I'm 60 ... at my age and my qualifications I'm getting double the minimum wage. [...] I'm relatively happy in what I do.'

Similarly, Tracy felt that there was little need for developing her literacy skills for her current job on the shop floor of the factory. Though she deals with graphs at work, she perceives that there is no use of maths in her job: 'I just get the computer to add them up for us'. She learnt how to use this technology at work without going on a formal course. Underpinning her participation in workplace courses lies a general interest and a wish to bolster her confidence which (as mentioned above) has been sorely bruised by negative educational experiences.

Mike's motivation for doing the course was 'for general interest, general knowledge, and to improve myself. I think as long as you're stimulated by learning different things, seeing different things then you'll always stay active and your brain's always alert and as long as your brain is alert I'm sure you'll get no problems.'

He took great pleasure in his newly acquired computer skills which allowed him to book his holiday online. His motivations for learning continued to be associated closely with his interests in history and languages: 'I still want to learn the language ... It's arrogant of us to think that everybody should speak English, we should be able to communicate in their language also, you know, to be fair.'

Victoria, Kathleen, Melanie and Bennie were motivated to engage in workplace learning by a complex interweaving of motivational factors in which career-oriented considerations were a significant but by no means dominant component. The experience of undertaking the English course equipped Victoria with a greater appreciation of reading and a more conscious knowledge of the English language: 'I'm more into reading. [...] I pay particularly attention to the construction of the sentences and that sort of thing. [...] I love to write, that is my *main issue*, share my experience with other people, even between friends you know.' The courses boosted Victoria's confidence at both home and work, underlining the difficulty of making clear-cut distinctions between 'job-specific' and 'generic' outcomes and motivations for learning: 'think ... it give the, the employee er–, what's the word, confidence, you know you go to your work or doing whatever you're doing with your head up'.

Kathleen outlined an attitude to learning that emphasized the value of knowledge for its own sake whilst also embracing the potential for learning to have career benefits (though not necessarily in the short-term or according to a well defined programme). Kathleen has recently left the company having been offered voluntary severance. She is undertaking a computer course funded by the local council and is planning to stay at home, whilst also undertaking temporary jobs, in order to support her children until they have reached sixth form level at school. She is planning to eventually embark on a course in psychology in response to a long-standing interest in this subject and retains her enthusiasm for learning: 'I've never stopped learning which I've said to the kids until you're buried you're still alive so do something, so you know, keep your brains ticking, keeps you active, you're meeting people, so yeah, I'm not giving up.' In boosting her 'cultural capital', the course has facilitated Kathleen's transition to a stage where she is no longer working full time but is still open to the possibility of short-term work: 'now I've got this qualification behind me then I feel more confident ... if anyone's pushing, questioning me "have you got the qualification for this" or whatever, I could say, well yes, I've got something to show that I've been through the wheels and I've done this'.

Bennie outlined an appreciation of learning for its own sake that was also accompanied by job-specific considerations. The increasing 'textualisation' (Scheeres 2004) of the workplace has challenged his previous capacity to cope in the workplace: 'everybody have to read and write or fill forms in which we never use to do before. We have the time sheets ... fill forms and read different things ... I was struggling a bit'. The course 'just came 10 years too late but it helped a lot'. According to Bennie, the formalization of health and safety procedures, has been particularly instrumental in increasing the use of literacy in the workplace.[4] Though Bennie has subsequently taken early retirement (following back problems) he plans to maintain his educational interests. In terms of the future, Bennie mentions that 'I just want an easy life and [to] my help myself with my education and help other people if I can'. Bennie is now reading books that his older children

Table 11.3 Future plans

Future plans	Frequency	Percentage
Same job at same company	127	48.1
Promotion in same company	46	17.4
Similar job at different company	17	6.4
Different job at different company	44	16.7
Retired	13	4.9
Full-time education	2	0.8
Other	15	5.7
Total	264	100

have studied as part of their college courses: 'I've got six kids and they all finished school already and they've got loads of books from the college and university and I take all of them because they're not using them. I took all of them and I put it on the shelf and I keep going through them so actually I am in university.'

Melanie was motivated to engage in workplace courses as a result of general interest, a wish to alleviate the above-mentioned negative educational influences and an awareness that literacy and numeracy skills were important for advancement within the workplace. She was promoted after the course to the position of 'hygiene coordinator' and she currently supervises approximately 20 people. As part of her job, she writes 'incident report forms', undertakes audits and uses email. She also uses maths in relation to meeting Key Performance Indicators (KPIs): 'its just like adding up how many hours in the day you've worked, how many trays you've produced, and what's your average trays per minute per hour and like, the percentage of your down time and the labour'. During the course of follow-up interviews in 2007, Melanie mentioned that her participation in workplace courses had facilitated her capacity to undertake public presentations: 'I can stand up in front of a load of people and talk or read or something and I could never have done that a long time ago.' She maintains a readiness to take on more responsibility where such opportunities become available: 'As long as I feel capable ... I would probably want to, sort of, you know, take on more responsibility'.

Trevor Woodford revealed that there were substantial job-specific outcomes from the workplace course. The course facilitated his capacity to fill in reports about accidents or incidents of graffiti on the estate. Trevor also asserts that he is 'a lot better at writing letters' and the course has also improved his capacity to undertake formal telephone conversations. During the course of follow-up in-depth interviews in 2007, Trevor Woodford revealed that he had taken on a more supervisory role as a caretaker and had proceeded to undertake various computer courses at the local 'civic centre'. He regarded the course as being useful in preparing him for the next stage of his career as an 'estate officer' which would entail more office administration and contact with contractors.

Responses to the question, 'In terms of your working life, where do you see yourself in two to three years from now if things go according to plan?' in the wider sample taken at in the second sweep of data collection (Time 2, N=264) showed that under half (48.1 per cent) saw themselves as being in the same job in the medium term, while approximately 40 per cent envisaged changes either in job or company. Only 16.7 per cent anticipated promotion within the same company.

Changing learning orientations

The longitudinal nature of the study allows us to track what happens in the working lives of those who are exhibiting changing learning orientations, as work events unfold for the employees who have engaged in workplace basic skills programmes (see Reder and Bynner 2008). While we cannot generalize our analysis of changing learning orientations on the basis of relatively few cases, our careful selection of cases with reference to prior experiences and current work position, together with the step-by-step analysis of interviews enable us to form a coherent picture of the ways in which these adults' orientations to learning have changed through workplace engagements, how they are acting to realize their different personal and work goals, and what happens when external factors such as redundancy intervene. Furthermore, these cases can be benchmarked in relation to characteristics of the wider research samples from which these subsamples are drawn (see Table 11.4).

In changes in learning orientations, distinctions can be drawn between those for whom the changes are seen as specific to current work and to career goals, and those for whom the changes in learning orientation are seen in much wider, personal development terms. For example, Bill Williams, Tracy Beaumont and Mike Philips were motivated to learn by factors that were entirely unrelated to their jobs, while Victoria Appiah, Kathleen Croft, Melanie Taylor and Bennie Thomas embarked on workplace courses in order to pursue a range of learning objectives that were only partially tied to the realm of work. Trevor Woodford stands out as being an individual whose learning goals are most closely tied to the goal of improving work performance and furthering career opportunities.

The career behaviours exhibited by the wider sample of employees who engaged in the workplace basic skills programmes can be categorized as: 'aspirational' (seeking skills development and wider experiences), 'struggling to overcome barriers in day-to-day work' and 'content with status quo at work' (often associated with family and other out-of-work priorities).

The career behaviours of Kathleen Croft, Trevor Woodford and Melanie Taylor can be described as 'aspirational' in nature in so far as these individuals revealed a commitment to skills development and self-improvement that incorporates (to differing degrees) a commitment to advancement within the workplace.

Victoria Appiah, Bill Williams and Mike Philips can be described as being 'content with status quo' in so far as they are content with their current job roles and harbour no plans for promotion. Bill's mockery of his job title (as 'seasoning technician') together with his rather far-sighted and eagerly anticipated perspective on retirement betrays a career disposition in which priorities are invested heavily in life outside work.

Tracy Beaumont and Bennie Thomas may be described as 'struggling to overcome barriers' in so far as both these individuals struggle to fulfil aspects of their

Table 11.4 Summary of learner data

	Kathleen Croft	Victoria Appiah	Tracy Beaumont	Bill Williams	Trevor Woodford	Melanie Taylor	Mike Philips	Bennie Thomas	Overall sample
Gender	F	F	F	M	M	F	M	M	65% Male 35% Female
Age Age at leaving school	b.1956 16	b.1950 16	b.1968 16	b.1961 15	b.1982 16	b.1968 16	b.1953 15	b.1945 15	Mean age: 42* Mean: 17.2 Mode: 16 Median: 16
Qualifications on leaving school	CSEs including English and Maths	No qualifications	None	5 CSEs (not Grade 1)	None	GCSEs	No qualifications	No qualifications	No qual.: 55% Some quals.: 44%
Literacy Level	Level 2 or above	Level 1	Level 1	L2 or above	Level 1	L2 or above	L1	E3	Below E2: 5.5% E2: 3.4%; E3: 19.6; L1: 45.6 L2 or above: 25.7
Likes/Dislikes Job (on a scale of 1–7 with 1=dislike, 7=like a lot)	7	7	7	6	6	6	6	4	5.8
Likes/Dislikes the Course (on a scale of 1–7 with 1=dislike, 7=like a lot)	5	7	7	7	6	7	7	7	6.7

	Kathleen Croft	Victoria Appiah	Tracy Beaumont	Bill Williams	Trevor Woodford	Melanie Taylor	Mike Philips	Bennie Thomas	Overall sample
Likelihood of doing a further course at work	Not very likely	Very likely	Very likely	Very likely	N/K	D/K	D/K not sure but has subsequently embarked on workplace computer course)	Quite likely	Not at all likely 4.6% Not likely 4.9% Quite likely 22.4% Very likely 55.6 D/K-not sure: 12.5%
Likelihood of doing a further course outside of work	Very likely	Not at all likely	Not at all likely	Not at all likely	Quite likely	Very likely (currently doing course)	D/K- not sure	Very likely	Not at all likely 23.3% Not likely 16.5% Quite likely 29.2% Very likely 17.4% D/K-not sure 6.8%
ELLI growth orientation/ challenge	3.5	3.8	3.1	3.1	2.6	3.2	Did not undertake ELLI	3.45	Mean: 3.0
ELLI dependence/ fragility	1.9	2.2	1.7	2.0	2.4	2.2		1.55	Mean: 2.3
ELLI imagination/ creativity	3.3	3.4	2.7	1.5	2.0	3.5		3.4	Mean: 2.6

*Mean age is 42. (18–24 3.5%; 25–34 23%; 35–44 32%; 45–54 24%; 55–64 15%; 65 + 1.5%)

job. Bennie's struggles are related directly to poor literacy and numeracy skills which have been increasingly exposed as a result of the greater use of report writing in the workplace.

The actual career events that can potentially follow on from engagement in learning can be categorized (according to previous work with young adults) as: 'progressive' (promotion, planned move to a better job), 'upwards drift' (gradual enhancement of work, overcoming difficulties, increased responsibilities), 'downwards drift', 'stagnation' and 'interruption'. Trevor Woodford's and Melanie Taylor's career events in the period after their participation on the workplace course may be described as 'progressive' in nature in so far as they have both taken on more supervisory roles. Victoria's career events may be described in terms of 'upwards drift' as participation in workplace courses has bolstered her position at work and increased her confidence. Tracy Beaumont's, Bill Williams' and Mike Philips' career events fall into the category of 'stagnation'. Previous participation in workplace courses has assisted both Kathleen Croft and Bennie Thomas in their current phase of career 'interruption'. Kathleen has drawn on her experience of studying in order to pursue hobbies and embark on further learning whilst she looks after her children. She underlines the significance of her qualifications in allowing her to pursue potential career opportunities in the future. Bennie has drawn upon his experience of workplace learning both in order to support his children's educational development as well as pave the way for a more fulfilled retirement.

Far from being propelled along the long-term predetermined learning trajectories proposed by Gorard et al., these cases show how adult workers can change orientations over time. This underlines the point that orientations are not manifestations of deep-rooted personal characteristics but are shaped by learning and labour market experiences, both positive and negative. Furthermore, these changes are best understood not simply as outcomes of individual agency or of organized programmes, but as part of a social ecology of learning that can operate in and through workplace-provided programmes of the kinds offered under 'Skills for Life'. These findings are also consistent with Evans and Heinz's findings on young adults' transitions, which showed that while trajectories and behaviours had structural foundations in gender and social class, young people could move out of their 'predicted' trajectory and this was dependent upon the interplay of transition behaviours with organizational structures and environmental influences.

There are affordances for (and impediments to) learning in all workplace environments. Some affordances are more accessible and visible than others. The intention of employees to act in particular ways in pursuit of their goals and interests, whether in their jobs or personal lives, makes the affordances for learning more visible to them. Shifting orientations to learning and efforts to compensate for early educational disadvantage allowed the above individuals to recognize and seize affordances for learning within the workplace. The know-how associated with literacy practices such as report writing or finding better ways of expressing oneself, and the confidence of 'knowing that you can' often develop further as the person engages with the opportunity. For example, Trevor Woodford experienced a surge of confidence in response to his enhanced capacity to cope with writing letters and reports at work, which provided enhanced learning opportunities

Table 11.5 Summary of learner trajectories

	Orientation to career	Orientation to learning	Careers
Kathleen Croft	aspirational	general and job-specific	interrupted
Victoria Appiah	content with current position	general and job-specific	horizontal development
Tracy Beaumont	struggling to overcome barriers	general and job-specific	horizontal development
Bill Williams	content with current position	general	horizontal development
Trevor Woodford	aspirational	job-specific	vertical development
Melanie Taylor	aspirational	general and job-specific	vertical development
Mike Philips	content with status	general	horizontal
Bennie Thomas	struggling to overcome barriers	general and job-specific	interrupted

through increased exposure to these duties. The process of making the affordances for learning more visible itself can generate some employees' will to act and use those affordances and new knowledge results. For example, Coopers' open learning centre has developed a wide range of learning opportunities (e.g. online courses and the loan of laptops) that can be flexibly incorporated into the employees' lives at work and home. In shifting orientations to learning, the changing levels of know-how and the confidence that comes from 'knowing that you can' both stimulate action and the seeking out of affordances within and beyond the workplace in the form of further opportunities. Mike Philips' progression to a computer course, Victoria's recent involvement in a creative writing course and Tracy's and Bill's participation in a large number of online courses at Coopers' learning centre are diagnostic of an increased yearning for a wide range of learning opportunities that has grown out of initial participation in workplace courses. Even where redundancy follows, as in the case of Kathleen Croft and Bennie Thomas, the change in learning orientation is sustained, allowing the individuals to adapt to and enhance the quality of their life in these new circumstances.

Conclusion

The above individual case studies, as well as data from the broader sample of learners, reveal a wide range of motivations for learning as well as shifting attitudes towards learning over the lifecourse. The advantages of workplace learning in being more accessible, convenient and free from negative associations of formal learning, have been significant in engaging learners who have been failed by previous forms of provision. The poor experience of school described by such individuals as Tracy Beaumont and Melanie Taylor is mirrored by many other employees in our broader sample. The courses in many cases have responded effectively to a greater proclivity towards learning on the part of employees than in previous stages of their career. Bill's statement that he is now 'older and wiser' and Trevor Woodford's assertion that he is more able to apply himself than he was at school are suggestive of the significance of growing aptitude for learning over the lifecourse. The timing of workplace courses is therefore key to their potential effectiveness in responding to shifting attitudes to learning on the part of the individual since leaving school.

In upholding the significance of literacy and numeracy skills at all levels of the economy, 'Skills for Life' strategy is driven by highly economic imperatives. Yet the motivations for engaging on these courses on the part of employees and the subsequent changes over the lifecourse are rarely focused exclusively on the development of job-specific skills. Whereas Melanie and Trevor are launched on 'aspirational' career trajectories, Bill, Victoria, Tracy, Bennie, and Mike have chosen not to follow a promotional career path. These differences in life, work and career priorities are broadly reflective of the larger sample.

The wide range of motivational factors behind participation in workplace learning (which includes, for example, the wish to learn foreign languages in response to travel abroad as well as assist children who are now embarking on university education) together with individual efforts to overcome early educational disadvantage need to be understood within the broad context of two key features of contemporary society: the salience of 'reflexive' knowledge consumption together with the weakening hold of structural constraints on individual behaviour. Models of adult learning that emphasize the structural determinants of the individual's early life become increasingly problematic in this context.

A 'social ecology' of learning in the field of adult basic skills leads us to consider the relationships between the affordances of the workplace (or those features of the workplace environment that invite people (or act as impediments to them) to engage and learn, the types of knowledge afforded by literacy and numeracy learning (including knowing how and 'knowing that you can') and the agency or intention to act of the individual employee, reflected in their diverse motivations.

These are triangular relationships and mutually interdependent sets of interactions. There are affordances for learning in all workplace environments. Some are more accessible and visible than others. The intention of employees to act in particular ways in pursuit of their goals and interests, whether in their jobs or personal lives, makes the affordances for learning more visible to them. The know-how associated with literacy practices such as report writing or finding better ways of expressing oneself, and the confidence of 'knowing that you can' often develop as the person engages with the opportunity. The process of making the affordances for learning more visible itself can generate some employees' will to act and use those affordances and new knowledge results. In the shifting attitudes to learning, the changing levels of know-how and the confidence that comes from 'knowing that you can' both stimulate action and the seeking out of affordances within and beyond the workplace in the form of further opportunities.

These reflexive relationships, as epitomized by the cases considered in this chapter, illustrate the significance of workplace programmes in supporting shifts in adults' learning orientations. In avoiding an unnecessary stress on the structural constraints of learning trajectories, and encompassing an exploration of the interactions between individual motivations and institutional affordances and constraints, the 'social ecology' approach can help to illuminate an understanding of individual efforts to navigate transitions in the workplace and beyond.

Notes

1   Although Gorard *et al.* acknowledge the lack of weight accorded to individual agency, and have sought to address such a weakness through their work on 'learner identities' (e.g Gorard *et al.* 2001), they still cling to an overarching theoretical model in which individual choices fall within structural determinants that are predictable from the individual's early life.
2   All the individual and organizational names cited in this chapter are pseudonyms.
3   Learndirect is a national, government initiative to provide online learning courses which can be undertaken at learning centres or through individual study on computers at home.
4   See also Barton *et al.* (2008: 22) who underline the effect of more stringent regulatory frameworks in necessitating higher level literacy skills amongst employees in certain sectors (such as care work).

Bibliography

Ananiadou K., Jenkins A. and Wolf, A. (2003) *The Benefits to Employers of Raising Workforce Basic Skills Levels: a Review of the Literature*, London: National Research and Development Centre.

Barton, D., Tusting, K., Hodge, R. and Appleby, Y. (2008) *Learners' Experience of Work*, London: National Research and Development Centre for Adult Literacy and Numeracy.

Beck, U. (1992) *Risk Society: Towards a New Modernity*, London: Sage.

Edwards, R. (1998) 'Flexibility, reflexivity and reflection in the contemporary workplace', *International Journal of Lifelong Education*, 17: 377–88.

Evans, K. and Heinz, W. (1993) 'Studying forms of transition methodological innovation in a cross-national study of labour market entry in England and Germany', *Comparative Education*, 49: 145–58.

—— (1994) *Becoming Adults in England and Germany*, London and Bonn: Anglo-German Foundation.

Evans, K., Behrens, M. and Kaluza, J. (1999) 'Risky voyages: navigating changes in the organisation of work and learning in Eastern Germany', *Comparative Education*, 35: 131–50.

Evans, K., Waite, E. and Admasachew, L. (2008) 'Enhancing Skills for Life? Workplace learning and adult basic skills', in S. Reder and J. Bynner, *Tracking Adult Numeracy: Findings from Longitudinal Research*, London: Routledge.

Giddens, A. (1990) *The Consequences of Modernity*, Cambridge: Polity Press.

Gorard, S. and Rees, G. (2002) *Creating a Learning Society?* Bristol: The Policy Press.

Gorard, S., Rees, G. and Fevre, R. (1999) 'Learning trajectories: analysing the determinants of workplace learning', paper presented at the ESRC seminar series Working to Learn, University of Surrey, June 1999.

Gorard, S., Rees, G., Fevre, R. and Furlong, J. (1998) 'Learning trajectories: travelling towards a learning society?' *International Journal of Lifelong Education*, 17: 400–10.

Gorard, S., Rees, G., Fevre, R. and Welland, T. (2001) 'Lifelong learning trajectories: some voices of those "in transit"', *International Journal of Lifelong Education*, 20: 169–87.

Reder, S. and Bynner, J. (2008) *Tracking Adult Literacy and Numeracy Skills: Findings from Longitudinal Research*, London/New York: Routledge.

Scheeres, H. (2004) 'The textualised workplace', *Reflect*, 1: 22.

12 Older workers' transitions in work-related learning, careers and identities

Jenny Bimrose and Alan Brown

Introduction

This chapter examines how older workers, aged over 45, have moved through different work and learning contexts as their careers and identities have developed over time. The strategic biographies of five older workers are traced, as they responded to the challenges of continuing to develop their work-related learning, careers and identities. These five have been chosen from a research sample of over 100 individuals in order to illuminate three broad patterns of response: up-skilling, re-skilling and disengagement. The cases demonstrate the value of learning while working as this helped individuals keep their skills, knowledge and competences up-to-date and maintain a positive disposition towards learning. Access to opportunities for learning and development is crucially important, though some individuals were much more proactive than others in taking advantage of these opportunities.

Older people are becoming an ever-larger proportion of the population and recent employment legislation has been in part designed to encourage older workers to continue working, with workers over 65 having the 'right to request' a constructive dialogue with their employer about that option. However, without a cultural change that values older workers' contribution there could be huge waste of human resource and potential (Fitzpatrick 2006). Distinctions between work and retirement are also likely to become increasingly blurred by the notion of semi-retirement as a way of easing the transition from work to full retirement, with employees moving into self-employment, taking short-term contracts, reducing their working hours or moving away from their previous main line of work (Humphrey *et al.* 2003). So with changing expectations of how long many people will work, and as the workforce ages, there are challenges of supporting the continuing education and development of older workers, as workers may need to maintain a set of work-related competences and manage effective work transitions for much longer than has been customary in the past.

Research interviews were used to construct 'strategic biographies' of the learning and development of over 100 individuals, who were working or had worked for long periods in the engineering, telecommunications or ICT industries. These occupational settings were chosen for two reasons. First, they were relatively knowledge-intensive, with the assumption that workers would be expected or encouraged to update their work-related skills, knowledge and understanding. Second, some respondents had pointed out that it was sometimes difficult to enter, or progress within, some forms of employment in these sectors once you were over 40 because of employer prejudice – especially from a position of being unemployed. This finding is in line with other reports of age discrimination (Age Concern 2005).

From these biographies five exemplars of individuals' 'strategic biographies' of learning and development were chosen to represent different approaches to up-skilling, re-skilling or disengagement, which illustrate the role of individual agency in managing change. Some broader policy implications are also considered.

Work-related learning, careers and identities of older workers

Brown (1997) identified the importance of the degree of challenge in work activities, the nature of interactions with other people at work and motivation and commitment in how individuals viewed their developing work-related identities. For older workers the biographical dimension of an individual's past and their current understanding of their past experiences of work, learning, careers and identities (their career story) was also likely to be significant. The dominant representation of the work-related learning, careers and identities of many of the 100 older workers interviewed was that they identified with their work, although sometimes with reservations. However, in view of the attention often given to those facing substantive problems, it is important to emphasise that our research identified many older workers who not only strongly identified with their work, but who also saw learning and development as a 'normal' and continuing part of their job.

In order to understand the approaches to work-related learning and development of older workers it is useful to break up their biographies into different time periods or segments and to identify those phases when there is more or less intensive learning and development. This is because the extent with which workers engage in learning varies over time, so it is important not to assume that individuals follow a single trajectory. It is also important to recognise that individuals can and do engage differently with learning and development over time, with people's overall skill development moving between periods of relative stability, incremental development, intensive development and decay. Furthermore, different sets of skills, knowledge and understanding could be moving in different directions at the same time. The advantage of looking at learning in different phases is that this could be used to represent the extent of changes in development of particular skill sets rather than just overall development – with development being more or less intense at different times.

In our research, the focus was on substantive learning: that is, learning that produces a significant change in skills, knowledge, understanding, values, attitudes or behaviour, including in individuals' approach to learning. When workers engaged in substantive learning and development, their work-related learning could be represented as being primarily concerned with up-skilling (within a current occupation and/or organisation) or re-skilling (linked to an actual or proposed career change) with the step change in development of work-related skills, knowledge and understanding in either approach being intensive or incremental. Additionally, workers could be disengaged from the whole idea of work-related learning and development. These patterns of behaviour can be conceptualised in terms of strategic action. Analysis of the interviews highlighted how the relationship between older workers and their work-related roles could be represented in terms of their patterns of strategic action across a range of structural, cultural and social contexts (compare Pollard *et al.* 2000). Their experiences could be mapped in terms of their patterns of relationships, orientation and adaptive response to work and it was possible to trace the dynamic development of individuals' characteristic repertoires of strategic action – their 'strategic biographies' (Brown 2004).

Identifying different forms of strategic action did help give meaning and shape to our interviewees' career histories by outlining some typical and relatively coherent repertoires of strategic response to the challenges posed by the development of their work-related learning, careers and identities. The two proactive responses from individuals of up-skilling and re-skilling could make use of primarily intensive or incremental development and examples of workers representing each of these four trajectories will be presented. The fifth case illustrates where an individual became progressively disengaged from any attempt to develop his work-related skills and knowledge

Intensive up-skilling

Aaron is in his mid-fifties and works for a small specialist aircraft and submarine engineering company which employs 60 people and where technically qualified workers play a key role. Five years previously, Aaron, a chief inspector at the time, was appointed as a 'change agent' to implement an approach to continuous process improvement that was being supported by the lead company in their supply chain network where Aaron previously worked as an inspector for 10 years. The 'change agent' training and subsequent application of what had been learned involved Aaron in the development of new techniques, training of other workers, changes to the organisation of work and organisational culture that required considerable skills in the 'management of change'.

Aaron had completed an engineering apprenticeship, but the nature of his technically demanding work and progression through a series of jobs with increasing responsibility meant he was used to learning while working and was not daunted by being given highly challenging work that was pivotal for the future of the company. The company had no hesitation in giving this key role to a worker in his fifties, even though he had not engaged in formal education and training for over twenty-five years. Rather, Aaron's depth and breadth of technical understanding, work-process knowledge and problem-solving abilities meant he was considered ideal for this key role.

The 'change agent' training had led to personal development and Aaron commented: 'I have become more interested in problem solving. [...] I still want to carry on learning and gain further qualifications.' One of the key aspects of Aaron's role was to facilitate the learning of others when cascading the approach to continuous improvement within the company and this required a deep commitment to continuing learning and development. It is particularly striking that for Aaron the greatest development in his skills, knowledge and understanding at work had taken place in his fifties. The training (a one-week workshop plus a series of follow-up one-day workshops and application visits to other companies in the supply chain) was very helpful, but the greatest development came through meeting the challenges associated with his day-to-day work of implementing continuous process improvement over several years. These work activities, by their very nature, were highly challenging and required utilisation of a full range of skills, knowledge and experience from all those involved in the development teams that Aaron had to facilitate. Additionally, the resulting transformation of how Aaron viewed his own continuing learning and development meant that he was going to study for further qualifications.

Four broader issues are noteworthy, here. First, learning while working is often the most painless way to develop skills, knowledge and understanding, as learning and development are fully integrated with working. Second, this case highlights the importance of not pathologising the problems that older workers face in learning new skills. Aaron and his contemporaries were chosen as 'change agents' because they had extensive work-process knowledge and strongly identified both with the company and their jobs, and were able to operate in cross-disciplinary and cross-hierarchical work teams. Third, being involved in substantive learning and development often acted as a spur to a transformation in the self-perception and self-confidence of older workers. Fourth, the interaction of training and creating opportunities for significant learning experiences at work meant it was possible to support learning and innovation in small companies, where traditionally it has often been difficult.

The developmental nature of work activities undertaken by Aaron influenced his positive orientation to learning and development and his commitment to up-skilling, which, over time, had been largely accomplished through incremental skill development, with learning being seen as a 'natural' part of work. Yet Aaron has also had periods of intensive up-skilling, when changing jobs, getting promoted and acting as a 'change agent'. Over his work career there were four distinct periods (each lasting a few years) when work presented a particularly strong learning challenge and resulted in intensive up-skilling. The rest of the time, learning and development continued incrementally. This differential pacing is important in relation to the policy rhetoric about lifelong learning – it may be more helpful to acknowledge substantive learning is often periodic rather continuous over a career. Even in a long career with continuing technical development in a knowledge-intensive industry, Aaron had often not been required to make any special effort to up-skill. Learning while working on challenging activities, together with a commitment to work, made this type of learning seem routine. The work activities themselves were challenging and Aaron experienced a sense of achievement in meeting these challenges.

Aaron's work activities involved multidisciplinary, inter-organisational and non-hierarchical teamwork as well as rich and varied interactions with other employees, managers, suppliers, customers and members of the supply chain and his own personal networks. Such relationships provided support, recognition that his expertise was valued and an opportunity to support the learning of others – a role he relished both at work and in his private life (he had taught chess for many years).

In relation to his work identity, Aaron exhibited very high organisational and occupational commitment. Everyone recognised that he possessed valuable expertise, based on his extensive work-process knowledge, and this contributed to Aaron being highly motivated and exhibiting a strong attachment to and identification with work. Overall, Aaron's work activities, interactions and identities acted powerfully together in concert producing a strong sense of agency in his approach to learning and development. He was committed not only to up-skilling, but also to broader aspects of learning and development.

Substantive up-skilling does not necessarily occur in the workplace; some individuals engaged in education-based mid-career professional development. For instance, some older workers in engineering, telecommunications or ICT had completed Master's degrees or other qualifications in their thirties or forties. Some other interviewees, however, who were also following strong work-based up-skilling trajectories, did so incrementally, through career progression that involved switching companies and/or jobs in order to broaden their experience, as well as taking on more challenging roles. One case of a person following such a trajectory will now be presented.

Incremental up-skilling over a long period

Substantive up-skilling can be incremental, where an individual, after completing initial education and training, relies for their learning and development almost exclusively on meeting changing requirements at work. An example of someone following this trajectory was Cliff, who had progressed from being an apprentice, technician, production engineer, claims adviser and had moved ultimately into a management position. Cliff was in his early fifties and had been with the same company, a car and truck manufacturer, for well over 30 years. He, however, had adapted to work in the company rather than maintaining a strong work identity. He completed an apprenticeship, continued learning on and off the job, eventually gaining a Higher National Certificate in Engineering and became a production engineer. Cliff then worked as a junior, then senior, claims assessor, deciding how much it would cost to repair company vehicles under warranty, authorising repairs (or writing off the vehicles) and deciding the value of a claim under warranty. Cliff was promoted further through a succession of management posts in merchandising, sales and marketing. However, by the time Cliff became a manager he did not identify with the company, no longer had a (technical) occupational attachment, and had no sense of needing or wishing to take any further qualifications. Cliff felt that once you reached management level the company tended to be quite ruthless in terms of what they expected from you: 'They certainly don't care about their employees' domestic and family circumstances.'

While Cliff routinely worked in three different locations for the company that he could travel to from home, three times he had also been relocated to offices over a hundred miles away. Particularly when drafted into positions such as regional manager, Cliff felt he had no choice but to agree to these relocations, even though this meant living away from home for between eighteen months and three years at a time. He felt keenly that whilst he had made sacrifices, the company had gained: 'You have no social life, so you might as well work all hours God sends.' Family was seen as unimportant by the company: 'Don't worry about the family. Just relocate and get the job started.' The only concession was leaving work early on Friday and arriving a bit later on Monday, but only when no meetings were scheduled.

He had no intention of 'putting the company first', as did some of his colleagues. Instead, he preferred to put his children first, trying to ensure they had stability whilst at school. This had become 'a bone of contention with his manager'. He had been told that he needed to be mobile to get ahead in a large company, because: 'only a very few – the three per cent who are high fliers – get their careers planned and for the rest it is a scramble'. Not only was he under pressure to relocate, where and when the company required, it was not always easy to get back into a preferred job on return from a temporary assignment. Fortuitously, one of the temporary relocations had led to a further permanent promotion in the local area. He was under no illusions that the company was just interested in getting the job done well. He received no support and dealt with problems alone.

Cliff had built a career over time with the company, but based upon adaptation to, rather than identification with, the company. He made extensive use of formal part-time education opportunities early on while developing his technical career, but since then a succession of managerial jobs, including temporary assignments, had provided plenty of opportunities for learning while working, extending and broadening his skills and knowledge base. Cliff had made a conscious decision not to engage with his work in a way that would maximise the likelihood he would be promoted. No 'extra' effort was put into either work activities or interactions. Although he worked hard, this had still created tensions with his manager. This constrained commitment, coupled with a critical understanding of how the company 'used' people, meant Cliff's sense of identity was strongly family-oriented rather than work-based. Additionally, Cliff did not want to undertake any additional learning and development activities above the minimum necessary to do his work effectively, even though this made him dependent upon the company since he knew he would struggle to find another job with the same level and status. Then again, work was not a central life interest, with Cliff feeling that he would be able to cope with any change in status. This constrained commitment and incremental up-skilling meant that Cliff had not used potential opportunities as a platform for further learning and development. The next case provides a contrast to this approach by illustrating how some older workers engage intensively in re-skilling.

Intensive re-skilling

Up-skilling involves individuals remaining within a single occupation, or following clearly signposted progression paths from a particular occupation – as illustrated in the two cases presented above. Some older workers, however, may have already embarked upon, or are seeking, a major career change, that involves re-skilling (that is, the development of skill sets different from those they already possess). Intensive re-skilling usually involves a major career reorientation. Often, this requires considerable personal commitment, with either a major shift in identity or a recasting of current identities.

Sally is in her late forties and works as a production manager in a car components factory. Although she is only a few years younger than Cliff, she represents a stark contrast in her approach to work-related learning. Sally did not become very purposeful about her own career development until after the age of 30. Initially, she completed a Sports Science degree, worked in outdoor pursuits for a year and then trained as a PE teacher. However, her teaching career lasted less than a year: 'I discovered I didn't like kids!' Next, she worked in a local authority leisure facility for five years. On leaving that post, she planned to live abroad, but this did not work out. She needed work, so took temporary office jobs for a couple of years. One of these jobs was with a small automotive components manufacturer. She took the job because she needed the work and it seemed to be a reasonable company.

Starting as a temporary clerical worker, Sally soon got a permanent job, in 'customer scheduling', calculating and costing customers' requirements, keeping track of what was being produced and what had been dispatched. Sally worked in this department for three years, but found the work undemanding as it was not utilising all her skills, nor giving her the type of challenge or responsibility for which she felt ready. She was, however, good at her job and was soon promoted to 'Head of Logistics', managing six clerical staff. Then in her mid thirties, she had not had any formal work-related education or training, having acquired the relevant work-process knowledge from the work itself. Her work activities and interactions were still not personally challenging, but she determined to use this opportunity to start to build a career. No company training had been forthcoming, despite the promotion to a supervisory role. So she embarked on a self-directed approach to her own learning and development. At her own instigation, she asked to go to the head office (in Germany) for a two-week period to orientate herself to the work of the company as a whole. She was given the time, but left to structure her own programme. Walking around the factory, talking to people helped her to find out what was being done, by whom and for what reasons.

Sally was promoted twice in quick succession – first to logistics specialist and then to production manager for a major customer group, with responsibility for resourcing the production and delivery of orders. Even though her (then) bosses encouraged her to apply for these posts, she experienced problems: 'I encountered huge difficulties as I had no knowledge of engineering production whatsoever. I knew nothing of production planning or engineering prioritising. Nothing!'

Her first new post involved managing 100 permanent, mostly full-time, staff on a three-shift system, plus seven support staff based in the office. She ordered and controlled all materials, as well as having responsibility for the production process itself, staff management and customer liaison. The challenges of the new job were considerable. Sally had had no substantive training relevant to her new job: 'My skills acquisition at this time was mainly on-the-job; finding out as I went along.' On her own initiative, she had enrolled for two evening classes: one on the Japanese view of the auto industry; the other on leadership and self-management.

The company did, eventually, provide training opportunities to help her cope with her new responsibilities, and as she began to 'get a handle' on her job she decided to do an Engineering Master's degree to give her a greater understanding of the technical underpinning of her management role: 'I wanted to understand what lay beneath what I was seeing on the shop floor and what I was controlling in my job.' The company paid for the course and much of what she learned was relevant at three levels – business, technical and operational. She had now fully grown into the job as a production manager.

When Sally reflects on her career she says: 'My career has gone every which way. It has gone differently to what might have been expected. I think there was a lot of luck involved in finding myself as a temp at my present company – being in the right place at the right time.' She is very satisfied with her salary and enjoys her job, although there are frustrations linked to working in what is still a man's world. 'It's not so much a glass ceiling as a huge steel ceiling!' If it had not been for gender prejudice, she felt she could have done much more. Indeed, the prevailing environment continues to constrain her: 'I find myself coping with it by taking on some of the male attitudes, and this makes me feel guilty. I think I confront it with aggressive behaviour, and people don't always understand why this is happening.'

Sally had never expected to enter the engineering world. 'The last place I wanted to work was a factory [...] but what I have come to realise is that it doesn't much matter what the workplace is, or where it is, or what it makes. Most of the processes for getting something resourced, produced and delivered are the same.' She is still looking to develop her skills, maybe in assertiveness to deal with the gender problem: 'some influencing skills training is probably what I need'. She also wants to follow up on work she did on the Master's around leadership and dealing with frustration: 'I need to learn how to deal with getting shouted down if I confront issues around gender discrimination.'

For the last ten years, Sally has been very proactive in building her career. She has exhibited a powerful commitment to re-skilling, intensively, when presented with new challenges and has achieved a great deal. However, she would not have wanted to miss doing Sports Science, being at university and working in the leisure industry. Sally's approach to learning and development made use of learning while working, major education-based technical training, taking formal training opportunities and being self-directed in seeking out other learning opportunities. In this case, although work activities, interactions and identity were strongly in alignment, these were being held together by a strong sense of personal agency in pulling everything together and driving her career forward. To return, briefly, to a comparison with Cliff, it is interesting that a mid-career change had given Sally an enthusiasm to drive her career forwards, while at more or less the same age, after over thirty years in the same industry, Cliff was seeking to wind his career down.

Incremental re-skilling over a long period

Some older workers had changed career frequently. Here, re-skilling typically occurred more incrementally, particularly where an individual was developing a career strategically, with a strong attachment to their own development. One example of this was Edward, who graduated in engineering and worked for an engineering company, but then moved every five years or so. These moves were into different areas that required the development of different skill sets: contract electronics, technical management, supply chain development and general management. They also required Edward to work in a wide range of different organisational contexts.

Edward was in his early fifties. He had completed an engineering degree and while at university was sponsored by a large company, for which he then worked for seven years. He was involved in a range of project work, also undertaking a manufacturing management conversion programme for engineers. Then he returned to another division, to a job in logistics and supply chain management. Edward, however, had become increasingly interested in electronics and decided, strategically, that he wanted to work in the expanding electronics industry. He worked in contract electronics for a couple of years, learning while working on different contracts in a variety of different settings. One of the contracts involved working with a global IT company and eventually he moved with the contract as the company took the work in-house. He stayed for two years, and then joined a large company as a supply chain manager. The company expanded considerably through mergers and acquisitions and, initially his IT expertise coupled with his proven ability in business development and experience of leading project teams, had been rather rare. However, since then (partly as a consequence of rationalisations following mergers) the standards of the company had gone up. He had been told: 'You're working with some very, very capable people, very motivated people, and you have to work hard to keep ahead or to keep up to them. This is a competitive environment.'

Edward was highly committed to his work and regarded the company as a 'very good employer, a good company to work for, I enjoy working here and they reward you well'. He transferred to London where his work involved being part of specially formed project teams with an international remit. He increased his experience in areas that were business oriented, rather than technical, although he recognised he has much less international market experience than others in the commercial field. On the technical operations side, Edward had gone as far as he was likely to go, because his previous manager, who had 'sponsored his career development', had left the company. Politically, he was then 'badged as one of his men'.

Edward represents a classic example of a strategic careerist, with decisions to enter and exit a career in IT being taken for career-related reasons. His progression has also been strongly linked to a willingness to engage with learning in a wide variety of forms: formal education; self-directed learning; training; learning while working; and particularly learning through taking on new challenges. The re-skilling aspect of his career has been important, because on at least three occasions he consciously chose to follow a particular route, rather than follow a clear up-skilling path, as he judged that the latter would narrow his options.

Both types of predominantly work-based re-skilling, intensive or incremental, have a strategic dimension. Because the re-skilling of both Sally and Edward was occurring from a base of high-level performance in their current work, with their new skill sets in great demand, the re-skilling was relatively risk-free. In contrast, major career change for older workers that requires a disjunction from existing employment represents a challenge of a different order. Where demand for existing skill sets changes and/ or there is a degree of prejudice against older workers, then individuals who have become, for whatever reason, disengaged from work-related learning and development for a significant period of time are in a vulnerable labour market position. This is the type of the case we will now examine.

Disengagement

John, in his mid fifties, left school at 16 with good qualifications. He then completed a telecommunications technician apprenticeship with a major telecommunications company and worked as a telecommunications engineer for just over a year. He was then offered a job with another major 'blue chip' company, this time in the growing IT industry. His new skill set was in demand and he was very well paid. A decade after leaving school, in his mid twenties, he was more highly paid than many graduates.

John's career initially went very well. He learned through a mixture of on-the-job learning and short periods of company-specific training. He became a senior engineer, working from a service centre. A couple of years later, however, the company decided to withdraw from offering support services in favour of independent contractors. John then worked for the company as a trainer of these new independent contractors: 'I suppose I was really working myself out of a job.' At this time, he demonstrated a strong organisational identity, shown by his willingness to move over to a training role and an expectation that the company would find him new employment.

When the company closed down the service centre he was offered either relocation to the head office or a fairly generous redundancy package. He chose the latter because he did not want to relocate for family reasons and he thought he would find alternative employment reasonably quickly, even if not at his previous salary level. In fact, it proved very difficult for John to get another job: 'although I was only just 40, and there quite a lot of jobs advertised, many employers thought I was too old for work in IT'. In a discussion of older workers' employment transitions, John's case is interesting, since he was considered 'too old', just after he reached 40 and despite reasonably high levels of initial skills training and continuing professional development. Subsequently, his career spiralled downwards and he became progressively more disengaged from any attempt to return to highly skilled work.

Eventually he was able to find work with the computing services arm of a large entertainment conglomerate. The work was not attractive, repairing computerised systems in pubs and clubs, and the salary was half what he had earned previously. 'It was 10.30 p.m. one New Year's Eve and I was working repairing a computerised till in a pub miles from home. It was hot, noisy and crowded, and there were strobe lights flashing while I was trying to solder a connection, and I was supposed to be at a party somewhere else and I suddenly thought: I've had enough of this!' John was disillusioned, so quit this line of work altogether. His company pension was at a level that meant he only had to do some work to top this up to a level on which he could live and 'give myself enough time to go fishing'.

From this time on, John did not feel he had an active occupational identity: he simply saw himself as a 'former computer maintenance technician'. John's commitment to work had been quite high, but learning at work was only ever directly linked to the evolving job. When the structure of work activities initially changed, he was able to develop 'bridging skills' that enabled him to train other people for a couple of years. Then came the complete break from his former work and as soon as he was no longer linked to the organisation, he had no further engagement with substantive work-related learning and development. After a spell out of work, he tried to continue in the role of computer maintenance technician in a different context. However, by this time the status, pay, conditions and most importantly the nature of the work had all changed fundamentally. The skill element had declined significantly, as computers had become much more reliable and technological change so rapid that if anything major went wrong it was almost always cheaper and more effective to replace it. He was then working in a maintenance role. His skill set was declining, and his work commitment and identity were becoming eroded.

Subsequently, he had other jobs, but these did not make any use of his technical skills or knowledge. He had worked as a taxi driver, mainly at night, in the suburbs of London. The work was challenging in a completely different way from the early part of his career: 'It was very high stress – you could have a fight every night if you wanted.' He also worked part-time as a forklift truck driver – his major reason for choosing the work being that it was local. He was effectively semi-retired in his early fifties. Personal circumstances, age discrimination and being tied to a particular geographical location made it very difficult for John to recover from a major career setback. From then on work was always about short-term adaptation rather than identification, and other events in his life reinforced a feeling that you had to 'make do the best you can in the face of events you cannot control'.

Where demand for existing skill sets changes and/or there is a degree of prejudice against older workers then individuals who, for whatever reason, have become disengaged from work-related learning and development for a significant period of time are in a vulnerable labour market position. This is the territory explored by Sennett (1998): there is an initial high commitment to work with a large company; but the major form of engagement with learning is through learning at work, with the expectation that the company will look after you. However, when circumstances change individuals can find themselves locked into work identities in decline. Then both work identity and work commitment start to slip away.

Discussion

Like all workers, those over 45 may be faced with changes in the patterns of employment, transformation of some occupations and changes in the organisation of work. For some, their work may remain essentially the same, with the extent of change easily accommodated within normal patterns of learning while working. For others, even though their work changes considerably, this might be easily accommodated by means traditional to the organisation or occupation, particularly if the job itself requires considerable learning while working. For a third group whose careers develop with increasing responsibility and challenge then engaging in substantive learning is a central component of their career. Problems are most likely to arise in two particular contexts. First, when demands at work change suddenly after a long period of relative stability and workers feel they have not engaged in substantive learning for some considerable time. Second, learning new skills can seem challenging when workers are faced with a major career transition, particularly if they are not in work or are about to be made redundant.

Most of the exemplary cases discussed and the wider set of biographies repeatedly demonstrated the value of learning while working in helping individuals keep their skills, knowledge and competences up-to-date and maintain a positive disposition towards learning. Access to opportunities for learning and development emerged as important. To some extent, these opportunities were more likely to be made available to individuals showing a strong commitment to work. However, it was also clear that some individuals were much more proactive than others in taking advantage of these opportunities. Further, those who were proactive in this sphere seemed more likely to take advantage of other learning opportunities. Even those who had not engaged in much substantive learning for some time could find that when they were involved in substantive learning and development, this often acted as a spur to a transformation in how they perceived themselves and what they believed they could do.

From our research, issues around the capacities and potential of older workers because of their age never arose directly, although reasons for reduced capacity were sometimes health-related. Many respondents were active in their own learning and development, although this was easiest if directly linked to learning while working. There are still, however, issues around cultural norms and values with a number of participants commenting that it could be difficult to recover from a career setback because of the perceptions of others that older workers could not adapt so easily as younger workers. Most of our interviewees had 'successful careers', but even some of them pointed out that it was possible to find your skills were no longer in demand and that with increasing age it became more difficult to overcome a career setback.

Many workers also exhibited a strong sense of attachment to their work, although others had found it was possible to continue in work as a form of short-term or long-term adjustment. In most circumstances, strong attachment to work brings considerable benefits, including a sense of career stability and having a career 'anchor'. However, there is the question as to whether a strong commitment to work also acts to hold individuals in 'chains', preventing them from attempting an appropriate career transition until it becomes more and more difficult to achieve. One way of considering an occupational identity to which we are adjusted and that is relatively stable over a period of time is as a psychological 'home'. 'Home' in this context is a 'familiar environment, a place where we know our way around, and above all, where we feel secure' (Abhaya 1997: 2). Viewed in this way it is easy to understand the sense of loss and dislocation that people may feel when they are made redundant, with little prospect of regaining their former occupational identity (Sennett 1998). On the other hand, religion, literature and film abound with stories of people 'breaking free' and 'loosening attachments to "homes" of many kinds, be they psychological, social or ideological' (Abhaya 1997: 2). In this sense, after a period of stability, an occupational identity may come to be viewed as a confinement from which the individual longs to escape. That is, what is initially experienced as interesting and exciting may, with the passage of time, lead to 'a sense of profound dissatisfaction with the comfortable limits' (Abhaya 1997: 8) of the existing way of life.

Dewey (1916) saw an occupation as giving direction to life activities and as a concrete representation of continuity: a 'home' with clear psychological, social and ideological 'anchors'. What should be of concern is the process for some individuals where the 'anchors' become progressively perceived as 'chains' that hold individuals close to their current roles, even if these are in decline. Interestingly, a strong attachment to a current work role could act as a career 'anchor' from which it was possible for individuals to continue their career development (e.g. through their willingness to engage in 'up-skilling' activities). However, where attachment was acting more as a 'chain' it often required an external stimulus such as a guidance intervention to help individuals to manage their career transitions, in some cases by viewing aspects of their current skill sets as 'anchors' that could be taken with them on a journey and utilised in a new setting, even if other aspects of their occupational or organisational identities were left behind.

The exemplary cases highlight how individuals are actors who shape important aspects of their own occupational trajectories and careers, with many individuals taking an active role as coordinators of their personal work biographies. A five-year complementary longitudinal study into the career transitions of adults indicates how older workers' biographies often involved elements of growth, learning, recovery or development as individuals moved between images of what they were, had been in the past or thought they might become, thereby emphasising biographical continuity (Bimrose *et al.* 2006; Bimrose and Barnes 2006). While major dislocations in individual careers could obviously be traumatic, where individuals had been able to construct coherent career narratives and 'move on', this had proved to be psychologically valuable. Career guidance often played an important role in that process.

From the research findings, there are clear indications for policy direction in the future. For example, policy could encourage individuals to engage in mid-career learning and development and give individuals the right to independent careers guidance after working for twenty years, in order to help them develop coherent career narratives that may help them thrive rather than just survive in what may be another twenty years of work. Additionally, workplaces and educational institutions could consider how best they can effectively support older workers' learning, development and work transitions. This could include identifying appropriate learning strategies and pedagogic practices that will assist the development and maintenance of older workers' capacities for working, learning, development and transitions. There is also a case for identifying good practice in policy measures, workplace practices and educational programmes in support of the continuing development of older workers' workplace competence and learning dispositions. Finally, the right to a 'career break' of, say, six months to be taken at any time after twenty-five years in work would support and encourage adults to remain active in managing their own career development.

The five cases outlined exemplify different patterns of behaviour in the development of work-related learning, careers and identities. The relationship between individuals and their work-related roles were represented as patterns of strategic action in their patterns of relationships, orientation and adaptive response to work. Two dimensions of individuals' response to challenges of development of their learning, careers and identities were apparent from their narrative biographies: attachment to work and the nature of the opportunities they had for, and their approach to, learning and development. Interestingly a strong attachment, or adjustment, to a current work role could act as a career 'anchor' from which it was possible for individuals to continue their career development (e.g. through willingness to engage in 'up-skilling') or else as a 'chain' that restricted their perceived freedom of action (e.g. through unwillingness to engage in substantive 'up-skilling' or 're-skilling'). Complementary research evidence provides a strong indication that guidance can help individuals manage career transitions by helping clients view their current skill sets as 'anchors' that can be taken with them on a journey and utilised in a new setting, rather than as 'chains' that hold them close to their current roles (Bimrose *et al.* 2006; Bimrose and Barnes 2007).

Bibliography

Abhaya, D. (1997) *Leaving Home: E .M. Forster and the Pursuit of Higher Values*, Birmingham: Windhorse Publications.

Age Concern (2005) 'Report finds that ageism is the most common form of discrimination in Britain', *ReportAge: England's Political Bulletin*, 11(8). Available online at www.ageconcern.org.uk/AgeConcern/Documents/reportage_oct_05.pdf (accessed 29 April 2008).

Bimrose, J. and Barnes, S.-A. (2007) *Navigating the Labour Market: Career Decision Making and the Role of Guidance*, Coventry: Warwick Institute for Employment Research and Department for Education and Skills.

Bimrose, J., Barnes, S.-A. and Hughes, D. (2006) *Developing Career Trajectories In England: the Role of Effective Guidance*. Coventry: Warwick Institute for Employment Research and Department for Education and Skills.

Brown, A. (1997) 'A dynamic model of occupational identity formation', in A. Brown (ed.) *Promoting Vocational Education and Training: European Perspectives*, Tampere: University of Tampere.

—— (2004) 'Engineering identities', *Career Development International*, 9: 245–73.

Dewey, J. (1916) *Democracy and Education. An Introduction to the Philosophy of Education* (1966 edn), New York: Free Press.

Fitzpatrick, J. (2006) 'Preparing for a new age', speech on the Age Regulations, CBI Conference, 19 June 2006.

Humphrey, A., Costigan, P., Pickering, K., Stratford, N. and Barnes, M. (2003) *Factors Affecting the Labour Market Participation of Older Workers*, Department for Work and Pensions Research Report No. 200, London: DWP.

Pollard, A., Filer, A. and Furlong, J., (2000) *Identity and Secondary Schooling: a Longitudinal Ethnography of Pupil Careers Phase 5*, full report of research activities, Swindon: ESRC.

Sennett, R., (1998) *The Corrosion of Character: the Personal Consequences of Work in the New Capitalism*, New York: Norton.

13 Managing and supporting the vulnerable self

Kathryn Ecclestone

Introduction

Depictions of educational transitions as discernible events, experienced in a linear sequence of progression through funding, institutional and achievement structures, create normative expectations of higher levels of participation, retention and achievement of formal qualifications. In parallel, new labels emerge for those failing to make successful transitions as, variously, disaffected, disengaged, vulnerable and at risk, thereby treating transitions as problems experienced by individuals and isolating them from broader structural conditions.

A view that transitions need to be both managed more closely and supported more sensitively for better personal, work or educational outcomes creates new formal and informal roles alongside those of 'mediators of learning', 'learning managers' and 'learning support workers', retention officers in colleges, mentors and coaches, and guidance and advice workers. These roles also involve parents, siblings and a growing number of children, young people and adults trained in counselling and mentoring to act as 'buddies' to peers, new or younger students. In various ways, those acting as what we might term 'transition workers' help others to simplify the navigation of new structures and systems, contribute to procedures for initial assessment and tracking progression through the system, and support the emotional or psychological demands of transitions.

In a policy context of concern about transition, research in this area reveals very diverse perspectives about what transitions are, how and why they are problematic, and about which groups experience particular difficulty in navigating them. There are different views about whether institutions and government agencies, teachers or support workers, or individuals experiencing transitions are the main actors in managing them. There is also disagreement about the best sort of curriculum content, assessment and support systems and institutional structures needed to manage and support transitions.

Different ideas about the nature, effects and management of transition depend on the emphasis given, explicitly or implicitly, to the respective roles of identity, agency and structure. (Of course, outside research, these concepts are rarely used directly.) It is noticeable that contemporary research interest tends to prioritise identity as a major concern, reflecting a shift in both interest and emphasis over the past ten years or so. In many education studies, researchers often acknowledge the effects of class, gender and race, and economic and social conditions but they often do so in a general reference to the importance of environment or context. Only two chapters in this book highlight structural conditions as a key shaper of identity and agency and point to the inequalities of transition for particular groups.

This chapter extends some ideas I began to develop in another paper on transitions (Ecclestone 2009a). It draws on some of the contributions to this book and on other studies. It explores the implications of different strategies for managing and supporting transitions and relates them to a broader rise throughout the education system of what I and a colleague have analysed as 'therapeutic' approaches to curriculum content, pedagogy and assessment. By 'therapeutic', I mean the application of ideas, principles, claims and practices associated with different branches of counselling, therapy and psychoanalysis to specific interventions, general teaching activities and diagnostic and summative assessment activities. Such activities may embody specialist therapeutic principles, activities or claims or, as is increasingly the case, they may embody populist, reductionist therapeutic characteristics that can be applied by non-specialists (see Ecclestone and Hayes 2008 for a detailed discussion).

In this chapter, I argue that, in different ways, concerns about the effects of transition, and suggestions for how to manage and support them better, cannot be isolated from broader political and public concerns about the negative emotional and psychological effects of an increasing range of life, work and learning events (see for example, Furedi 2003; Layard 2005). This context means that strategies to manage and support transitions can slide easily into therapeutic and disciplinary approaches, whether advocates wish this to happen or not. This not only emphasises the self as a major focus for curriculum content, pedagogy and assessment but it also brings more and more aspects of the private self within the remit of educational institutions.

Developing a positive learning identity

Navigating different identities

A number of studies have focused on the ways in which children navigate the different demands of home, school and peer relationships and how these navigations require them to create and maintain a sense of self as a learner, a son or daughter, and a peer or sibling. Some researchers call for schools and parents to pay more overt attention to the artefacts, activities and knowledge that children use at school and home, and to recognise how different uses of these might create more congruence between home and school identities. This helps children, parents and carers, and peers evolve a constructive learning identity that is congruent between the two contexts (see Hughes et al., this volume).

Such interests also link to the idea that teachers and other 'transition workers' in educational institutions, guidance and advice systems need a closer, more overt understanding of 'typical' identities and the sorts of problems that children and young people face in constructing and maintaining them. For example, Lam and

Pollard (2006) argue that understanding what children encounter during the transition from home to kindergarten, and knowing what makes a positive experience for them can be achieved by 'transition policies' and 'transition practices' for a 'smooth' transition.

In higher education, some researchers argue that 'non-traditional' entrants to higher education need both support and a reorientation of curriculum content to develop 'functional capabilities' in order to construct and manage a viable 'learning identity' (see, for example, Walker 2006). For disabled students, although universities have become better at providing systems that encourage students to disclose disability and seek support, tensions remain between the need to provide better social and emotional support for some students, and a traditional view that once at university, young people are adults and therefore independent. This can hinder students from either creating a disabled identity, or from coming to terms with that identity, thereby preventing them from being able to take full advantage of a university experience (Wheedon and Riddell, this volume).

Understanding identity narratives and agentic orientations

There is a long history in adult education research of interest in the purposes and applications of life history and biography, both as a research tool and as a progressive pedagogy (see, for example, Alheit 1995; ESREA 2008). Some researchers are interested in the ways in which adults evolve a sense of agency and how agency relates to different lifecourse transitions; and there appears to be a growing enthusiasm for using research methods and processes as pedagogical interventions that enhance self-awareness and reflexivity. In a project exploring the links between life events, learning, agency and identity, Biesta and Tedder argue that life history interviews, and the construction of a life narrative, can be used to discuss ideas and themes with interviewees because they have the potential to help people to learn about the particular composition of their agentic orientations and how they 'play out' in an individual's life. This can help people to understand agency better and to think of ways in which to use it more effectively (see Biesta and Tedder 2007; also Tedder 2009).

Some researchers might acknowledge that adults' life histories and narratives might be, variously, valid and authentic, artificial and factually incorrect or be a form of 'performativity' and that, as a result, they have limitations both as a pedagogy and a research tool (see Biesta *et al.* 2005). Nevertheless, the idea that they can be used as a pedagogy with adults in order to enhance self-understanding, to enhance collective understanding by sharing stories with others or to become more agentic is becoming increasingly popular (see for example ESREA 2008). These approaches are readily translatable into formal modules in personal development and summative assessment that requires students to reflect on their experiences. Of course, the long-running, increasingly endemic use of reflective journals and personal development portfolios in further and higher education means that such notions are not new or controversial. Nevertheless, there is a new emphasis on reflexive exploration of personal, learning and working identities or agency in order to enable students to develop skills for lifelong learning by being able to deal more effectively with transitions now and in the future (see, for example, Buckley and Fielding 2007).

In a similar vein but with a more specialist therapeutic approach drawing from a long-running interest in psychoanalysis amongst adult educators, some advocate the incorporation of principles and approaches drawn from psycho-therapy and psychoanalysis as ways of helping adults understand patterns of action and reasons for them. This is especially important because many adults return to formal education at the point of a major life transition or find the processes of formal learning and assessment deeply unsettling. One response is for teachers to embed exploration of behaviours, responses and possibilities for change through education in reflective assignments, tutorial reviews and processes such as biographical creative writing (see, for example, Hunt and West, 2006).

In primary education, findings from the Home–School project, discussed by Hughes *et al.* in this volume, also led to interest in psychodrama techniques where theatre educators in the role of 'transition workshops' helped children, parents, peer mentors (or 'buddies') and teachers to act out and explore feelings and responses to the impending transition to secondary school and to help each other develop coping and managing strategies (see Ecclestone and Hayes 2008, Chapter 2 for discussion).

A relatively new turn in these ideas is that a crucial aspect of teachers' profes-sionalism is for them to become 'reflective' and 'self aware' as part of being 'psycho-logically healthy' and therefore better able to develop children's well-being (see General Teaching Council of England 2009).

Encouraging critical consciousness

In contrast to ways of supporting and managing transitions that might be seen as helping people adapt as individuals to the demands of transition, a more radical, politicised approach comes from a long-standing tradition in further and adult education that aims to help people to understand how structural factors of class, race and gender shape agency and identity in particular ways (see Avis 2007).

Advocates of critical pedagogy place questions about structure at the heart of analysis of identity and agency, and relate these to curriculum content and teaching, and learning activities. For example, a study of young women learning emotional labour as nursery nurses leads Colley (2006: 25) to argue that curric-ulum content and teaching should enable students to see how 'structure and agency combine to produce and reproduce social inequalities'. The creation and exploitation of emotional labour comes both from the demands of the formal curriculum, the socialisation demanded by the workplace and the ways in which young women's own dispositions, experiences and attitudes interact with these 'fields of action':

> [T]he concept of gendered habitus holds powerful structural influences within its frame. Gendered habitus includes a set of complex, diverse predis-positions. It involves understandings of identity based on familial legacy and

early childhood socialisation. As such, it is primarily a dynamic concept, a rich interfacing of past and present, interiorized and permeating both body and psyche.

(Colley 2006: 26)

A focus on classed, gendered or racial habitus that combines identity, agency and structure offers two possible interpretations of critical pedagogy rooted in the idea that 'the personal is political': one is a psycho-social analysis of how gendered habitus has evolved in individuals and groups and how it both creates and reproduces emotional responses and patterns. This might take the form of radical or critical therapy, advocated by well-known feminist psychotherapists such as Susie Orbach, for example. The other interpretation challenges students to 'ask critical questions about what [those] destinies both offer and demand; and to ask why their education contributes so often to the reproduction of social inequality' (Colley 2006: 27). Following this argument, Colley argues that curriculum designers, awarding bodies and employers also need to recognise the demands of learning emotional labour in caring occupations and also consider the content of the care curriculum so that students and teachers can challenge it.

Building on these ideas in relation to Kurdish women immigrants in Sweden, Colley argues that educators and transition workers need a very different understanding of how time and place affect such groups and how these influence their transitions to new cultures. In contrast to traditional, gendered notions of time, a more critical reading of how oppressed groups experience time, enables transition workers, teachers and students themselves to understand how 'processes of change *in* particular times, that is to say, in particular epochs, periods, or moments [are] mediated by gendered, racialised and classed practices which engender those times' (Colley, this volume).

A critical perspective on transitions therefore requires teachers and transition workers to understand them in very different ways from policy and mainstream professional depictions but also to encourage collective rather than individual understanding, and through this, collective resistance and struggle to change power relations within lifecourse transitions.

Aligning the demands of different contexts of learning

Narrowing the gap between different stages and contexts

A significant body of work around transitions in employment and workplaces focuses on how adults construct a learning identity and engage with the relationships, norms and expectations of a particular learning community of practice in order to develop both agency and a strong sense of identity and through this to deal with conflicting roles and demands (see Bimrose and Brown, this volume; Felstead *et al.*, this volume; Evans and Waite, this volume).

In educational transitions, this focus leads some researchers to advocate support through closer alignment between the formal systems and processes of different educational contexts. For example, Satchwell and Ivanič (in this volume) argue that dissonance between the literacy practices young people use competently and enthusiastically in their social, personal and work lives, and those demanded by competence-based and assignment-based assessment methods in vocational courses inhibits motivation and achievement. One implication is that teachers should incorporate more of the technologies that young people use confidently and effectively outside college, within everyday teaching and assessment strategies.

Alignment between systems and context also appears in the increasing use of dedicated modules or interventions to ease transition from one phase to another, such as primary to secondary, and school, college or work to university. These offer students the chance to reflect on themselves as learners, to identify 'learning to learn' skills, to evaluate strengths and weaknesses and to identify personal resources and strategies (see, for example, Claxton 2002; Park and Tew 2007).

Concerns about the risks, fears and anxieties experienced by children making the transition to secondary school, and subsequent dips in achievement for significant numbers of children, has led some schools to adopt practices and approaches of primary schools or to offer special 'learning to learn' activities to ease the transition. A school in Manchester has the same teacher for 11- to 14-year-olds 'for every lesson, every day, just as they are at primary ... the teacher will have a shepherding role ... they [sic] will have intimate knowledge of their class from their circumstances at home to what their special needs are ... Specialists will join the regular teacher for certain subjects' (Frankel 2007: 18). Some researchers argue that such strategies may be appropriate for other major transitions in the education system, including that made by non-traditional students to higher education (see, for example, Dixon and Alcock 2007).

Attending to the psychological climate of 'learning cultures'

Some researchers argue that institutional managers, transition workers and teachers should find ways to align the social and psychological features of learning cultures more effectively. A study of adults returning to formal learning through community-based further education illuminates the ways in which emotional and practical difficulties of adults who have had negative experiences of formal education are exacerbated by inequalities caused by class and gender.

Drawing on the ideas of Bourdieu, Gallacher and colleagues argue that these adults need and then come to expect particular types of relationships and approaches to teaching because they bring particular dispositions that both create and reinforce expectations and activities in a new habitus. This is a barrier in the transition to mainstream further education. Yet, the activities and understanding of some tutors and support staff who might not see themselves as, or be seen as, 'transition workers', such as receptionists, catering staff and cleaners, can make powerful differences to the emotional and psychological climate of different learning cultures to ease transition. Conversely, other features make that climate more difficult. Yet, the study also acknowledges that reinforcing the learning cultures of community education can create comfort zones, expectations of 'acceptable' behaviour on the part of both teachers and students and exclusion for those who do not fit (Gallacher et al. 2007).

Changing the curriculum

In contrast to calls for better alignment between institutional structures and processes, or attention to the dynamics and relationships of different learning cultures, Quinn offers a different critical view of how institutions might respond better to the realities of transition for 'non-traditional' and, in particular, working-class students. She argues that admissions and assessment procedures, and curriculum content in universities need to recognise the fluid nature of transitions and the 'multiple identities' involved in navigating them.

Countering fixed ideas of 'failed' transitions requires educational institutions to offer much more flexible types of support in order to help people make positive transitions. Flexible enrolment and funding and genuinely modular systems that enable movement into and out of the system at different points need, she argues, to be aligned with curriculum content that is much more tuned to students' own interests and to the idealised futures they imagine for themselves (Quinn, this volume).

From a critical perspective, images of identity and agency that suggest people can construct a linear, chronological and coherent account of themselves bear little relation to the transition of particular groups and therefore to the sort of systems and curriculum content they need. Yet, institutional structures and depictions of transition are only one aspect of the problem. For critical researchers a curriculum based on traditional subjects not merely institutionalises 'alien' or 'irrelevant' knowledge', but it also oppresses particular groups and individuals through the imposition of gendered, classed and racial forms of knowledge. Enabling students to engage effectively with education, to navigate the fluid nature of identity and to deal with structural disruptions therefore requires radical change to curriculum content as well as institutional structures.

Therapeutic and disciplinary assessment

Tracking targets

One effect of official depictions of transition is that formal assessment dominates people's experiences of transitions into, through and out of different sectors and qualification regimes. In post-compulsory education, for example, successful navigation and achievement through a growing number of courses require learners to participate in formal requirements for initial diagnostic assessment and guidance, to set, review and track goals and targets through Individual Learning Plans (ILPs) and to respond to detailed coaching and feedback on learning tasks broken into manageable parts and presented in detailed assessment specifications and criteria.

All these activities aim to ease students' transition through the requirements of summative assessments as painlessly as possible, an approach reinforced by teachers' concerns about maximising both personal development and educational achievement for young people and adults deemed to be 'second chance', 'non-traditional' or 'disadvantaged' learners (see Torrance *et al.* 2005; Ecclestone 2007).

An example of assessment used in formalised and ritualistic ways is the ILPs used with adults taking part in 'Skills for Life' literacy and numeracy programmes. As Hamilton shows, participation in processes around the ILP requires teachers and guidance workers to construct artefacts and procedures within fairly tight boundaries specified by funding bodies, awarding bodies and inspectors, beginning with diagnostic assessment that creates a detailed plan around targets and a set of normative expectations (Hamilton, this volume).

The artefacts, prescriptions and rituals of assessment and the detailed specifications of criteria that increasingly dominate qualification systems to maximise the chances of students getting through them successfully, create a series of mini-transitions within a taught programme. These have changed profoundly how tutors teach and assess students and the degree of influence they have on designing both the content and process of teaching. The requirement in growing numbers of programmes in post-compulsory education to track transitions into, through and out of qualifications in great detail not only produces official interpretations of good practice with which teachers must comply but also constrains teachers and students within mechanistic forms of pedagogy and assessment (see Torrance *et al.* 2005; Ecclestone 2009b). Resisting target-driven management of transitions requires forms of professional training and development that raise levels of professional competence, expertise and confidence.

Emotional support and disciplinary assessment

Closer technical and psychological alignment between sectors, institutions and programmes appears to be increasingly institutionalised for many children, young people and adults. Yet, certain groups experience much more intensive management through high levels of emotional support to encourage engagement and to build confidence and self-esteem which go hand in hand with disciplinary forms of target setting and monitoring. Although a combination of emotional and disciplinary assessment is a relatively recent turn in approaches to managing transitions, it has its roots in earlier initiatives for similar groups in the past (see Ecclestone 2009; Edwards and Usher 1991).

A particularly salient example is that of young people not in formal education, training or work (the so-called NEETs) (see Turner 2007; Colley 2003a). The introduction of the Common Assessment Framework (CAF) of Every Child Matters requires practitioners to share information about children and young people and their families with other professionals, and to target services and specific interventions at individuals identified as being at risk. Supported initially by a personal adviser who brokers welfare and education services and support systems and also carries out diagnostic assessments and reviews as part of the CAF, young people categorised as 'NEETs' may experience a range of personalised interventions, including cognitive behavioural therapy, motivational interviewing, brief solution-focused therapy and neuro-linguistic programming (Turner 2007).

In his analysis of assessment activities used by advisers in the ex-Connexions service of personal advice and guidance, Patrick Turner, a trainer of advisers and youth workers, shows how interventions based on 'solution-focused' therapy and counselling are meant to complement the main approach to fostering behavioural change for young people deemed to be at risk of transition, namely the Assessment Planning Implementation and Review tool (APIR). In this, a typical activity requires young people and their advisers to construct a personal version of a template in the form of a wheel with the 'client' at the hub and each spoke representing a different feature of their life-world such as friends, family, education and work. The adviser helps the young person subdivide these sections further, through a series of concentric circles radiating out from the centre and encourages him or her to 'map' for themselves where they are positioned in the major aspects of their lives.

A key feature in client change is to address difficulties that young people face through what Turner defines as the 'problem-as-opportunity-orientation' of solution-focused therapy. Here, 'the therapist facilitates the discovery of hitherto unknown resources for framing questions in such a way as to only elicit responses that provide tangible evidence of client self-efficacy' (Turner 2007: 152).

The idea that 'self-efficacy' is a resource that enables someone to identify other 'resources', such as friends, family, advisers, and mentors, is integral to 'personal capital' where psychological and emotional attributes are redefined as 'skills' that enhance opportunities and survival in life and the labour market (Turner 2007). Formalised therapeutic approaches to self-assessment were introduced in earlier initiatives in further education (see Ecclestone and Hayes 2008: Chapter 4; Ecclestone 2009c). They have become integral to the marshalling and development of personal capital deemed to be crucial for young people at risk of making poor transitions (see Social Exclusion Unit 1999, 2005).

Assessments that diagnose and develop 'personal capital' are inextricably linked with what Helen Colley has analysed as 'engagement mentoring' (Colley 2003b). This redefines old notions of providing 'advice, training and/or counselling by an experienced person to a junior or novice, through a relatively informal, dyadic relationship' into an intensive form of emotional support (Colley 2003b: 86). 'Engagement mentoring' targets young people seen as disaffected, alienated and difficult, and therefore 'unattractive' to mentors in other types of mentoring schemes, and searches out young people's own interests and perception of needs to create targets that 're-engage' them with institutionalised norms, structures and pathways. In her study of mentoring, Colley showed how high levels of emotional labour from mentors aim to bring about a significant shift in the values and motivation of the young people, their skills and abilities, and their interaction with the wider environment. In line with policy from bodies like the European Commission, the overall objective is to move the young person from a position of alienation and distance from social and economic reality, to a position of social integration and productive activity (Colley 2003b: 92).

Once in formal programmes such as Entry to Employment (E2E), young people deemed to be personally, socially and educationally 'at risk' experience a combination of emotionally intensive mentoring and coaching by tutors and disciplinary forms of assessment. This alignment of emotional and therapeutic support with strict and very detailed processes to set and review behavioural and attitudinal targets is highly personalised. It encompasses everything from eye contact, getting up in the morning to social skills and signs of basic motivation to participate in activities as potential targets for progress. Tutors regard evidence that young people both participate in and show positive attitudes towards a very detailed monitoring of themselves as 'learning' (see Ecclestone 2009).

Creating a curriculum of the self?

Therapeutic management of transitions

Interest in raising awareness about identities and/or agency in transition resonates with contemporary cultural expectations that we should be self-aware and able to offer coherent accounts of ourselves. Closer alignment between educational interests and practices and cultural narratives that regard self-awareness and a 'reflexive flexibility' in managing our identities as essential to emotional well-being, is reflected in Giddens' widely-cited view that 'reflexive self-awareness' on the part of the public and policy makers alike is a positive trend. He argues that psychoanalysis and therapy flowing from a quest for self-awareness provides a setting and a 'rich fund of theoretical and conceptual resources for the creation of a reflexively ordered narrative of self. In a therapeutic situation, whether of the classical psychoanalytical type or not, individuals are able (in principle) to bring their past into line with the exigencies of the present, consolidating a story-line with which they feel relatively content' (Giddens 1995: 31; see also Giddens 1991).

The rise of popular cultural interest in therapeutic ideas, explanations and activities has been charted in detail by sociologists and educational researchers, leading to arguments that political, academic and professional interest in identity and agency does not merely resonate with cultural expectations and interest. Instead, there is a powerful iteration between cultural expectations, policy and practice (see Furedi 2003; Ecclestone and Hayes 2008). This is evident in the ways in which policy makers have incorporated popular interest in emotional and psychological effects of social change in areas such as the Social and Emotional Aspects of Learning strategy and initiatives for young people at risk of transition (SEU 1999; DfES 2005; Oxford Review of Education 2009).

From some perspectives on identity, the idea that there is a coherent 'self' around which one can construct a coherent account is deeply problematic (see Quinn, this volume; Taylor 2008). Notwithstanding such objections, notions of the reflexive self permeate policy and practice. In the context of transitions, there are two possible implications for support, pedagogy and assessment. One is that biographical approaches, reflection on the self, or applications of psychoanalysis and counselling within pedagogy, require individuals and transition workers supporting them to explore and draw out 'agentic orientations' and perceptions of identity in order to develop better 'managing' strategies. An alternative, less interventionist view is that insights from this research can inform teachers' uses of teaching and assessment strategies rather than being the basis for direct interventions in people's perceptions of their identity and agency.

Focusing on emotional and affective aspects of transition

Whichever view is salient, the various strategies to support and manage transition discussed in this chapter are linked inextricably to the extension of counselling and mentoring schemes, growing interest in eliciting biographical narratives, smoothing or aligning learning cultures and relationships, and requiring students to take part in 'learning to learn' or 'reflective practice' modules in order to develop self-awareness (see Ecclestone and Hayes 2008). In this context, calls to change subject teaching and content, or to create special modules to encourage self-awareness and reflexivity, or to develop affective dispositions, attributes and attitudes, also become part of a wider therapeutic turn because they reinforce the idea that people need formal support, not just for making transitions but simply in order to learn at all (see Ecclestone and Hayes 2009).

A broader therapeutic turn also embraces techniques and arrangements that enable parents to know more about how their children navigate identity between home and school, help teachers to know more about children's identities and learning activities at home or that encourage students to take part in activities in order to understand the effects of transition. All of these strategies draw in emotional and psychological aspects of transition for support, monitoring and assessment.

In this context, even critical pedagogy can become therapeutic because, without being able to connect critical consciousness about structure, agency and identity to strong political movements, pedagogy or other interventions based on connections between agency, structure and identity can engender emotional rather than political responses. However compelling might be analysis about links between structure, agency and identity, an absence of political movements can mire 'the personal' in introspection about emotional responses. For example, the goal of raising consciousness about the oppression of emotional labour might not lead to empowered political insights but to pessimistic and emotional responses.

Preoccupation with the emotional and affective aspects of the self is also symbolised by an invisible strand in research on transitions, namely that of transition or progression in ideas, thinking and learning in relation to specific subjects, skills or crafts. While the self and its feelings and awareness about identity and agency is both a significant and dominant subject in debates about transitions, transition through the subject in its traditional cognitive or intellectual sense is curiously silent. The human subject is dominant in two senses: it is the focus of attention and its feelings, responses and identity are increasingly the content of curriculum, teaching and assessment (see Ecclestone and Hayes 2009).

Blurring the line between public and private spheres

Therapeutic forms of support and management can jeopardise the separation that some children, young people and adults use consciously to maintain different identities. As Hughes acknowledges in this volume, support and management blur lines between formal education and private life, and incorporate home life in the formal curriculum. As I have argued in this chapter, these lines are obscured completely for some groups and individuals for whom therapeutic and disciplinary practices are emotional support to place individuals' behaviours, attitudes and dispositions at the heart of target setting and assessment.

In different ways, then, not only do depictions of transition in both policy and research raise questions about the purpose, content and process of learning, but they also change the role of state agencies and institutions, and the growing numbers of transition workers who support and manage transitions. Activities that intervene more directly than at any time in the past, in the emotional and psychological dimensions of families, children, young people and adults, raise new and problematic questions about the line between public and private spheres of action and thought.

Conclusions

Most of, if not all, the researchers cited in this book are likely to reject the epithet of 'therapeutic' for their suggestions about how best to manage, support or challenge contemporary experiences of transition. Yet, I have argued in this chapter that it is important to connect the increased pathologising of transition in policy, professional and academic concerns, and a corresponding interest amongst researchers in identity and agency that is often divorced from structure, to a broader cultural preoccupation with emotional and psychological aspects of life and learning. Making these connections suggests that support and management for transition is taking a strong therapeutic turn, and that in some contexts and for certain groups and individuals, therapeutic and disciplinary forms of support and assessment are symbolic.

The perspective taken in this chapter places the sociologist C. Wright-Mills' much-cited injunction for researchers to explore the links between 'private troubles' and 'public concerns' in a new light (Mills 1970). This popular rallying call was frequently cited by researchers in the seminar series that led to this book (see Ecclestone et al., this volume). Yet, contemporary depictions of transition raise new questions about how education helps people think and act for themselves, but, crucially, what they think and act about. I have aimed to highlight how different concerns about transition shift old debates about what constitutes useful, worthwhile or emancipatory knowledge, pedagogy and assessment, onto a new, much more personal, private and emotional terrain.

If arguments here are valid, aligning technical aspects of transition, creating better links between home, school and the self and between curriculum content, pedagogy and assessment, or encouraging a politicised critique of knowledge and curriculum, require much wider and sharper debate. Not least, we need to know more about the ways in which these strategies shape people's sense of self and agency, about the conditions that shape identity and agency, and about our potential to shape those conditions. Finally, managing and supporting the self in transition raises new questions about the role of state agencies in the increasingly blurred therapeutic spheres of public and private thought and action.

Bibliography

Alheit, P. (1995) 'Biographical learning: theoretical outline, challenges and contradictions of a new approach in adult education', in P. Alheit, A. Bron-Wojciechowska, E. Brugger and P. Dominicé (eds) *The Biographical Approach in European Adult Education*, Vienna: Verband Wiener Volksbildung.

Avis, J (2007) *Education, Policy and Social Justice: Learning and Skills*, London: Continuum.

Biesta, G. and Tedder, M. (2007) 'Agency and learning in the lifecourse: towards an ecological perspective', *Studies in the Education of Adults*, 39: 132–49.

Biesta, G. J. J., Hodkinson, P. and Goodson, I. (2005) 'Combining life-history and life-course approaches in researching lifelong learning: methodological observations from the "learning lives" project', in Centre for Research in Lifelong Learning, *What a Difference a Pedagogy Makes: Researching Lifelong Learning and Teaching*, Stirling: Centre for Research in Lifelong Learning.

Buckley, C. and Fielding, S. (2007) 'Building bridges for lifelong learning', paper presented at the Researching Transitions in Lifelong Learning Conference, University of Stirling, June 2007.

Claxton, G. (2002) *Building Learning Power*, Bristol: TLO Ltd.

Colley, H. (2003a) *Mentoring for Social Inclusion: a Critical Approach to Nurturing Mentor Relationships*, London: Routledge.

Colley, H. (2003b) 'The myth of mentor as a double regime of truth: producing docility and devotion in engagement mentoring with disaffected youth', in J. Satterthwaite, E. Atkinson and K. Gale (eds) *Discourse, Power, Resistance: Challenging the Rhetoric of Contemporary Education*, Stoke-on-Trent: Trentham Books.

Colley, H. (2006) 'Learning to labour with feeling: class, gender and emotion in childcare, education and training', *Contemporary Issues in Early Childhood*, 7: 15–29.

DfES (2005) *Guidance to Teachers on the Social and Emotional and Aspects of Learning Strategy for Schools*, London: Department for Education and Skills.

Dixon, M. and Alcock, H. (2007) 'Managing the transition of pupils at the primary–secondary interface: lessons for other major systemic transitions?' paper presented at the Researching Transitions in Lifelong Learning Conference, University of Stirling, June 2007.

Ecclestone, K. (2007) 'Compliance, commitment and comfort zones: the impact of formative assessment on vocational students' learning careers', *Assessment in Education*, 14: 315–33.

Ecclestone, K. (2009a) 'Lost and found in transition: the educational implications of "identity", "agency" and "structure"', in J. Field, J. Gallacher and R. Ingram (eds) *Researching Transitions in Lifelong Learning*, London: Routledge.

Ecclestone, K. (2009b) *Transforming Formative Assessment in Post-compulsory Education*, Buckingham: Open University Press.

Ecclestone, K. (2009c) 'From Youth Opportunities Programmes to emotional well-being in further education: the emergence of therapeutic and disciplinary teaching and assessment', internal manuscript, Oxford: Oxford Brookes University.

Ecclestone, K. and Hayes, D. (2008) *The Dangerous Rise of Therapeutic Education*, London: Routledge.

Ecclestone, K. and Hayes, D. (2009) 'Changing the subject? The educational implications of emotional well-being', *Oxford Review of Education*, rev. edn, 35(3): 371–91.

Edwards, R. and Usher, R. (1991) 'Disciplining the subject: the power of competence', *Studies in the Education of Adults*, 26: 1–14.

ESREA (2008) 'The emotional dimensions of learning and researching lives: a neglected species?' Life history and biographical research network conference, Canterbury: Christ Church University, March 2008.

Frankel, H. (2007) 'Surviving the leap year', *Times Educational Supplement*, 15 June.

Furedi, F. (2003) *Therapy Culture: Creating Vulnerability in an Uncertain Age*, London: Routledge.

Gallacher, J., Crossan, B., Mayes, T., Cleary, P. and Smith, L. (2007) 'Expanding our understanding of learning cultures in community-based further education', *Educational Review*, 59: 501–17.

General Teaching Council for England (2009) *Draft Code of Conduct*. Available online at www.opm.co.uk/gtc/GTCE_draft_code.pdf

Giddens, A. (1991) *Modernity and Self-identity: Self and Society in Late Modern Age*, Oxford: Polity Press.

Giddens, A. (1995) *The Transformation of Intimacy: Sexuality, Eroticism and Love in Modern Societies*, Oxford: Polity Press.

Hunt, C. and West, L. (2006) 'Learning in a border country: using psychodynamic ideas in teaching and research', *Studies in the Education of Adults*, 38: 160–76.

Lam, M. and Pollard, A. (2006) 'A conceptual framework for understanding children as agents in the transition from home to kindergarten', *Early Years*, 26: 123–41.

Layard, R. (2005) *Happiness: Lessons from a New Science*, London: Allen Lane.

Mills, C. W. (1970) *The Sociological Imagination*, London: Penguin.

Oxford Review of Education (2009) Special edition on 'well-being' in schools, 35(3), October 2009.

Park, J. and Tew, M. (2007) 'Emotional rollercoaster: calming nerves at times of transition', *Curriculum Briefing*, 5: 21–8.

Social Exclusion Unit (1999) *Bridging the Gap: New Opportunities for 16–19 year olds not in Education or Training*, London: SEU.

Social Exclusion Unit (2005) *Transitions for Young People with Complex Needs*, London: SEU.

Taylor, M. (2008) 'A clumsy road to well-being', paper presented at the ESRC Seminar Series, Changing the Subject: Interdisciplinary Perspectives on Emotional Well-being and Social Justice, Oxford Brookes University, December 2008.

Tedder, M. (2008) '"Almost a therapy": taking part in a life history research project', paper presented at the ESREA Conference, The Emotional Dimensions of Learning and Researching Lives: a Neglected Species?, Canterbury, March 2008.

Torrance, H., Colley, H., Garratt, D., Jarvis, J., Piper, H., Ecclestone, K. and James, D. (2005) *The Impact of Different Modes of Assessment on Achievement and Progress in the Learning and Skills Sector*, London: Learning and Skills Development Agency.

Turner, P. (2007) 'The transition to work and adulthood', in D. Hayes, T. Marshall and A. Turner (eds) *A Lecturer's Guide to Teaching in Further Education*, Buckingham: Open University Press.

Walker, M. (2006) 'Functional capabilities in managing transitions in higher education', paper presented at the ESRC seminar series 'Transitions Through the Lifecourse', London, May 2006.

Index